Contents

Introduction   4

Chapter 1 – The Rise of Supermarine   10

Chapter 2 – The Struggle to Survive   18

Chapter 3 – Post-War Flying Boats   25

Chapter 4 – Flying Boat Torpedo Bombers   32

Chapter 5 – Last of the Flying Boat Racers   39

Chapter 6 – The Southampton and Beyond   45

Chapter 7 – The Air Yacht   56

Chapter 8 – Giants   65

Chapter 9 – The Seamew   74

Chapter 10 – Replacing the Southampton   78

Chapter 11 – Four Engine Military Flying Boats   84

Chapter 12 – Flying Boats for Imperial Airways   90

Chapter 13 – High Speed Flying Boats   102

Chapter 14 – Replacing the Walrus Part 1   110

Chapter 15 – Replacing the Walrus Part 2   116

Chapter 16 – Last of the Line   121

Chapter 17 – The (Oh So Slow and Painful) End of an Era   125

Appendix – How to Construct a Linton Hope Hull   129

Author: Ralph Pegram

Design: Burda Druck India Pvt. Ltd.

Publisher: Steve O'Hara

Published by: Mortons Media Group Ltd, Media Centre, Morton Way, Horncastle, Lincolnshire LN9 6JR

Tel. 01507 529529

Printed by: William Gibbons and Sons, Wolverhampton

ISBN: 978-1-911639-94-7

Acknowledgements

Locating information relating to inter-war aircraft projects is proving to be both a rewarding and intensely frustrating endeavour, often in equal measure. On the one hand I have been astounded at the amount of original drawings, brochures, reports and data, in various forms, that are still out there in the world, unseen and ignored for many years just waiting to be unearthed, while on the other hand some of these material turn up in the most unlikely of places, making tracking it down a challenge to say the least.

In the past I have, on occasion, raised an eyebrow at the errors and omissions in many older books on aviation history, but given that the only aids available to these authors were the telephone, the writing of letters, a few helpful librarians and the memories of cooperative individuals, I take a different view now.

The advent of digital resources and the internet has turned research on its head. Paper ledgers and card indexes have been replaced by their digital equivalent in a great many libraries, archives and collections, with many then placed on their websites in searchable form. Who would begrudge a small fee for access and copies if you know what it is you will receive? This is all most welcome and those that have chosen not to do so, and there are many that should know better or are unaware of the benefits both to themselves and researchers, are encouraged to follow suit. There is still a great deal of material yet to see the light of day in many collections; properly catalogued and accessible you have an archive, without it you have a hoard.

The National Archive at Kew and the Department of Research and Information Services at the RAF Museum Hendon are a goldmine of original material but unexpected nuggets can be, and have been, tracked down at numerous museums and libraries around the world to fill gaps in the narrative. Mention should also be made of online antiquarian booksellers and auction site sellers, a further great resource, if a bit pricey at times. The internet also brings with it the ability to dialogue with other researchers, authors and enthusiasts to share information. Questions can be answered in minutes that a few decades ago would have taken weeks.

So, I would like to acknowledge the assistance I have received from the staff at the RAF Museum Hendon, my volunteer colleagues with the Royal Aero Club Trust, fellow authors Tony Buttler and Chris Gibson, and knowledgeable contacts Chris Michell, Dave Key, and many others.

Ralph Pegram

Introduction

Flying boats hold a particular fascination for many aircraft enthusiasts in a way that no other type seems to manage. For some reason they conjure up an image of romance and adventure often quite out of step with the roles for which they were designed, and as with any class of aircraft there were good 'uns and bad 'uns, and everything in between. Naturally a great many stayed firmly on the drawing board, the 'what if' projects that make up the majority of any designer's portfolio.

It is distinctly ironic that Supermarine, the company responsible for the design of the Spitfire fighter, an aircraft produced in far larger numbers than any other in Britain, was a business that had been launched with the specific intent to build flying boats. For many years expectations were high that there was a lucrative global market just around the corner for such types, both civil and military, yet it would turn out that flying boats were to represent well under 1% of total British aircraft production. On the positive side, around half of these flying boats were designed by Supermarine but, as is so often the case for aircraft companies, the majority of its projects were destined never to see the light of day.

For the purposes of this review of Supermarine's flying boat designs, the term 'secret project' will encompass not just those unfulfilled 'paper' projects, of which many were submitted as brochures and unsuccessful tenders to airlines and the military, but also those that were stepping stones on the way to the design of aircraft that the company actually did construct. Among these are a number of 'one-off' prototypes built with high expectation for sales and spin-off types, but which underperformed in one way or another and thwarted the company's plans.

But before embarking on the tale of Supermarine and the flying boat, we must first define what we mean by the term 'flying boat' as it tends to vary through time and from country to country. In the early days in Britain there were, among other names, hydro-aeroplanes, waterplanes, seaplanes, float planes, boat seaplanes and flying-boats.

By the end of the First World War, the standard terminology used in British technical reports was to refer to marine aircraft as seaplanes when they were supported on the water by a float or floats that were separate from the main body of the aircraft, and many of these where the direct counterparts of their land plane equivalent where some form of float had been substituted for the wheeled undercarriage. When the aircraft was supported on the water by the main body of the aircraft, generally referred to as a hull, as in a boat, the term used was flying boat. Occasionally, with the intent for greater clarity, official documents would refer to float seaplanes or boat seaplanes. Supermarine produced both seaplanes and flying boats, the former including their celebrated series of racing aircraft for the Schneider Trophy, but their primary focus was always on the latter.

The name Supermarine is inextricably linked with that of the man who served as chief designer for 17 years and director for ten, Reginald Joseph Mitchell, but there are many others who contributed to the success, and a reasonable number of failures, of the company. So, to start, we have to look at the founder of the company and the direction he intended for it to take.

Noel Pemberton Billing

The years immediately prior to the outbreak of the First World War saw the establishment in Britain of a fair number of partnerships and companies all seeking to capitalise on the anticipated demand for both civil and military aircraft. The Army and Navy had both started to take an interest in the new technology, the Army using its Balloon Factory at Farnborough as a base to support early experiments by aviation pioneers Samuel Franklin Cody and John William Dunne in 1908. The facility was renamed as the Army Aircraft Factory in 1911 and service trials of potential military aircraft were held at Larkhill in 1912. The Navy soon followed suit with an establishment on the Isle of Grain.

Several of the new aircraft companies were established as subsidiaries of, or associated with, existing businesses, the most prominent being Vickers, Short Bros, Grahame-White, and the four companies formed by Sir George White in Bristol, while others were set up by the pioneers of flying in Britain, financed, in the main, by wealthy family members or friends. This route was taken by Blackburn, Verdon Roe, Handley Page and others. One who would have loved dearly to have been in this latter group was Noel Pemberton Billing.

It is hard to grasp what exactly Billing was aiming to achieve in life. Overwhelmed with self-confidence and a distinct tendency to exaggerate or even veer towards fantasy, yet possessing a fair degree of inventive imagination, he had made a reasonably comfortable living through a variety of jobs, both in England and South Africa, and by marketing the rights to the various patents he held, the most profitable being for a form of typewriter. On the other hand he was also arrogant, tempestuous, prone to be combative and, unfortunately, easily distracted, lacking tenacity and always on the look-out for the next new venture rather than knuckling down to nurture the one in hand. And so, in late 1908, for reasons none too clear, he determined to enter the world of aviation, not content to be just one of the growing cadre of pioneers but to create for himself a role as a leader and facilitator.

It has to be said that Billing never thought small, not for him the graft of working his way up from the bottom, so his master plan was to establish a "Colony of British Aerocraft" with himself in the forefront. A trusty band of likeminded aircraft builders would beaver away to establish of a fleet of aircraft, which he intended to call the "Imperial Flying Squadron".

He published a new magazine, also named Aerocraft, to help publicise the venture and as a base for the 'colony' he purchased 3,000 acres of wet reclaimed land crossed by numerous drainage ditches at South Fambridge in Essex, adjacent to the tidal stretch of the River Crouch. On this site there were several useful buildings; large workshops formerly used by an engineering concern, a few bungalows, a hotel and club house, a general store and an electricity plant. Billing saw this as a viable base for his venture, everything that would be required for the colony was already in place. It was a grand plan which he hoped would attract many pioneer aviators, and to further advertise the opportunity he managed to get it described in a Flight magazine feature.

The colony was not to be, however. Many of the more prominent and successful pioneers, the Short brothers, Dunne, Charles Rolls and several others, preferred to base themselves at the Aero Club's grounds at Shellbeach and later nearby Eastchurch, where the airfields were firmer and not liable to flood. Billing's venture folded within a year and South Fambridge had to be abandoned. Billing's own attempts to build and fly an aircraft had also failed, the result being a few brief hops and a crash that put him in hospital. He now lost interest in aviation, or "relaxed his efforts", as he was to put it later, took up property speculation at Shoreham on the south coast and enrolled to study law. In 1912 he had shifted focus yet again and set up a new venture running a yacht charter business on the River Itchen in Southampton.

What goes around comes around and once the charter business was up and running in the capable hands of his assistant, Hubert Scott-Paine, his mind wandered and returned again to aircraft. On a visit to Grahame-White's burgeoning flying ground at Hendon in 1913 he got into an argument with pioneer aircraft constructor Fred Handley Page over how easy it would be to learn to fly. Handley Page claimed that his latest aircraft was so stable that anyone could learn to fly on it within a day. Billing scoffed, countering that a competent person could do that on any machine, and a bet was made as to who would be the first to earn their aviator's certificate.

Heading to Brooklands race circuit and airfield, where his brother ran a restaurant, Billing purchased a Farman biplane and at the crack of dawn engaged the services of Harold Barnwell from the Vickers School to teach him the rudiments of flying. By breakfast time, after little more than a couple of hours training, he decided that he was prepared sufficiently and cajoled the Aero Club examiner to observe his test flights. These he completed and was duly awarded his certificate, the story reported, once again, in Flight. Handley Page, who had yet to even start, paid up.

Billing was now officially an aviator and determined to make a second attempt to join the pioneers. This time he would become a constructor of aircraft and spotting, or possibly being urged to address, a niche that had yet to be filled, he decided to concentrate on marine types. He submitted patent applications for various inventions associated with flying boats. Across the Itchen from his yacht charter business, at Oak Bank wharf in Woolston, there was a ship's chandler and gravel merchant business that had fallen into receivership. Billing acquired their site on which there were a couple of large sheds, a wharf, several lesser buildings and a small tidal basin. Here he established Pemberton-Billing Ltd.

Pemberton-Billing Ltd.

Billing's new business began to take shape over the winter of 1913-1914. The sheds were repaired

The Pemberton-Billing Ltd Supermarine Works at Oak Bank Wharf, Woolston, on the River Itchen opposite Southampton Docks in 1914

and extended and named as the Supermarine Works. Construction of the first Pemberton-Billing aircraft, a small single-seat flying boat named as the Supermarine P.B.1, began there at once. Billing produced a souvenir silk-bound brochure to publicise the start-up in which he itemised his grandiose plans: three types of built to order flying boat, a school to teach the subtleties of flying from the water, a tidal dock capable of housing up to 12 flying boats, and an Aerial Marine Navigation passenger service flying to and from the Isle of Wight. The sketch artwork within the brochure gave a grossly exaggerated idea of the size of the site and facilities, a fine match for the equally fanciful text.

The name 'Supermarine', which Billing had applied first to the works and then to the aircraft he intended to build, had been conjured up by him "… to convey to the mind a craft capable of navigating the surface of the sea as also the air… (his) ultimate object was directed not to the production of a flying machine which under favourable weather conditions could rest on the surface of the water, but to the construction of a sea-worthy boat capable of attaining flight…"

The Supermarine P.B.1 was completed, albeit without an engine, in time to be displayed at the Aero and Marine Exhibition held at Olympia in London during March 1914. Unfortunately, when prepared for flight testing in the early summer, it failed to lift from the water even after a radical modification. It is hard to judge whether there were any fundamental flaws in the design – it certainly appeared sound – but it was definitely underpowered as the only available engine was Billing's aging 50hp Gnome rotary, plundered from his Farman biplane.

Neither the P.B.2 nor P.B.3, larger flying boats described in the brochure, ever materialised but a completely new and unrelated design, P.B.7, which incorporated Billing's patented 'slip-wing' system, was the subject of advertisements in the aviation press in July. Two were reported to be under construction for the German military. The 'slip-wing', a term coined by Billing years later, was a system whereby all the aircraft's flight surfaces could be detached from the hull by a quick release mechanism thereby allowing it to function as a conventional motor launch.

The Supermarine P.B.1, minus its engine and propeller, is launched from the tidal flats adjacent the Supermarine Works in the late spring of 1914

The main shed at Woolston with Billing's Farman at the back and the modified Supermarine P.B.1 in front

The Supermarine P.B.2 as shown in the company's souvenir brochure. It was never built

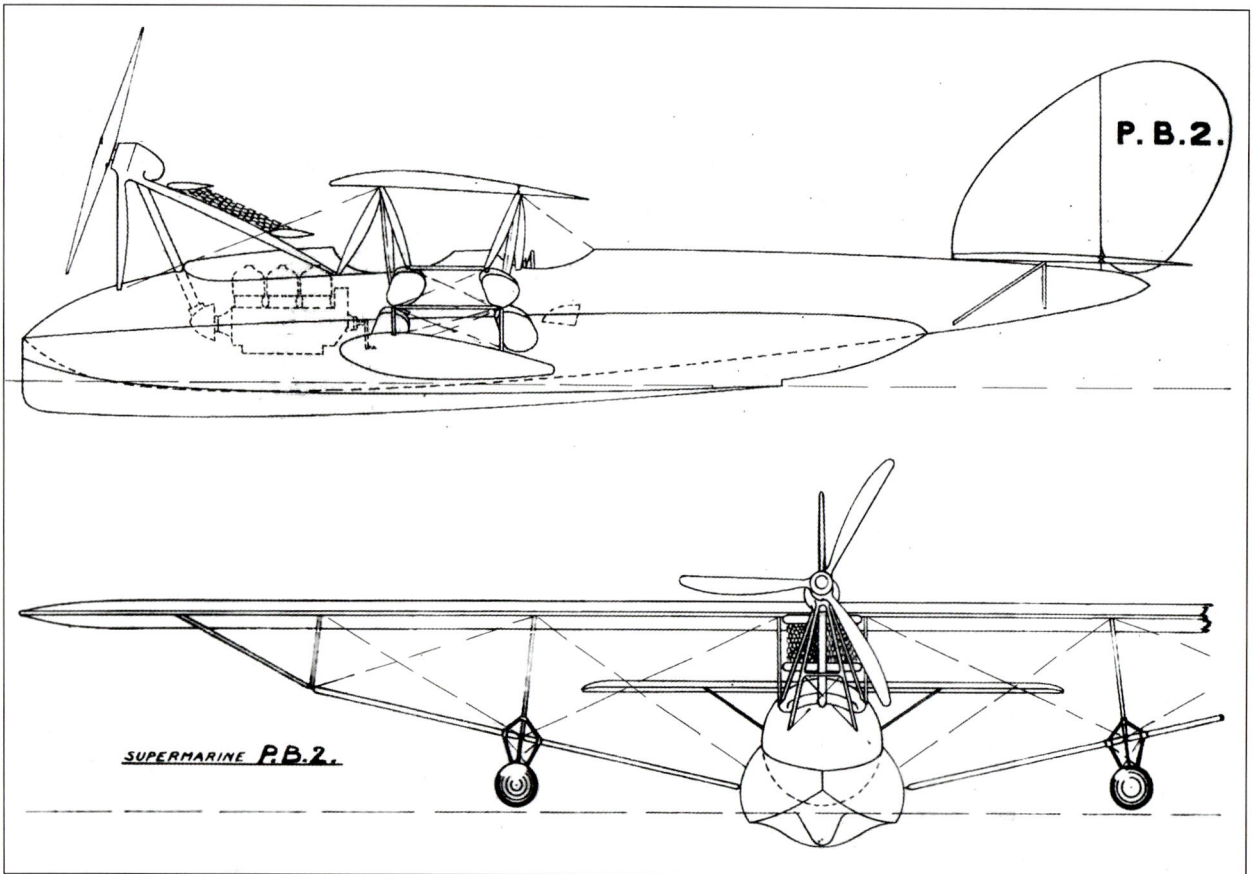

Side and front views of the Supermarine P.B.2 from the brochure

Flying boat construction, what little of it there was, came to an abrupt halt with the outbreak of war and Billing rushed off to join the Royal Naval Air Service (RNAS). Desperately short of funds, the factory was left in the lands of Scott-Paine. Billing participated in the raids on the Zeppelin factories at Friedrichshafen on the shores of Lake Constance in late 1914 but his military career was cut short when he resigned his commission at the end of 1915.

He returned to Woolston to develop his ideas on defensive and offensive aircraft but by now his zeal for the business was on the wane and he had determined to enter Parliament. His campaign was based on the notion that the whole war in the air was mismanaged; politically, technically and strategically. After fighting one by-election unsuccessfully he was elected at his second attempt and entered parliament as the member

This photograph taken in early 1914 shows two hulls under construction, probably for the P.B.7s. Although the aircraft were never completed, the hulls were repurposed later as flying boat tenders

PEMBERTON-BILLING, Ltd.

Illustration demonstrating the latest type of SUPERMARINE, P.B.—7. Span, 57 ft. 6 ins. Overall Length, 34 ft. Weight, 3,000 lbs. Engine, 225 h.p. Speed, 45-70 m.p.h. Fuel capacity, 4 hours. Under stress of weather, at the will of the pilot, the aeronautical impedimenta is instantly detachable, leaving an ordinary High-Speed motor craft, which contains the engine, pilot, passengers, petrol, instruments and gun, and is equipped with water propeller and rudder, having a distance range of 200 miles and speed of 35 knots. Built under Pemberton-Billing's patents at his Southampton Works. Applications for licences to build under the French, German, Russian, Italian, Belgian, Norwegian, Australian, American, Japanese, and other Foreign and Colonial patents, are invited.

SOUTHAMPTON, ENGLAND.

Pemberton-Billing advertisement for the 'slip-wing' P.B.7. July 1914

for Hertford East. He also published his views in a book, Air War: How To Wage It, and sold out his part-ownership of Pemberton-Billing Ltd to Scott-Paine in order to avoid any accusation of a conflict of interest. His Parliamentary career was controversial to say the least and he lost his seat at the first full post-war general election in 1921. Thankfully he was to play no further part in the future of the aircraft manufacturing company he had established.

1
CHAPTER

The Rise of Supermarine

Much of the initiative for the formation of Pemberton-Billing Ltd as a manufacturer of flying boats had come from Hubert Scott-Paine – as later events would make fairly clear. In his youth he and his brothers had built small speed boats at Shoreham in Kent and he had an affinity with the sea and a love of speed. Much of the organisation of Billing's yacht charter business, including the recruitment and management of the yacht crews, had been in Scott-Paine's hands. Furthermore, many years later, Scott-Paine wrote a letter to Flight claiming that the design of the Supermarine P.B.1, with its sleek monocoque-style hull, had been his work and this was not refuted by Billing.

The business had been in a dire state when Billing left to join the RNAS; no sales had been made, funds had been depleted through the purchase of stock from defunct aircraft businesses, notably Radley Gordon-England, several workers had left to join the forces and the remainder could not be paid until Billing's business partner, Alfred de Broughton, agreed to inject more money into the company.

Scott-Paine now rose to the challenge. A far better manager and negotiator than Billing had ever been, he used his contacts and skill to acquire contracts to repair damaged military aircraft and this proved just sufficient to keep the business afloat. He was also successful in obtaining further contracts from the Admiralty Air Department (A.A.D) to build both a seaplane and a flying boat of their design. Billing's return had thrown a slight spanner in the works as some resources were shifted to pursue his ideas on air defence fighters, but that had come to an end when he departed, leaving Scott-Paine free to forge a closer link with the A.A.D. It was a partnership that would provide a firm foundation for the new company.

Once he had full control, Scott-Paine promptly discarded the increasingly tainted Pemberton-Billing name and instead used that which had been applied to the works; henceforth it was to be the Supermarine Aviation Works Ltd. With new contracts in place, the workforce could be expanded

and newly-qualified engineer William Abraham Hargreaves was employed as chief designer in the first weeks of 1916.

Supermarine was now in close contact with the A.A.D aircraft design team, headed by Harris Booth and Harold Bolas, and this included naval architect and hull designer Linton Chorley Hope. One of the first contracts acquired by the company in late 1915 was for the construction of a small batch of A.D. Flying Boats. This was an experimental two-man machine designed primarily to evaluate Hope's monocoque-style hulls, a type derived from his extensive experience with the design and construction of racing yachts and motor launches. The first batch of hulls, however, would be constructed not by Supermarine but by Southampton-based shipbuilders May, Harden and May, part of George Holt Thomas' expanding Airco group. Supermarine was responsible for the detail design and construction of the flying surfaces and for final assembly, under the supervision of A.A.D staff.

Hope's hulls were constructed in two parts; the main body, typically cigar-shaped, and the boat-like lower surfaces that provided stability and smooth running on the water, known as the planing bottom. The main structure was designed to distribute static and shock loads to avoid local concentration of stress, the construction allowing for a small degree of flexibility. It was made by shaping thin wood stringers and hoops around a jig of lateral formers and then applying the skin as thin, narrow planks, usually of mahogany, butted together.

This process was labour intensive and required skilled woodworkers to produce a watertight hull. The planing bottom was then attached to the completed main hull structure, thereby creating a double skin and sealed buoyancy chambers. The curved shape of the bottom surface was designed to let the flying boat run smoothly, to minimise bow-wave and spray, and to increase the angle of incidence of the aircraft as it approached take-off speed and then rose clear of the water. Experience both with high speed launches and early marine

The A.D. Flying Boat – the inspiration and template for many of Supermarine's early designs

aircraft demonstrated that the planing bottom would perform better if it terminated with a clean step at the rear, usually vertical, which broke the water surface tension force resisting the take-off of the aircraft. It was also usual to have a small secondary surface and step towards the rear of the hull for the same purpose.

As Hope's construction techniques for aircraft were still experimental, the hull of one of the third batch of A.D. Flying Boats was allocated for strength testing at the Royal Aircraft Factory. Between September and November 1917 it underwent a series of tests to check distortion under various loads, which were minimal, and it was then inverted in a sand bed and the planing bottom loaded with bags of lead shot until, under a load of 13,800lb or about 8.8lb per sq inch, the hull began to collapse around the cockpit aperture. This form of hull construction had therefore proven to meet all the claims for distribution of stress and high strength made by Hope and his supporters.

While work progressed at Woolston on the A.D Flying Boats, other contracts awarded to the company covered construction of a large patrol seaplane designed by the A.A.D, the A.D. Navyplane, and both Short 184 seaplanes and Norman Thompson NT2B flying boat trainers. There was much from which an alert and competent design team could learn.

Supermarine's first flying boat – the Baby

The company's first opportunity for a complete in-house design came in early 1917 with the issue of Admiralty Specification N.1(b) calling for a Single Seat Marine Fighter. Supermarine's submission was the Baby, a pusher biplane flying boat with a 24ft hull, 6ft shorter than that of the A.D. Flying Boat but of similar cross section. Its design was led by Hargreaves and heavily influenced by the work already carried out by the company with and for the A.D.D, particularly with regard to the Linton Hope hulls.

A contract was awarded to the company for three examples and they were allocated the registrations N59, N60 and N61. N.59 flew in February 1918. It is not entirely clear whether Supermarine had built any of the Hope hulls for the later batch of A.D. Flying Boats or whether this was to be their first attempt at one, but the company certainly implied in later years that they had indeed built some.

Meanwhile, the first A.D. Flying Boat had run into serious handling problems on the water,

The Supermarine N1b Baby flying boat fighter, claimed by the company to be the fastest flying boat in the world. They may have been right

where a divergent pitching motion, a phenomenon known as porpoising, was proving difficult to resolve during both take-off and landing. The A.A.D experimented with various modifications to the planing bottom and position of the step which improved the situation but failed to eliminate the problem completely. Supermarine dealt with the changes suggested by the Admiralty designers, watched and learned.

The Baby was fortuitous not to experience porpoising to the same extent but was prone to ship water into the cockpit; bow-wave and spray being the other persistent bugbear of hull design, especially for small aircraft with an open cockpit sitting close to the water. The planing bottom was extended forward to a point ahead of the main hull as a quick fix but the problem was not resolved completely and various modifications or alternative designs were suggested for the second and third machines.

At this stage, hull and planing bottom design was almost as much an art as it was a science. As a result, the alternative designs were based to a large extent on boat building experience and, it has to be said, inspired guesswork. Supermarine had no large tank of its own within which to evaluate

models. The National Physical Laboratory (NPL) had initiated a programme of systematic research into the characteristics of many hull profiles in 1917, which included the A.D. Flying Boat, but the results were yet to be published or otherwise percolate back down to industry.

Neither N60 nor N61 were completed before the end of the war when the contract was cancelled. N60 is thought to have been almost ready to fly while work on N61 may have been in the very early stages of hull construction.

During the closing years of the war the growing confidence of Scott-Paine, Hargreaves and the rest of the team, which now included Reginald Mitchell acting as deputy works manager, encouraged them to develop and propose entirely new designs of their own. This led to two speculative flying boat projects passing over their drawing boards.

Supermarine S.S.1

The first original scheme drawn up the company, designated S.S.1, was a revised version of a project first considered in the final days of the Billing era. Billing himself had referred to it as the P.B.31 (the actual P.B.31E was a quadruplane anti-Zeppelin

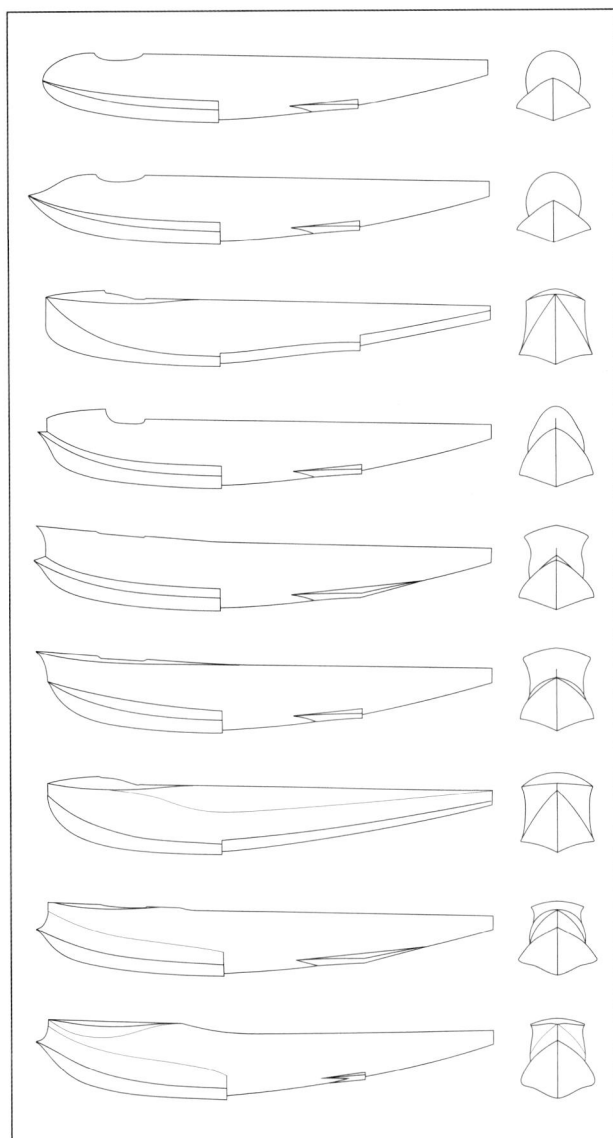

Many alternative hull profiles were considered for the Baby. From top to bottom; the original Baby hull, Baby as modified after the initial flights, six alternative hull profiles suggested in mid-1918, and finally the hull for the Type A and Sea Lion, patented in 1919

fighter). The S.S.1 was a single-seat light bomber flying boat equipped with a 'slip-wing' that the company had devised for operation from a submarine. The original intent of Billing's detachable wing system, as described in his 1913 patent, had been as a safety feature for use after landing in rough weather, a point at which the flying boat could be destabilised and capsized if the wings were still attached. Several alternative layouts were illustrated in the patent, two of which show features adopted for the S.S.1. However, for the S.S.1 the use of a 'slip wing' had little to do with safety.

The engine of the S.S.1, a six-cylinder water-cooled type, was to be installed within the hull, which was of basic flat-sided boat form and not of

Linton Hope construction. The pilot, in a cockpit ahead of the engine, could engage a clutch and gearbox system to direct power either to a standard marine propeller beneath the hull or to the air propeller via a chain drive. The top end of the chain gear drive for the tractor propeller was installed mid-gap in the biplane wings at the front end of a boom that supported the tail surfaces.

The boom was built with a vertical hinge in the middle so it could be swung sideways and then stowed tightly against the trailing edges of the wings. The drive to the air propeller was equipped with some form of quick-release mechanism as part of the 'slip wing' process that detached the wing structure and tail boom, although how this would function is not evident from surviving drawings.

The ambitious mission concept suggested by Supermarine for the S.S.1 was for it to be stowed, hull detached and tail boom folded, in a special watertight container fitted on the deck of a submarine. The submarine would approach the enemy, a ship at sea or a target located on the coast, under cover of darkness. At a safe distance, it would surface and stop. The S.S.1 would be unpacked, assembled and flown, the submarine then submerging. After locating and attacking its target, the aircraft could either return to the submarine to be recovered or fly on to a suitable safe landing spot.

If necessary the aircraft could land, discard the 'slip-wing' structure and proceed as a high-speed motor boat. One suggestion was that if the aircraft was under attack, the discarded flight structures might act as a decoy and draw fire away from the motor boat. It was the only unbuilt flying boat project to be featured in a company brochure of 1919, in which Supermarine commented, "The authorities, however, were not impressed with the idea, and construction of the machine was not completed." This is not particularly surprising as the type of one-off clandestine 'special-ops' mission envisaged hardly justified the modification of a submarine and development of a specialised new aircraft, especially one which, half a century later, might have seemed like something created by 'Q' division for James Bond. The thought of the submarine's crew standing exposed on the deck in the open sea, in the dark, manhandling and assembling the S.S.1 is rather jaw-dropping.

A few drawings of the project were retrieved from the archive in 1920 and retraced, so it is plausible that some thought was being given to resurrecting the concept at that time. The Air Ministry did issue a Specification in 1924, 16/24, for an aircraft to be carried by a submarine, but this was for the diminutive Parnall Peto fighter

Supermarine key players pose with the N1b Baby in early 1918. From left to right are Basil Hobbs (RNAS test pilot) Cecil Richardson (chief draughtsman), Hubert Scott-Paine (director and general manager), Cecil Dominy (director), William Hargreaves (chief designer), Victor Paine (publicity)

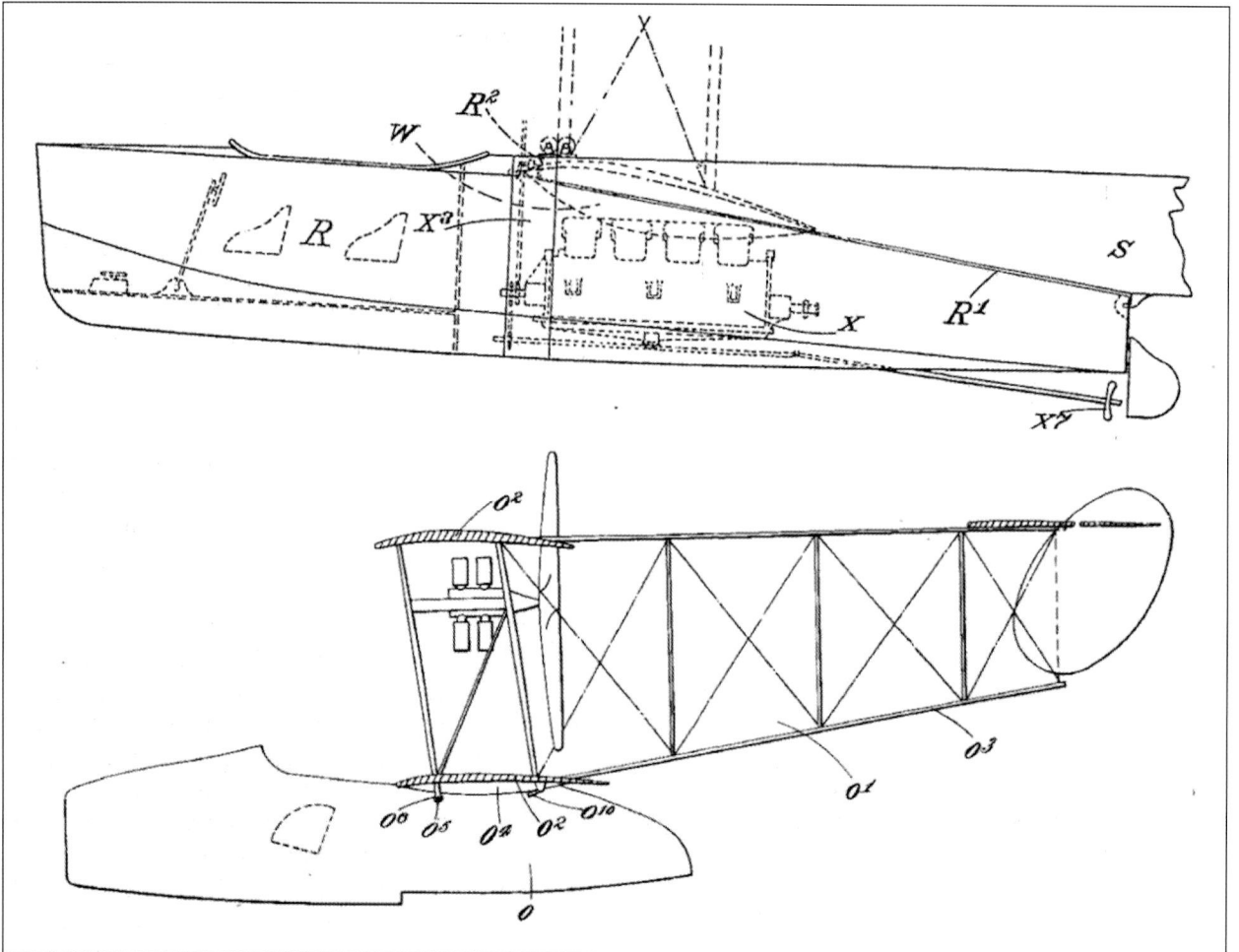

Two of the illustrations from Billing's 1913 patent for detachable wings, later referred to as a 'slip-wing'

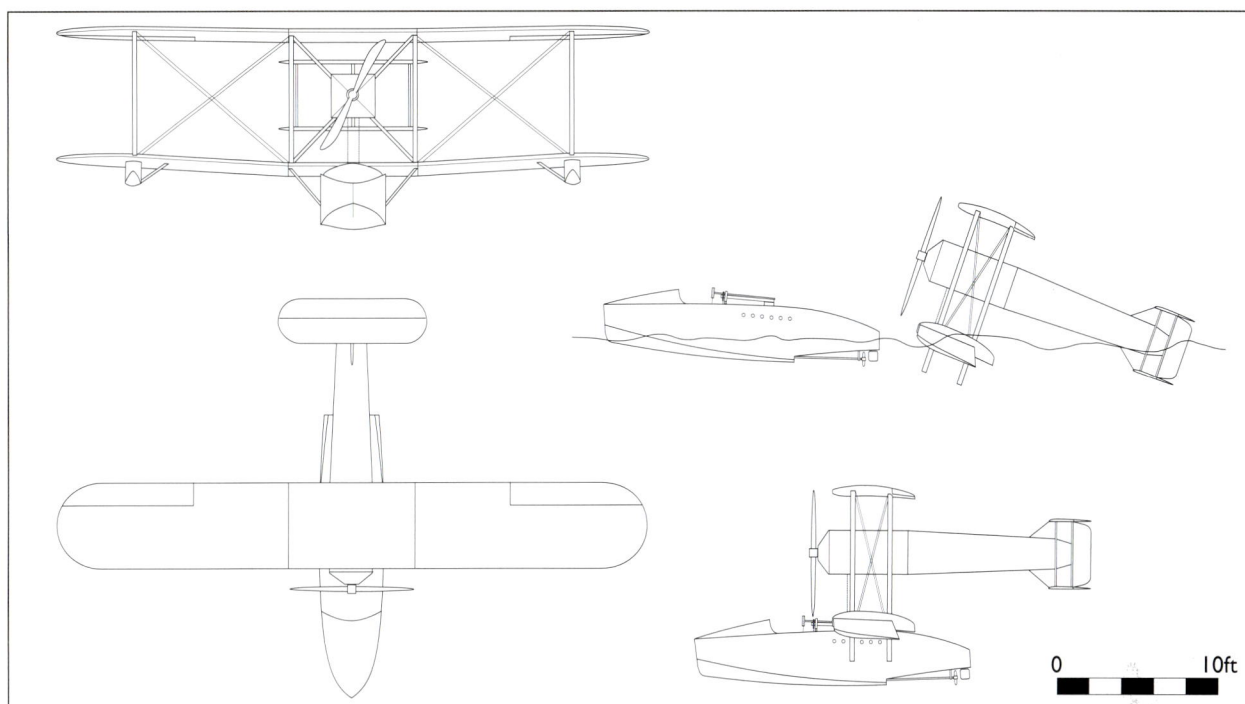

The Supermarine S.S.1 'slip-wing' bomber flying boat

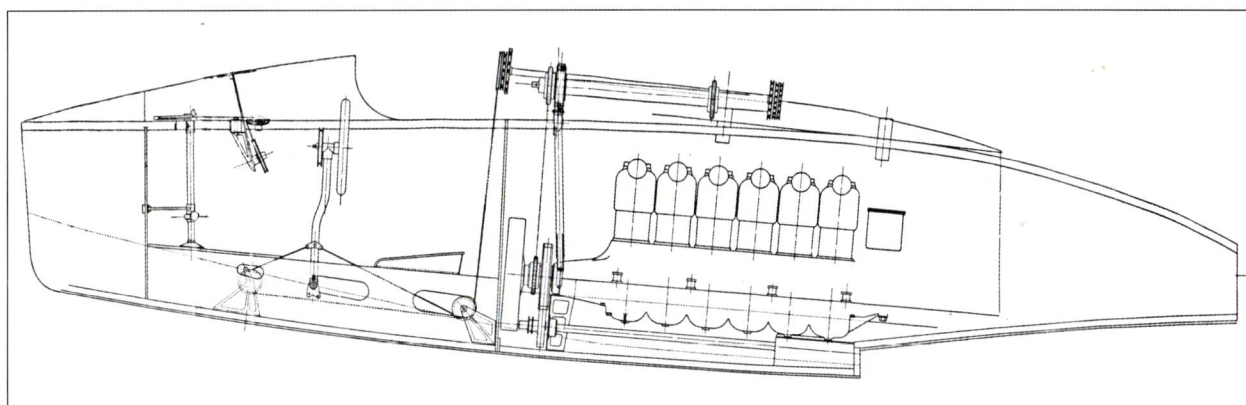

The hull of the S.S.1 showing the engine and twin drives – drawing retraced in 1920

for defence purposes. The experiment ended in tragedy when the converted submarine, M2, sank with the loss of the entire crew when water flooded in through the hangar doors as the aircraft was being prepared for flight.

Metal hulls

The second innovative design, dating from the summer of 1918, was a small flying boat with a fully enclosed cockpit for which the hull was to be constructed entirely of metal. Of roughly the same length and span as the Baby but lacking any clear indication of military features, it may have been intended as a civil two-seater or trainer. Stylistically the basic concept for the hull appears to have been inspired by the Norman Thompson NT2B, a small two-seat trainer with an enclosed cockpit, examples of which Supermarine were engaged in building

under sub-contract for the Admiralty. However the proposal to employ metal construction was a somewhat bold idea for Supermarine given their total lack of expertise in working with this material and growing commitment to wooden boat-building methods.

Fabrication in metal was not a simple process, especially when light aluminium alloys were to be used. The metal plates needed specialised equipment so that they could be heat treated to prepare them for shaping and then given a coating against corrosion, possible by electroplating. This all required time, money and expertise. One can only speculate that someone within the Supermarine design office may have worked at some time on the construction of small metal boats; a possible candidate could be F.T. Pearce, whose initials appear on many Supermarine hull drawings in the late war period. The aircraft

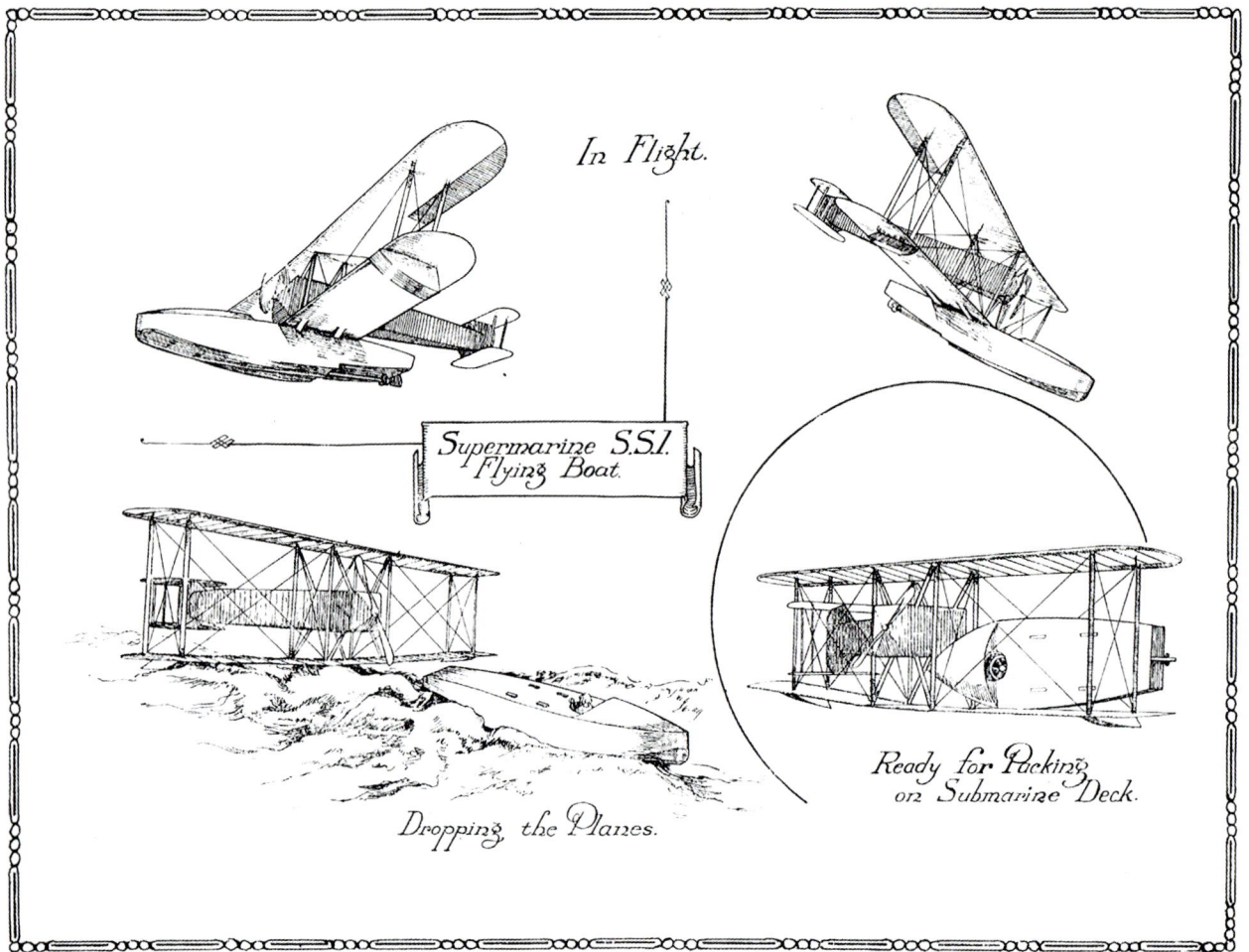

The S.S.1 was featured in Supermarine's 1919 brochure

The Supermarine S.S.1 as it would have looked afloat

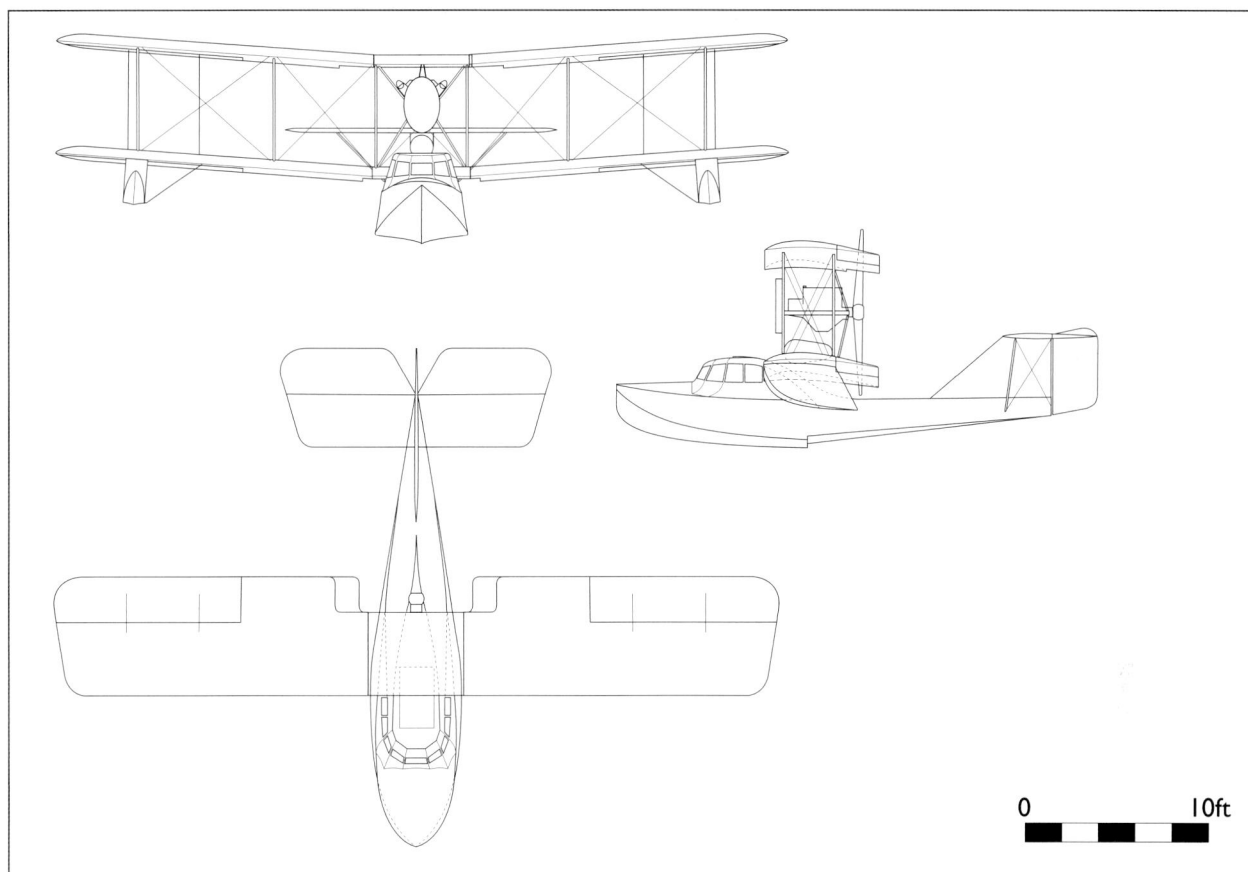

Supermarine unnamed metal hull flying boat scheme – 1918

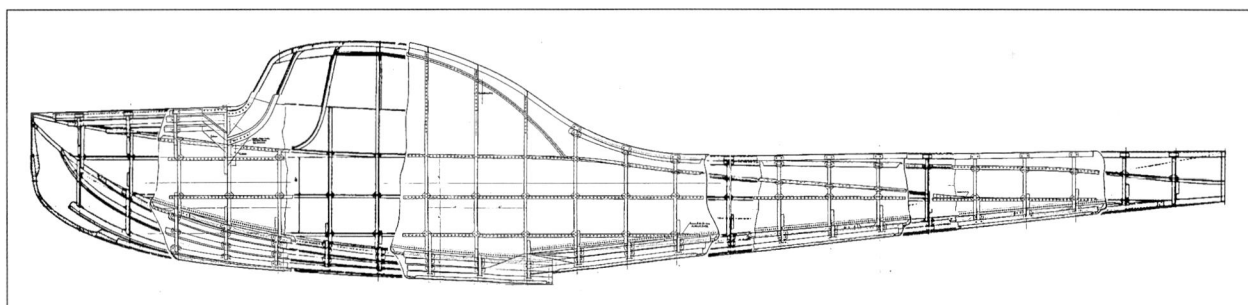

The internal structure of the unnamed metal flying boat

was intended to be powered by a 150hp Hispano-Suiza engine. The span was 40ft, hull length 24ft and weight fully loaded 2880lbs.

Design of the Supermarine flying boat's metal hull had reached a surprisingly advanced stage by August 1918. Details of the internal bulkheads and stringers, arrangement of plating, rivet sizes and patterns had all been finalised, but it went no further and no other metal hull projects were to be proposed by Supermarine until the advent of the Southampton II in late 1925. Quite why a project of this nature had been contemplated just as the war was drawing to a close remains enigmatic. However, if Supermarine had had the resources to proceed with it, which would have required serious commitment, there has to be an outside

chance that the whole future of Supermarine could have developed in an altogether different direction – committing to metal hulled types some seven years earlier than was actually to be the case.

While there had been a small number of metal aircraft, including flying boats, built by German companies during the war no other British aircraft constructors are known to have been contemplating all-metal construction at this time although Short Bros would champion the concept in Britain in the following year and fly their first all-metal aircraft, the Swallow, in 1920. Engineering giant Vickers would commence design work on a vast metal flying boat, the Vigilant, in late 1919 with the intention to build it in their Barrow shipbuilding yard.

2
CHAPTER

The Struggle to Survive

The armistice of 11th November 1918 was more than welcome after four years of carnage and despair but regrettably brought with it a huge wave of unemployment and plunged the country into economic depression. The aircraft industry was hit particularly hard as almost all military production contracts were cancelled abruptly and those that survived, of which there were few, were cut back drastically.

There was no prospect of a civil market yet either since a ban on all non-military flying remained in force. Consequently, large parts of the industry workforce had to be laid off. Scott-Paine was determined to keep Supermarine in business and took immediate steps to help secure its future. First, he invited James Bird, the former Admiralty regional officer responsible supervising aircraft building in the greater Southampton area, to invest and join the board – an offer he accepted. Bird, a qualified naval architect, had established good contacts within the military and government ministries and therefore took his place based in the company's London office to facilitate liaison.

Second, Scott-Paine bought back from the ministry, at little more than material value, a small number of surplus and unused A.D. Flying Boats, the two incomplete N1b Baby aircraft, and a quantity of components and spares. Third, he drew up plans to provide commercial and joyride flights around the south coast of Britain once civil flying resumed, utilising mildly modified A.D. Flying Boats. A

number of ex-RNAS pilots were recruited to fly these. Fourth, he formalised as a new department the portion of the works that had been responsible for building small launches and tenders.

Finally, he forged a marketing alliance with businessman and Member of Parliament Alan Burgoyne to help sell aircraft in foreign markets and to build car bodies for Burgoyne's planned

Supermarine established a Marine Department in 1919 to construct motor launches. One 24ft model was sold to act as a tender to the royal yacht *Victoria and Albert II*

The Sea Lion preparing to take-off for the 1919 Schneider Trophy Contest at Bournemouth

automobile venture. On top of that, he was quick to apply for a number of patents relating to Supermarine's modifications to Hope's hull construction methods (also patented by Hope as the war ended) and other aspects of flying boat design.

On the downside chief draughtsman Richardson had quit in mid-1918 and chief designer Hargreaves followed a year later – weakening the design department considerably. Scott-Paine looked around for replacements for both and also advertised for a draughtsman familiar with stress calculation.

Supermarine was a name and business largely unknown outside of Southampton and the Admiralty so it was important for the company to get noticed. A brochure was issued, titled *"Supermarine" Flying Boats and Seaplanes,* which described the work that had been undertaken by the company during the war and set out plans for the immediate future. Although largely factual, there was a faint whiff here and there of Billings-esque exaggeration. Also included in the brochure, as a first move to attract customers, was a description of a civil conversion of the A.D. Flying Boat, now named Channel, and

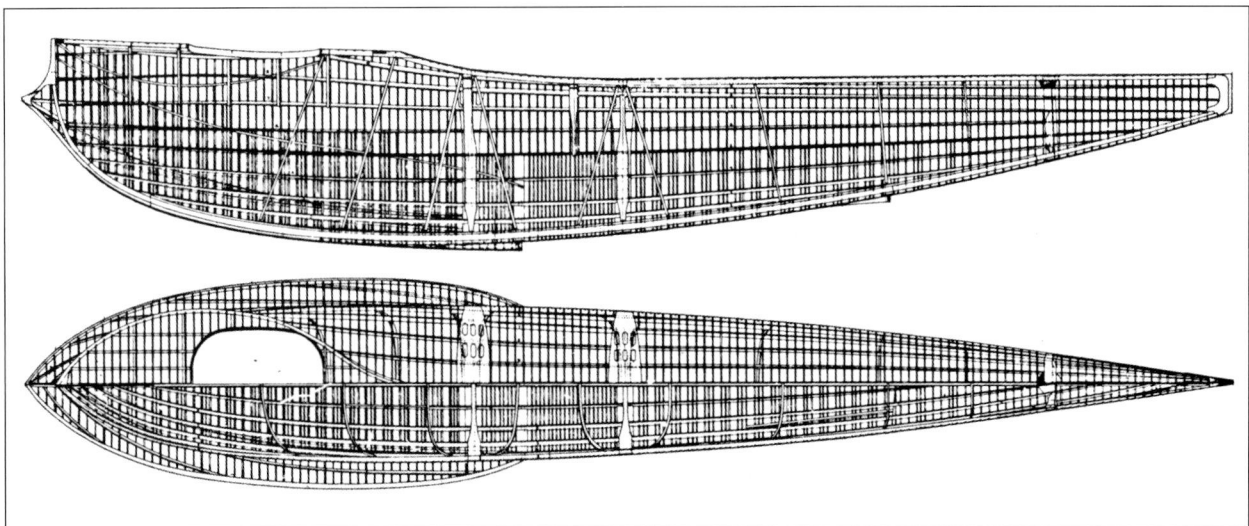

The interior structure of the Sea Lion hull showing the web of light hoops and stringers typical of Linton Hope-type construction

One of the Supermarine Channels provided joyrides for spectators at Bournemouth

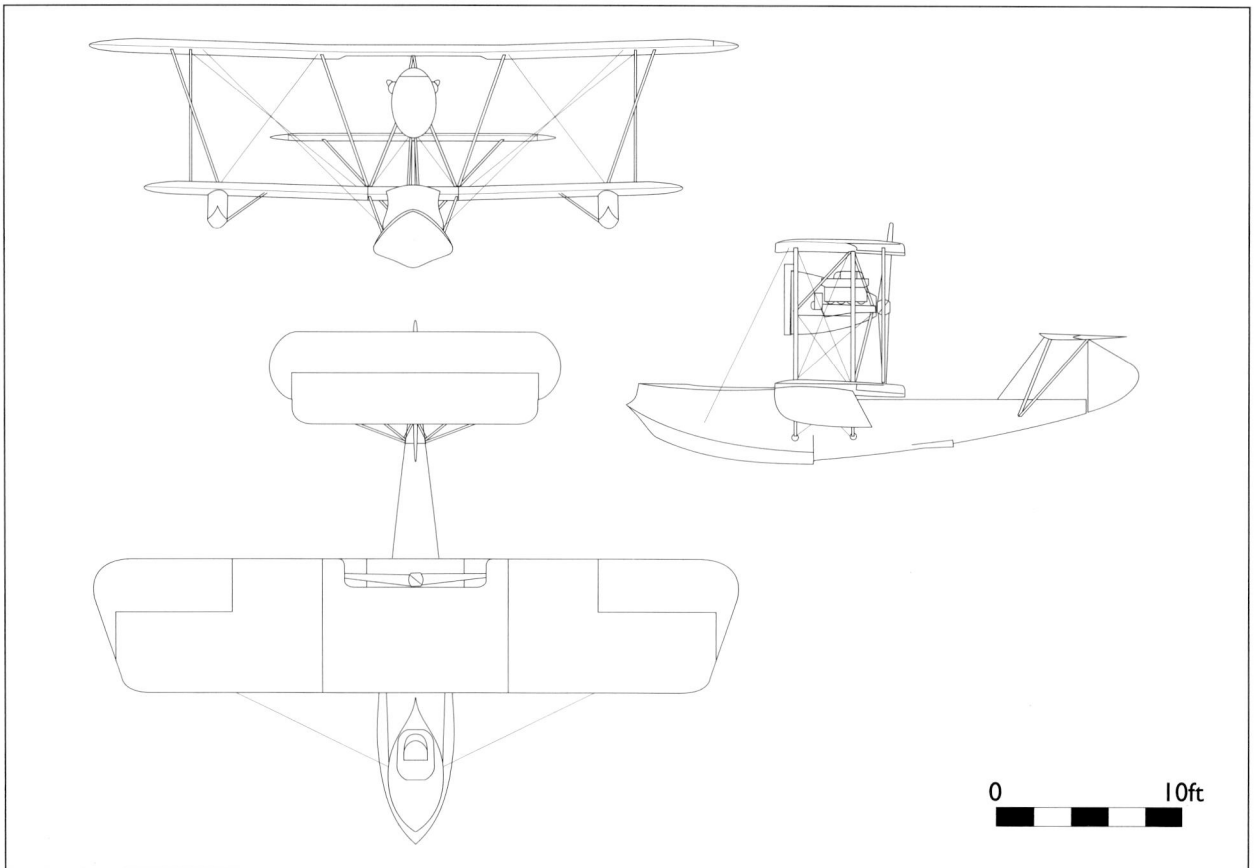

Type A single seat flying boat

examples of the motor launches offered by the Marine Department.

A key part of the brochure restated the company's intent to build a "seaworthy hull that will fly" and even expressed a degree of surprise that during the war, "Notwithstanding the fact that our policy was for the Flying Boat we were given another seaplane to design."

Scott-Paine was presented with two ideal opportunities to promote the products of the company in the late summer of 1919. The government's restriction on civil flying was

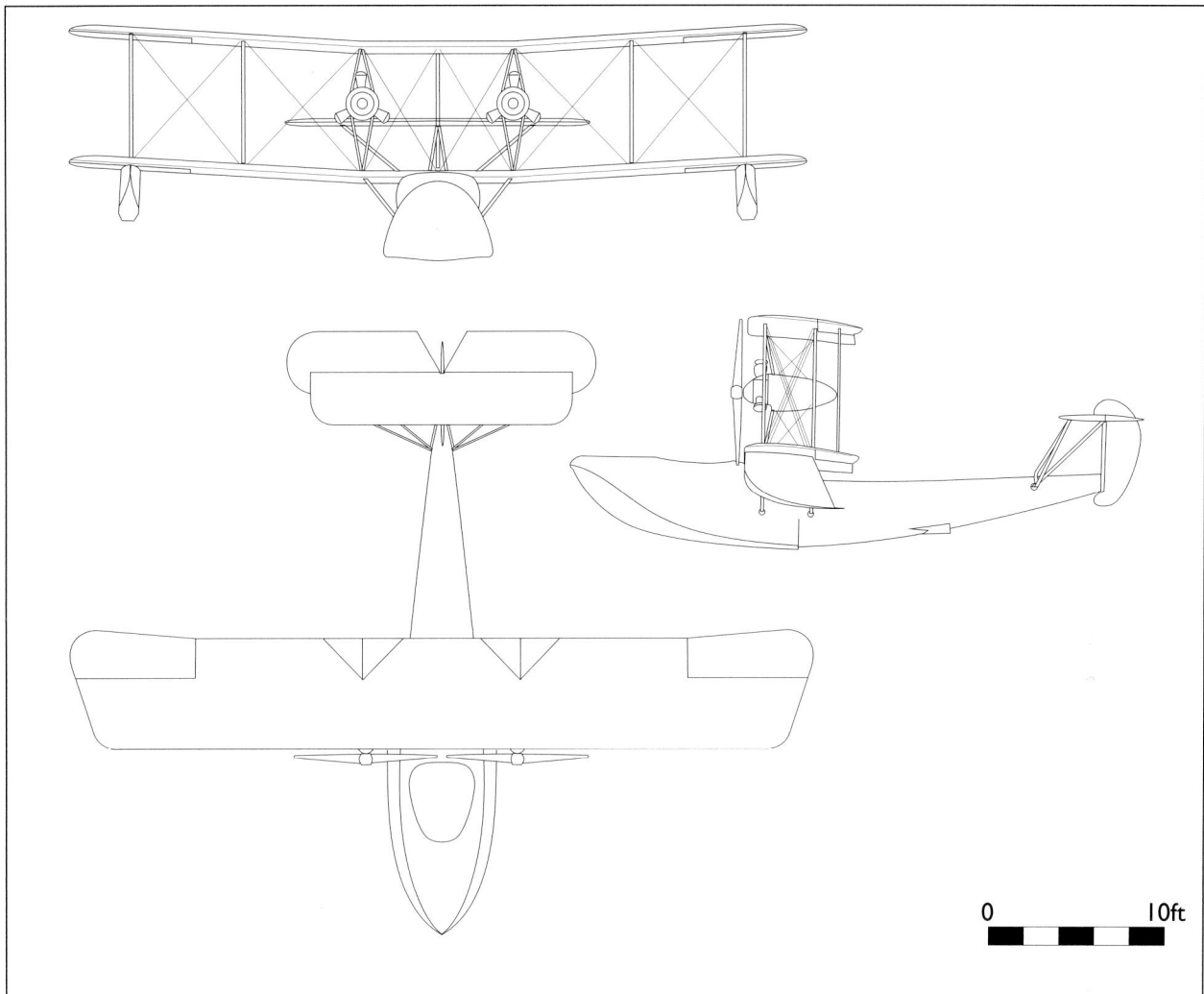

Type B, three seat flying boat

finally lifted in July, allowing him to place ten Supermarine Channels on the civil register and commence commercial flights under the banner of the Supermarine Transport Company. The A.D. Flying Boats had required minimal modification to turn them into Channels, mostly changes to the interior of the forward part of the hull where the pilot's seat and controls had been moved rearwards in order to accommodate three folding seats for the passengers in the bow. At the Cowes Regatta, held in early August, the company sold tickets for sightseeing flights and a few days later inaugurated a modest scheduled service flying between Southampton and Cowes on the Isle of Wight, followed by a second route to Bournemouth. A few charter flights were also made to ports on the northern coast of France. His claim that this was the first commercial flying boat service in the world is open to debate, but it was certainly in the vanguard.

In September the Royal Aero Club (RAeC) hosted the annual Schneider Trophy Contest. Howard Pixton had won the last event in 1914 flying a Sopwith Tabloid on floats and the contest had been postponed from 1915 on due to the war. The club had laid out a course in Bournemouth Bay, which was within easy reach of Supermarine's works, and Scott-Paine informed the contest organisers of his intent to apply for a place on the British team of three aircraft.

Napier provided a Lion engine and the new Supermarine racer, named Sea Lion, was more likely than not a quick and simple adaptation of the incomplete third Baby, N61; resources were too tight for it to have been a completely new build. The Sea Lion had to secure its place in the team via a fly-off against a seaplane entered by Avro, and while their speed in the air proved to be broadly comparable the superior water handling of the Sea Lion won the place for Supermarine.

The aircraft was accompanied to Bournemouth by a couple of Channels for the use of the support crew and to provide joyrides for the spectators and generate a little more income. Scott-Paine had

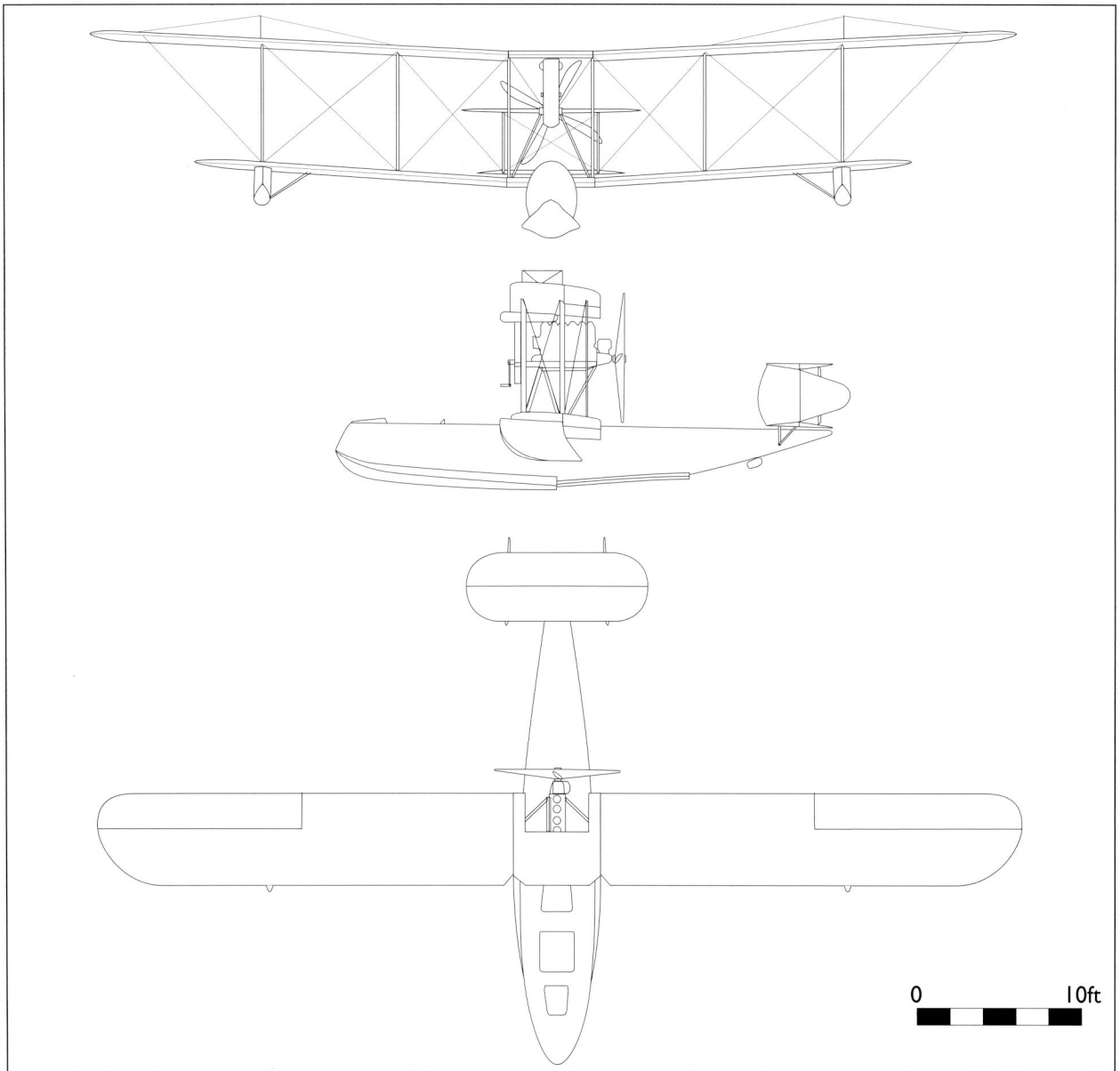

Type C, four seat Channel flying boat

arranged for the racer and one of the Channels to have SUPERMARINE painted in two foot high white letters down their sides. On paper, the Sea Lion could have been a serious contender for the contest win but fog and RAeC confusion turned the whole event into a farce. The Sea Lion was holed and subsequently sank when it hit a submerged object while taking-off after the pilot had been forced to land out on the course in order to get his bearings. The whole debacle ended with only one aircraft, the Italian Savoia S.13, completing the course. However, even this was judged subsequently to have skipped one turn marker on each lap and was disqualified, with the result that the entire contest was declared null and void. There was a great deal of criticism expressed by all the teams after the contest.

Supermarine's 1919 brochure was supplemented towards the end of the year by a two-part article published in issues of *The Aeroplane* which served to advertise other new aircraft types that the company offered. Type A was a single engine, single seat high performance flying boat, once again more than likely derived from the incomplete third Baby which had then flown in the Schneider Trophy Contest as the Sea Lion. Probably intended to be powered by a Hispano engine it would have a spritely top speed of 130mph.

Type B was an all-new twin engine, three seat flying boat for training purposes. Its hull bow profile, designed to deflect spray away from the cockpit and similar to the alternative Baby scheme used for the of the Sea Lion, was the subject of a patent. The engines were three-cylinder Cosmos

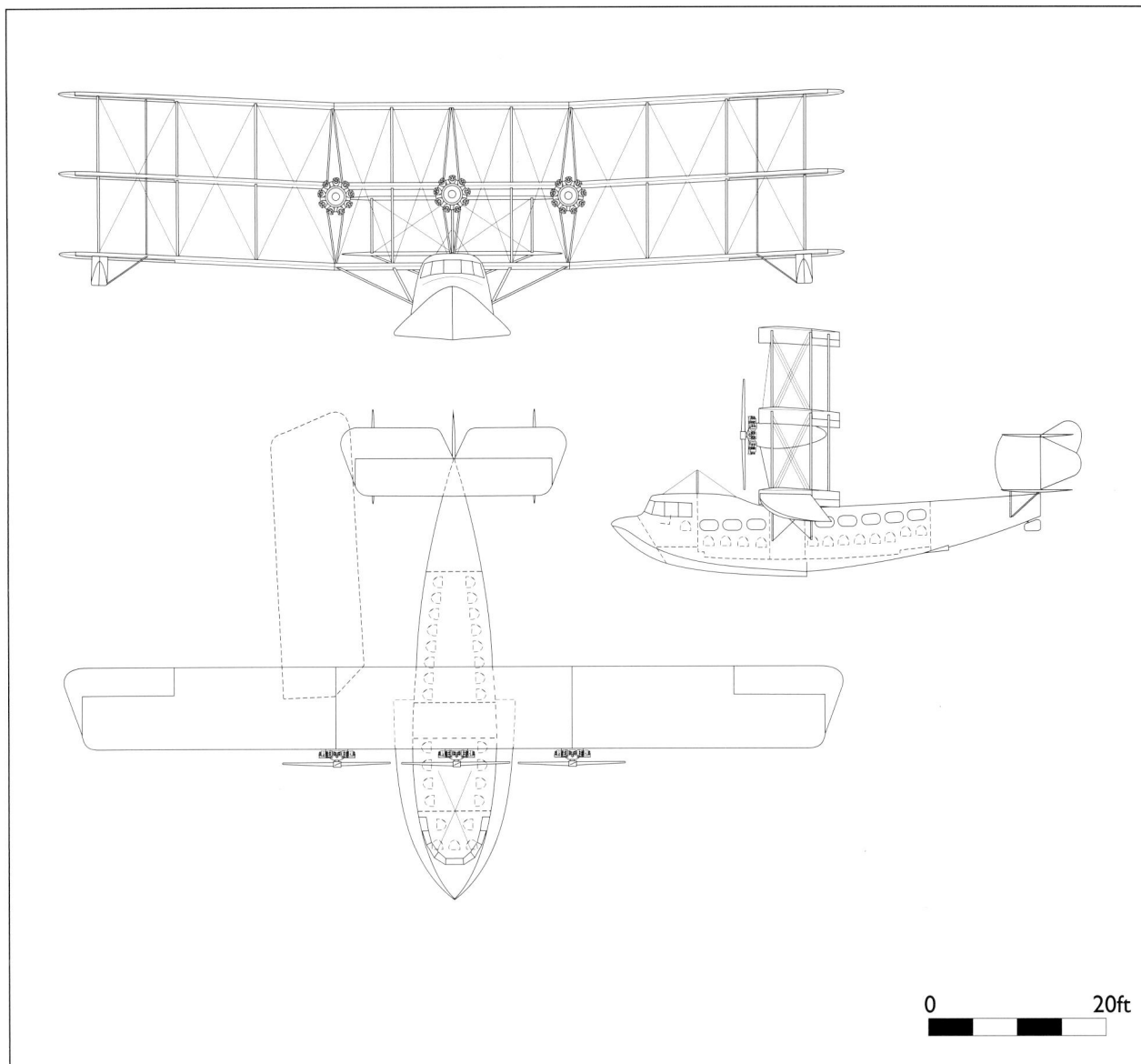

Type D 'Dolphin' 24-seat civil airliner

Lucifer air-cooled radials, giving the aircraft a speed of 90mph. Type C was the Channel, powered by a 160hp Beardmore engine.

While these three offerings were all ready to take orders straight off the drawing board, the article also mentioned but did not illustrate Type D, a long-distance mail and commercial triplane flying boat capable of carrying 24 passengers. The cabin was arranged with inward-facing seats along both sides of a wide central aisle. Cruising speed was estimated as 98mph and endurance was four hours, giving a range of around 350 miles. It was to be powered by three of the new Cosmos Jupiter nine-cylinder air-cooled radials or Napier Lion 12-cylinder 'broad arrow' water cooled motors.

The project was referred to in the article as the 'Dolphin type', although that name does not actually appear on Supermarine's drawing. A scaled-down

version of this design was drawn up in December and named as the 'Shark Type', and would appear to be the first project signed-off by Reginald Mitchell. It was to be powered by two Rolls-Royce Eagles and could carry 18 passengers. A military conversion was also considered with five gun positions and with torpedo carriers under each wing. It was the start of a design thread that would run for several years.

It is a sign of the highest optimism and aspiration that many aircraft companies chose to put forward ideas for large, in some cases extremely large, civil flying boats in 1919. Supermarine's offerings actually looked quite plausible alongside some of the others. The Phoenix Pulex, for example, was to be powered by eight engines coupled in groups of four to power two gigantic propellers. Vickers' all-metal Vigilant had its eight engines coupled in four tractor pairs. Gosport intended to build a civilian version of

The Supermarine Dolphin – one of several large civil flying boat types proposed by the British aircraft industry in 1919

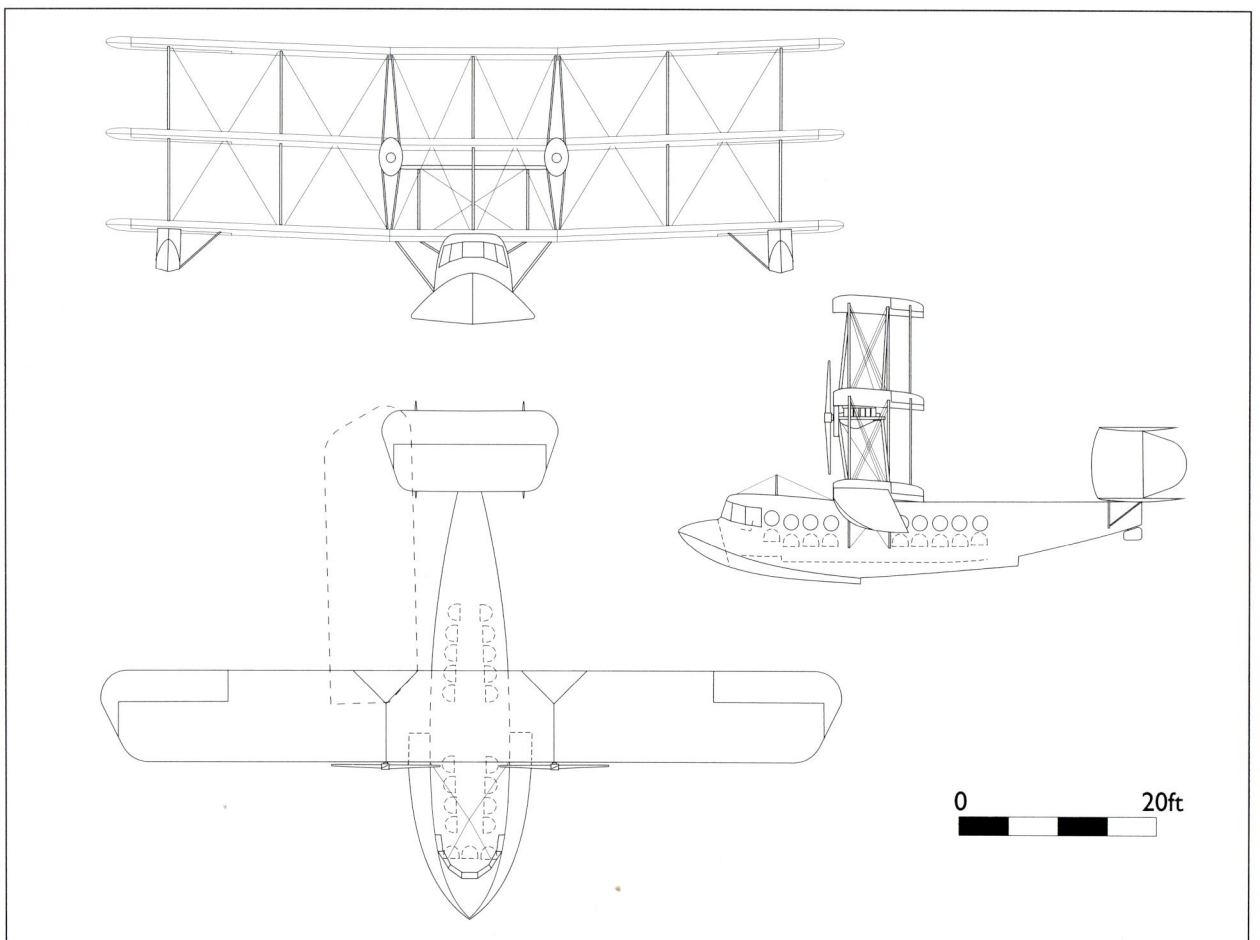

Shark Type 18-seat civil airliner triplane, also proposed as a torpedo bomber

the RNAS Felixstowe Fury, the largest flying boat yet flown, and Short Bros had a twin-hull triplane scheme which was designed to fly the Atlantic.

Neither of Supermarine's triplane projects progressed beyond initial layout drawings, their intent probably more to demonstrate ambition and capability than to find an immediate market.

And so 1919 drew to a close. Supermarine had managed to limp through the year but its future was still far from secure.

Post-War Flying Boats

3

During the war the development of flying boats in Britain had been dominated by the work carried out at the Admiralty's own facilities at the Isle of Grain and Felixstowe, under the leadership of John Porte. Porte had been invalided out of the Navy in 1911 after developed tuberculosis and then took up flying, obtained his Aviator's Certificate and acquired a job as test pilot with White and Thompson, a company based on the English south coast that had acquired a licence to build Curtiss aircraft in the UK.

Porte moved to the USA in 1913 and worked alongside Glenn Curtiss on a project to build an aircraft that could to cross the Atlantic. This flying boat, the Wanamaker-Curtiss Atlantic, was intended to win the prize of £10,000 put up by the *Daily Mail* for the first direct Atlantic crossing and would have been piloted by Porte had not war intervened. Porte returned to the UK immediately and re-enlisted to aid in aircraft development for the RNAS.

Perceiving the potential value of patrol flying boats to the service, he approached the Admiralty leadership to make his case and was granted approval to purchase two aircraft of the Atlantic type from Curtiss. These aircraft then provided the starting point for the vast majority of flying boats that were to serve with the RNAS, although after, it has to be said, a great deal of redesign and modification.

Porte worked hard to refine an aircraft type that was never intended for military service and, swapping ideas back and forth with Curtiss, this resulted in the Felixstowe family of twin engine flying boats and their Curtiss counterparts. Among the Admiralty's aircraft development staff, however, were a number of qualified naval architects and they were, to say the least, far from impressed with the construction methods that Porte and Curtiss had employed.

The Atlantic was described publicly, post-war, as "...extraordinarily heavy and badly built, but in addition she was a very poor hydroplane.." and "...probably the worst example of boat building that could be imagined...". This was harsh but not entirely surprising as Porte had never designed an aircraft of any sort before, let alone a flying boat, and Curtiss' experience with hulls came mostly from empirical experimentation and was not based on boat building standards.

Pressure was brought to bear on the Admiralty authorities by this group with the result that they authorised a parallel development programme within the A.A.D under Linton Hope to produce flying boats with hulls that drew their construction inspiration from racing yachts and motor launches. As noted previously, the first practical result of this programme was the A.D. Flying Boat.

In addition to Hope's direct design work with the A.A.D, which had terminated when the organisation disbanded under political pressure in 1917, Specification N.3(b) was issued by the Admiralty to industry in 1917 for a twin-engine flying boat to supplement or replace the Felixstowe types The first contract to be awarded was for the Phoenix P5 Cork, which had a Linton Hope-designed hull, followed by the Short N3 Cromarty and the Vickers Valentia. A second Specification, N.4, for a much larger four-engine flying boat for fleet cooperation and open-sea reconnaissance, was awarded to Fairey, in the role of project coordinator. Three examples were ordered, the hulls all subcontracted to shipbuilders and of differing designs. The second and third of these, *Atalanta* and *Titania*, also had Linton Hope-type hulls.

In addition to these specifications, further contracts went to Short Bros and to Saunders for experimental hulls for comparative trials fitted with Felixstowe F.5 flight surfaces. This all represented a considerable investment in flying boat research, both in terms of hull hydrodynamics and of construction methods. Only the P5 Cork had been completed before the armistice but construction of the other project prototypes was allowed to continue, albeit at a very low priority.

Once wartime reporting restrictions had lifted, several articles were published in the aviation press drawing attention to the deficiencies of the Porte and Curtiss hulls, as quoted above, repeating the arguments that had taken place earlier within the Admiralty. As wartime military aircraft the Felixstowe and Curtiss flying boats had served with considerable distinction and had chalked-up numerous successes in the last year and a half of the war – engaging and destroying submarines, Zeppelins and aircraft – but, the authors argued, as examples of marine aircraft construction they left much to be desired.

Foremost among these critics was David Nicolson, like Linton Hope a naval architect and former RNAS officer, who in the war years had been tasked with supervising aircraft construction and was now employed by the Air Ministry as chief production officer for flying boats. His word therefore carried considerable weight. Writing in 1919, he compared Porte's methods and designs to those of Hope, which he regarded as vastly superior. Hope himself also wrote on hull construction in 1920, judging Porte's type unfavourably against his own and those of other qualified boat builders.

Baker, on the staff at the NPL, summarised the results of the research work that the organisation had carried out in the large William Froude water tank using hull models, alongside comparisons with full-scale tests carried out at the RNAS station on the Isle of Grain. Porte was unable to reply to any of this criticism as in 1919 he succumbed to the tuberculosis he had fought for years. Hope, too, died the following year.

John Rennie, Porte's deputy at Felixstowe and future head of flying boat design with Blackburn, returned to the subject in 1923 to defend their work, only to be met with another barrage of negative comments. Porte had done important work in providing the RNAS with flying boats capable of effective patrol and enemy engagement, but he was undeniably less proficient in designing robust structures and hulls with good hydrodynamic qualities.

1920 – A new hope

In many ways 1920 looked as if it would turn out to be even worse for the industry than 1919, the tentative shoots of optimism that had sprouted around the resumption of civil flying were beginning to wither, the military market was negligible and the future appeared increasingly bleak. Both Sopwith and British and Colonial had been wound up under the burden of excess profit taxes and it would be some time before they re-organised as new companies, Hawker Engineering and Bristol Aircraft respectively. Grahame-White failed to regain his Hendon airfield from the government, which had requisitioned it for the RFC during the war, and threw in the towel as an aircraft builder. British Nieuport and others went much the same way. This was not the climate within which to allocate scarce design resources to speculative projects.

Supermarine was carrying a debt of £20,000, which was considered manageable for now, so Scott-Paine concentrated on selling the existing stock of Channels, starting with the ten that had joined the civil register in mid-1919. These were offered either as two-seat dual control trainers or three or four seat passenger carriers. The design of the removable metal framework that held the seats and controls within the hull made interchange between the two types a simple process that could be completed in a couple of hours.

Early sales were encouraging. Three civil Channels went to Det Norske Luftfartrederi and another four military types to the Kongelige Norske Luftforsvaret in Norway. Several demonstrations of the aircraft were made for government officials and for a delegation from Japan, which purchased one aircraft. Single customers in New Zealand, Sweden and Chile bought one each.

Reginald Mitchell was confirmed as the company's new chief engineer and designer in early 1920, replacing Hargreaves. One of his first tasks was to create a conversion kit which could bring the Channel up to MkII specification, allowing the installation of more powerful engines and bringing improvements to the method for mounting and bracing the wings to the hull.

It was also necessary to prepare two aircraft for exhibition on Supermarine's stand at the Olympia Aero Show that July. One was to be a standard three-passenger civil Channel fitted with a detachable cabin top with windows, while the other was a new single seater called the Sea King, to replace the Type A/Sea Lion – which was no longer available, having been holed, flipped onto its back and sunk during the Schneider Trophy Contest the previous year. Drawings of both aircraft were issued to the press for pre-show publication. Curiously, the Sea King depicted in these drawings, dated March, looks to be a standard Baby hull fitted with unequal span wings and fin, similar to those built for the Sea Lion, but this was not to be the aircraft that Supermarine actually exhibited. Judging from photographs, the Sea King looks in all probability to have been just the second Baby, ex-N60, to which a raised foredeck coving had been added around the cockpit to deflect spray. It was, as an article in *The Aeroplane* expressed it "…either a thoroughly sporting little vehicle for the single or unhappily married man, or is a useful small fast patrol machine for Naval work along troublesome coasts".

The most probable reason for the sudden change in exhibit became apparent in April when the Air Ministry issued the full rules and specifications for the civil aircraft design competitions it was

The Supermarine exhibits at Olympia in July 1920 – the Channel and Sea King

sponsoring, scheduled for September. The one that had caught Scott-Paine's attention was for an amphibian to carry a minimum of two passengers "...the best type of Float Seaplane or Boat Seaplane which will be safe, comfortable and economical for air travel and capable of alighting on and rising from land as well as water". This would require the rapid design and construction of a completely new aircraft, an updated Channel no longer being deemed to be appropriate, and this effort would occupy the full attention of the design and workshop staff.

Scott-Paine judged this opportunity to have a higher priority than the exhibits for Olympia, not least because the Air Ministry was offering cash prizes. Supermarine placed advertisements in the press seeking experienced woodworkers. To provide an indication of the amount of work involved and the urgency of the project, Supermarine said later that the hull for a Channel, broadly comparable to that of the new aircraft project, took five and a half weeks to build, employing three skilled men and two boys working a 47-hour week. The new Amphibian, by comparison, took just four and a half weeks for the entire aircraft from the point that drawing commenced until the aircraft was flown.

There was no time, nor, to be truthful, expertise, to consider anything other than a further variation of Supermarine's current aircraft type designs. Consequently it had to have a Linton Hope-type hull, with which the workforce were now quite familiar, biplane wings of unequal span like a scaled-up, two bay version of those on the Sea Lion, and a single fin and tailplane, also as on the Sea Lion. It is an interesting footnote that the layout drawings that the company issued to the press in September had been drawn personally by Mitchell. The aircraft was never given a name – Supermarine just referred to it as the Amphibian.

For the aircraft to be able to operate from land, Mitchell had to devise a retractable undercarriage. In his design the undercarriage would be attached to the same brackets on the hull and lower wing as the wing bracing struts. The whole undercarriage unit was hinged at its top end on the wing and when lowered it locked in place by engaging with catches on the hull brackets. In order to raise the wheels, the catches on the hull had to be released first – the then the whole undercarriage assembly could be pivoted outwards and upwards on the wing attachment hinges, pulled by a rather clumsy arrangement of cables and pulleys. It was the best that could be

The Supermarine Amphibian on the slipway at Woolston and afloat prior to the Air Ministry competition at Felixstowe

achieved in the short time available yet it was quite effective.

Only three aircraft made it to Martlesham Heath in time for the competition: the Supermarine Amphibian and Vickers Viking flying boats, and a Fairey III seaplane. Both of Supermarine's rivals were powered by 450hp Napier Lion engines, giving them an immediate advantage over the 350hp Rolls-Royce Eagle-powered Amphibian. The robust double-skin hull construction of the Amphibian meant that it was also some 500lb heavier than the others. Nevertheless its overall performance outstripped the Fairey with ease and it was inferior to the Vickers only in speed.

Speed had a relatively high value under the points scoring system devised by the Air Ministry, so once all the tests had been completed the Vickers Viking was deemed the winner. Nevertheless, the Amphibian had performed well and garnering high praise for being equipped with numerous useful features; consequently its prize money for second place was doubled to £8,000, a fine return for the diligent work of Mitchell and the Supermarine team. Plans were afoot to re-engine the aircraft with a Napier Lion prior to seeking sales with the airlines but it was wrecked in a landing accident, on land, on 13th October, just weeks after the contest.

Military flying boats

Following the Amphibian on Mitchell's drawing board was a new military flying boat in roughly the same class as the A.D. Flying Boat. It was an adaptable two or three seat design offered as an amphibian and appropriate for a wide range of shore or ship-based applications; fleet spotter/reconnaissance, bomber or fighter. Some who had flown the A.D. Flying Boat thought its hull had been too small, prone to shipping a lot of spray and rather low on reserve buoyancy. Apparently it had also proven to be 500lb above the original design weight and underpowered. All of these perceived weaknesses would be addressed by the new project.

An initial two-seat scheme with the engine as a pusher, as in the A.D. Flying Boat, was drawn up in October 1920 as an Amphibian Flying Boat for Ship's Work and remained unnamed. By November a refined version, with tractor engine and three seats, bears the name Seal MkII – although there appears to be no record of there ever having been a MkI. Unlike the A.D. Flying Boat, the Seal MkII had its engine, a 450hp Napier Lion, mounted as a tractor unit in order to be able to locate the second and third crew members to the rear of the wings. The hull had a single layer of mahogany planking, compared to the Amphibian's two, to reduce weight.

Mitchell also revised the design of his retractable undercarriage mechanism completely, the activation now via span-wise screw-jacks within the lower wing centre section that drew the top of the legs inwards, pivoting the undercarriage unit at the lower hull attachment end to raise the wheels. This system was both more robust and more reliable than the quick-fix cable-activated system on the Amphibian.

The Sea King MkII and Seal outside Supermarine's Woolston works

Stereo photographs of the first two Seagulls N158 and N159 nearing completion in the Supermarine Works

Contrary to what some have written, the Seal was neither based on nor derived from the Amphibian. The two shared no parts or design features beside both having Hope-based hull construction. It was a unique design and formed the basis for many projects to come.

When Supermarine submitted the Seal MkII design for consideration, the Royal Air Force (RAF) had only just passed its second birthday. Its leadership were working hard to define its role in the post-war world, while fending off pressure from the Army and Navy to regain control of their aerial forces. Stocks of fighters and bombers were high, indeed large quantities were surplus to requirements and there appeared, at first, to be little need for an amphibian. However the Navy was pushing ahead with plans for a small fleet of aircraft carriers and the best mix of aircraft types required to serve on them was, as yet, unclear. The Seal was given an opportunity to prove itself and an order was placed for a single prototype, Air Ministry Specification 7/20 being written around it. The aircraft, registered N146, flew in May 1921.

Early service tests found that the Seal was a little unstable in yaw, improved by the fitment of an enlarged fin. It was also noted that there was a slight tendency to porpoise under certain load and sea conditions. Neither issue was of serious concern, however, and test pilot reports were largely favourable. On the strength of these evaluations two further, and slightly improved, examples were ordered. These had a hull lengthened by 2ft 4in, beefed-up bracing of the fin and tailplane, and a small amount of sweep added to the wings to restore balance. The construction and

details of the two aircraft, both near complete and registered as N158 and N159, was documented by the company in a series of stereo photographs which were to be distributed to prospective customers. On these photographs the aircraft are identified as Seals but prior to launch, in early 1922, they had been renamed Seagulls.

With Seal and Seagull construction under way, the Sea King was brought back into the workshop and revised once more as an amphibian fighter. With new coving around the cockpit, improved fin and rudder, Seal-type retractable undercarriage, and a Hispano 300hp engine it was renamed Sea King MkII. Together the Seagull and Sea King would become the template for the majority of Supermarine projects in the early 1920s.

Military expansion

Notwithstanding all of the experimental work on flying boats now spread around numerous aircraft companies and shipyards, for a brief period during 1921 and 1922 Supermarine found itself almost without significant competition for new flying boat designs. Vickers and Saunders had dissolved their wartime collaboration and neither had yet managed to get their separated marine aircraft design divisions fully functional.

English Electric, formed from the amalgamation of Phoenix and other industrial companies, continued working on the P.5 Cork but was giving serious consideration to withdrawing from the aircraft business entirely, and Fairey, slowly completing its N.4 prototypes, showed a distinct preference to concentrate on aircraft other than flying boats.

Blackburn, later to be a major competitor, had as yet neither a marine aircraft design department nor an experienced designer for these types. That left only Short Bros and despite aiming to stay in the flying boat business that company was preoccupied with the development of metal construction methods. It was a time to grasp any opportunities that came along, although there was little optimism that anything significant would.

The RAF was now beginning to clarify its plans for the future, although it remained seriously constrained by both limited funds and manpower. Emphasis was placed primarily on a strategic bomber force, secondarily on defensive fighters, and then on more general purpose types earmarked for policing duties in overseas territories. Coastal defence flying boats barely got a look in, which left aircraft for the RAF's new carrier squadrons as the only obvious, but distinctly limited, market. The prototype contracts issued to Supermarine were welcome but whether this would result in a production order was still far from clear.

Carrier fighters

The Directorate of Research at the Air Ministry issued Specification DofR Type 6 in June 1921 for a single seat fighter amphibian to serve on aircraft carriers. At this point only HMS *Argus* remained in commission but two more, *Eagle* and *Hermes*, were

scheduled to join the fleet in a couple of years. The small number of in-service carrier fighters were Sopwith 2F.1 Camels, standard land fighter types that had been modified for naval service, and Parnall Panthers, built to Specification N.2A in 1917 and coming from the drawing board of ex-A.A.D designer Harold Bolas. Both were due to be replaced from 1922 by the Nieuport Nightjar, a modified version of the Nighthawk land-based fighter powered by a Bentley B.R.2 rotary engine as used in the Camel – which was both cheap and plentiful. This was the first specification issued post-war to call for a completely new design of navy fighter, rather than an adaptation of an existing land fighter. It was assumed that the projects tendered would be conventional biplane scout types with the option to replace the wheeled undercarriage with floats, but Supermarine had other ideas.

Despite the lack of interest shown by the RAF in the Baby, the Sea King MkII and the various projects derived from the same basic scheme, Supermarine remained undeterred from pursuing this line of fighter type. It was fairly obvious, however, that yet another design based on the template of the 1917 Baby was hardly likely to receive much in the way of consideration. Mitchell was therefore tasked with designing a small flying boat that would be more appropriate for the future.

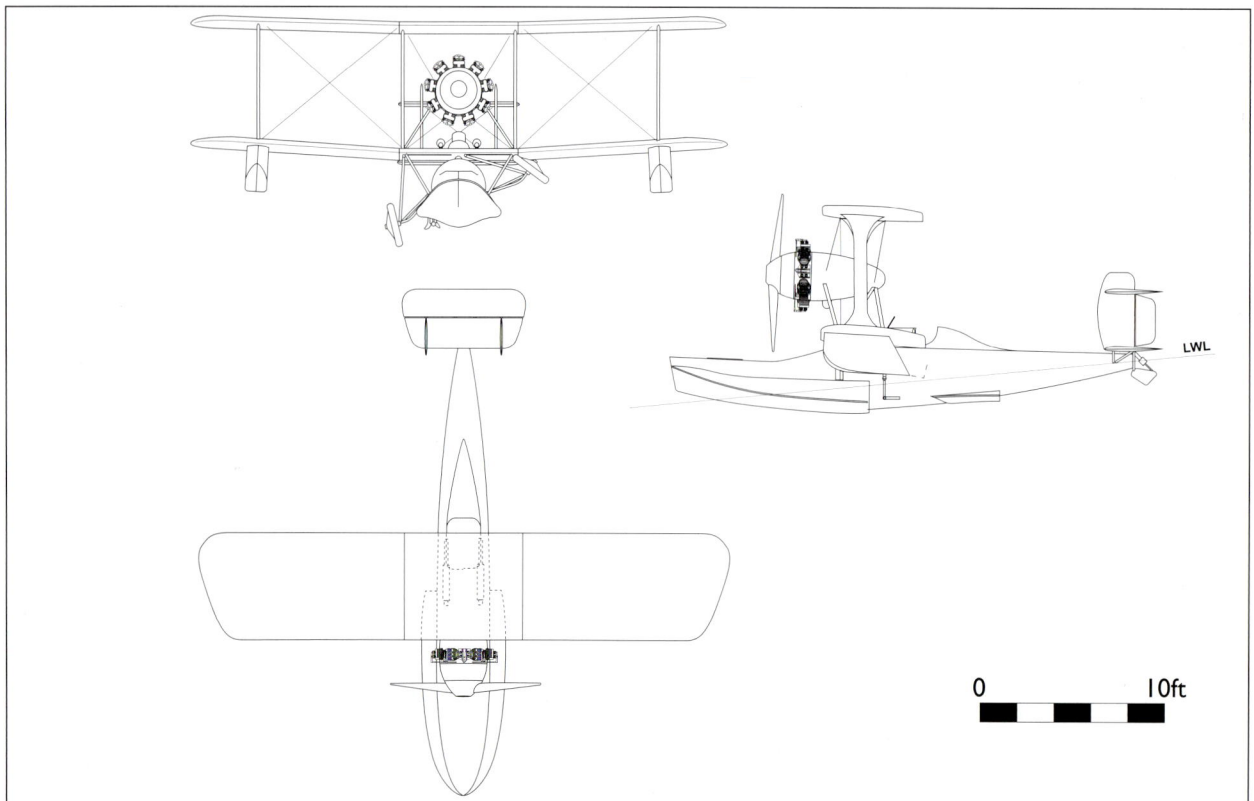

Supermarine amphibian shipborne fighter to meet the requirements of DofR Type 6

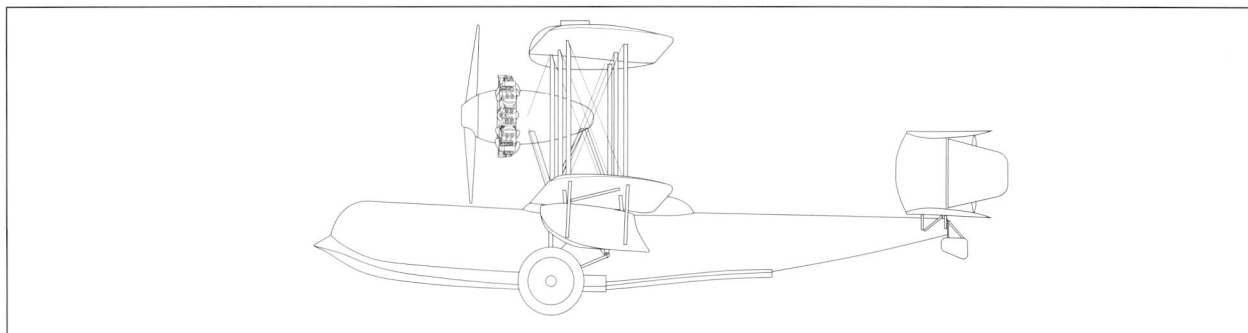

School Amphibian – a trainer to support the DofR Type 6 amphibian fighter

This was no easy matter. There were size limitations imposed on navy aircraft because they needed to fit within carrier lifts and hangers, and they had to be fast enough for combat yet able to go slowly enough for safe deck landings. They also had to meet the basic armament requirement and all of this left little room for manoeuvre design-wise. Yet Mitchell made a serious attempt to effectively break the mould. Superficially at least, he seems to have drawn inspiration from the company's firstborn, the Supermarine P.B.1.

The ubiquitous elliptical section, cigar-shaped Linton Hope hull had to undergo a radical rethink. The cockpit, in sharp contrast to that of the Baby-based family, had been moved from low in the nose to a position aligned with the trailing edge of the lower wing. The pilot sat slightly higher in the hull than in previous designs and was protected by streamlined fairings fore and aft.

While retaining the usual elliptical section hull profile rearwards from the cockpit to the stern, the fore section was re-profiled, the top sloping down dramatically ahead of the cockpit before extending forward to meet the planing bottom in a shallow boat prow. Total hull length was 24ft 9in, just 9in more than that of the Baby. The planing surfaces were a standard design, very similar to those on the Baby and Sea King MkII. Supermarine drawings show that the aircraft would have sat very low in the water.

The single bay equal-span biplane wings were not designed to fold. They had a span of 29ft, which was 1ft 6in less than the Baby, and were braced by 'I' struts, one inboard and one outboard on each side . The wingtip floats were of the standard Baby type, attached flush with the lower wing. The small tail surfaces were of biplane form with double fins and rudders that appear to have been derived from those of the Channel. As the aircraft was to be carrier-based it was fitted with Mitchell's usual form of retractable undercarriage, described as an improved type but looking to be of the same design as that fitted on the Sea King MkII.

The engine, a choice of either a 400hp Bristol Jupiter or a 300hp Siddeley Jaguar air-cooled radial,

was installed as a tractor unit in an egg-shaped nacelle mounted mid-gap and slightly ahead of the wings where it drove a propeller of 8ft 3in diameter. The nacelle also housed the oil and fuel tanks; in Baby-based aircraft the fuel was carried in a cylindrical tank within the hull beneath the wings. The two Vickers machine guns, one of 0.303 calibre with 800 rounds and the other of 0.5 calibre with 200 rounds, sat on the cowling ahead of the cockpit, their breaches within easy reach of the pilot.

HMS *Argus* was fitted with an experimental aircraft arrestor system that consisted of an array of long fore and aft wires spaced 9in apart that could be raised 15in above the deck. These served to keep the aircraft straight as it landed so as to prevent slewing off the deck. Special hooks fixed to the aircraft undercarriage caught these wires to further stabilise and slow it down. On Supermarine's flying boat these hooks were fitted to the hull sides as partially retractable units that were extended when the undercarriage was lowered.

It soon transpired that the arrestor wire system was fundamentally flawed. Pilots often couldn't tell whether the hooks had engaged or not – and if they engaged asymmetrically the aircraft could drop to one side, damaging a wingtip. Another idea tried aboard Argus was to lower its lift slightly, so the landing aircraft's undercarriage could bump down into it.

Inevitably both systems took their toll on aircraft undercarriages. No doubt the arrestor wires would have done a superlative job of slicing into the hull of the low-slung Supermarine flying boat. The fighter project was a non-starter.

Supermarine proposed that, in parallel to its fighter, a dedicated amphibian trainer derived from the Channel could be built – utilising the same Siddeley Jaguar engine as the fighter. But this, too, was rejected.

DofR Type 6 was updated first as Specification 7/21 and subsequently as 6/22, which was written to cover the two aircraft selected for prototype construction: the Fairey Flycatcher and the Parnall Plover, both conventional biplanes with fixed undercarriages.

4
CHAPTER

Flying Boat Torpedo Bombers

In 1916, following a suggestion from Porte, the Admiralty had ordered the construction of a number of specialised lighters designed to carry Felixstowe flying boats. These could then be towed out to sea behind a fleet destroyer, extending the range of the aircraft on board and bringing the German naval bases on the North Sea coast within reach. The lighter could be flooded at the stern to launch and recover the flying boat.

All the early tests of this process were deemed successful and a contract was issued to build 50 or so examples, delivery beginning in early summer 1918. A few operational sorties had been made prior to the Armistice, not all successful, but the practicality of lighter launch and recovery had nevertheless been proven. The lighters were also used, with the addition of a short deck, to carry Sopwith Camels as part of the UK defence system to counter the Zeppelin and bomber threat before they could reach the mainland.

Post-war the idea of a specialised bomber/torpedo flying boat that could be deployed with the

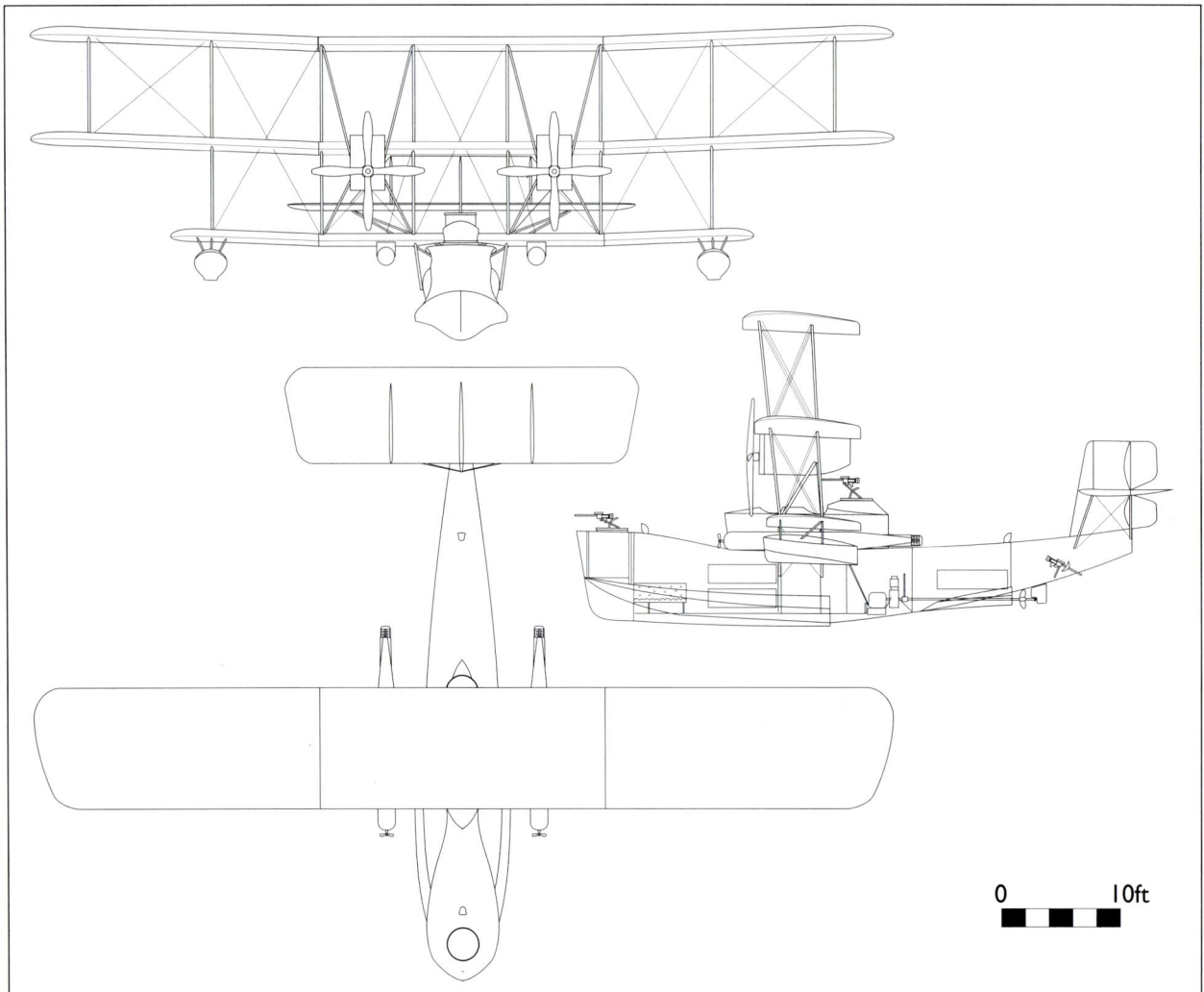

0   10ft

Supermarine triplane Torpedo Carrier 1921

fleet, possibly aboard lighters, had been bounced around the Admiralty. Such an aircraft would need to be both large and robust enough to function in the North Sea or beyond. In the first days of 1921, taking inspiration from the earlier Shark, Supermarine produced a preliminary design for a large triplane torpedo bomber powered by two 550hp Rolls-Royce Condor engines, the most powerful British engine available at that time.

Captions on the drawings produced the following year state that the project was associated with Air Ministry Specification DofR Type 10, the details of which appear to be unknown. The aircraft's large Linton Hope hull had a prominent lip around the raised bow, an enlarged version of the hull type first tried on the Sea Lion racer in 1919 and, judging from surviving drawings, Mitchell paid particular attention to the design of the boat bow profile. A robust boat shape was going to be paramount for a flying boat designed to land and take off in the open sea.

Machine gun rings were in the bow and in a turret on top of the hull, just to the rear of the wings. There would be a third gun position in the rear hull, firing through an aperture in the floor. The cockpit was a separate structure on the hull top just ahead of the turret. A standard torpedo could be carried on each side, suspended under the lower wings. The centre section was braced in two bays each side and included the engine mounts, braced between the upper and lower wings. The outer wing panels

were of unequal span, a shorter lower wing braced in a single bay, and longer mid and upper wings braced in two bays.

The bracing wires followed the simplified pattern originally conceived for the Pemberton-Billing anti-Zeppelin quadruplane fighters during the war years and which he had patented in 1916. The wires were secured to the upper and lower planes only and passed through and clamped to brackets on the middle plane. A small auxiliary petrol engine was installed in the lower hull to drive a marine propeller located behind the rear step with a water rudder. This would facilitate manoeuvring on the water, when docking and, feasibly, when operating with a lighter. It could also power a winch to lift the torpedoes into place on their racks and a dynamo to provide electric power to start the main engines, and to run the bilge pumps.

Specification 14/21, for a Five-Seater Boat Seaplane, was issued by the Air Ministry late in the year, drawn up around Supermarine's project.

By May 1922 the project had advanced to the stage of more detailed design and had been given the name Scylla. *The Aeroplane* reported that Supermarine "have under instruction for the Air Ministry a really large sea-going machine, intended to operate with the Fleet at sea under the most difficult of weather conditions … the Supermarine firm are confident that this machine, when completed, will be so great an advance on all previous machines of a comparable type as to

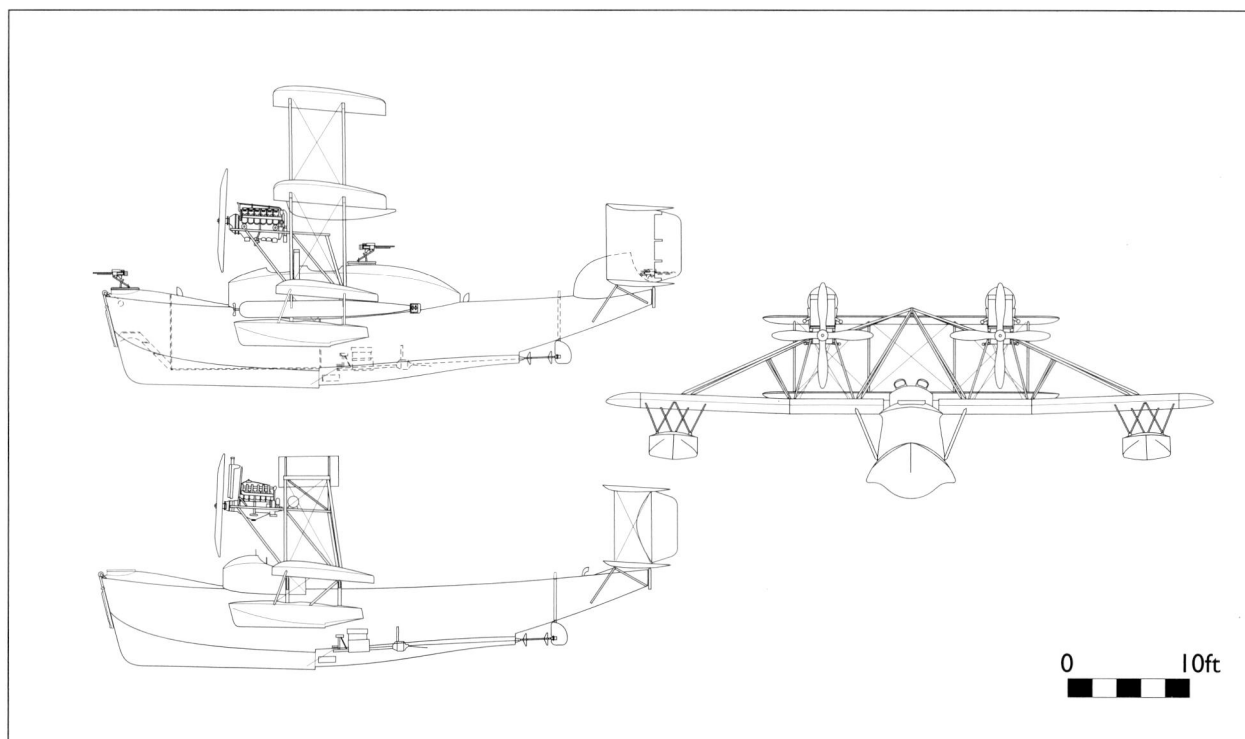

Supermarine Scylla Flying Boat Torpedo Carrier – as designed and as completed

render everything heretofore designed completely obsolete." Confident they may have been but the design was far from being advanced in any aspect.

Work on construction of the hull commenced around the same time and there is photographic evidence to show that Supermarine was in fact working on two hulls in adjacent bays in the workshop. The first, which was to be that used for Scylla, was constructed in the conventional Linton Hope manner with the planing bottom built onto the completed and fully-skinned hull as a separate unit, giving the final product a double bottom. The second hull had the planing bottom framework built as part of the primary structure prior to the whole thing being skinned. Photographs show this hull as largely complete, just requiring the sides and top of the hull to be skinned, but there do not seem to be any of it as a finished hull, so possibly it was never completed.

By late 1922 the requirement for a large torpedo bomber triplane must have lapsed. Alongside the layout drawings for the planned complete triplane aircraft, another drawing showed a stripped-back configuration with the wings discarded and replaced by a simple braced framework able to hold the wingtip floats and engine bearers, on which were installed two 360hp Rolls-Royce Eagle IX engines. Scylla was then finalised in this form and taken by trailer to Felixstowe where it is believed to have been used for taxiing trials, although no report of these trials, if indeed they took place, is known. The final fate of the Scylla is also unknown.

The Air Ministry's attitude to very large flying boats at this point is hard to understand. The first of the three large hulls built under Specification N.4, designed by boat builders C. Camper and Nicholson, and built by the Gosport Aviation Company, had been completed in 1919 but was never fitted with flight surfaces and was later scrapped. The second hull, *Atalanta*, was constructed by shipbuilders May, Harden and May on Linton Hope lines and was also competed in 1919 – but it wasn't fitted with its wings and flown until 1923. The third, *Titania*, was built at Fyfe on the Clyde and was also of the Linton Hope type. This hull was transported to Fairey's works at Hamble where the wings were installed. There it remained in storage until 1925, it is said, before being flown.

If these large aircraft were of such little consequence that they could sit unused for years, it is difficult to see why Supermarine received an order for yet another large flying boat hull. Why not simply utilise one of those already built?

The hull for Scylla was photographed outside the Supermarine Works during the winter of 1922-1923, lined up alongside those of the Sea Lion II and a Seagull.

Schneider Trophy contest success

The Sea Lion II, seen in the line-up of hulls, was the new name given to the Sea King MkII after it was refitted with a Napier Lion engine and had its undercarriage removed. Scott-Paine had authorised this work as he wanted Britain to be represented at

Supermarine's family of wooden Linton Hope hulls in 1922 – Sea Lion II, Seagull and Scylla

the 1922 Schneider Trophy Contest in Naples; no other potential entrants for the British team had come forward.

The previous two contests had been hosted by Italy and had been dismal affairs flown without any foreign competitors challenging for the trophy. One more contest win would mean that Italy would hold the trophy outright and the annual contests would be wound up. Both of the previous contests had been won by the Italian team fielding small flying boats that were little more than simple modifications of Italy's serving military types. Scott-Paine believed that a Lion-powered Sea King MkII would be at least as good as any of these. After early test flights in the hands of the company test pilot, Henri Biard, the only additional modifications found to be required were increases in the size of both the fin and rudder.

Scraping together financial and material support – the RAeC for the entry fee, Napier for the engine, Shell for the fuel and the General Steam Navigation Company for transportation – the small Supermarine team headed to Naples. Once there they saw that the Italian team did indeed consist of similarly modified flying boats plus one dedicated racing flying boat, the Savoia S.51, which looked like it was destined for an easy win. However fate took a hand when the aircraft capsized during preliminary trials and should have been disqualified.

No complaints were raised, however, when it was dried out and prepared for the contest proper. Flying around the triangular contest course laid out in the Bay of Naples, Biard easily outpaced the modified Italian flying boats. And the Savoia S.51, clearly suffering from its unscheduled bath, could not match the Sea Lion II's speed. Britain had taken the win, preventing Italy from winning the trophy outright, and would host the next contest in 1923.

It is worth noting that Biard wrote an autobiography, *Wings*, in the mid-1930s in which he includes a great deal chronicling his time with Supermarine. Alas, if his depiction of the 1922 contest is anything to go by his writing was significantly short on fact and long on fanciful anecdote. He describes how the Sea Lion II was built in secret and how he was astounded when he first saw it; remember, this was an aircraft that had actually been around the works in one form or another since 1919. He also told a lurid tale of the fraught start with all the contest participants taking-off together, how the Italians bunched up on the course to prevent him passing and how he eventually did so by zooming and diving around one of the turns. All pure fantasy. The aircraft actually took off individually a few minutes apart; it was a time trial not a race, and during Biard's laps around the course he encountered and had to pass just a single aircraft, and that on a straight and not a turn. As a consequence his descriptions of other

The Supermarine Sea Lion II afloat in the Bay of Naples prior to the 1922 Schneider Trophy contest

flights and aircraft in the book should be taken with a very large pinch of salt.

Commercial aviation

The Government and aviation world alike held great hopes for the development of commercial aviation in the immediate post-war world. Manufacturers pitched many ideas for what they believed new airliners should look like and some had even ventured to suggest that flying trans-Atlantic routes could be in sight, spurred on by the success of Alcock

and Brown in crossing the North Atlantic in a mildly modified Vickers Vimy bomber in 1919.

Cost and practical considerations, however, saw the development of less aspirational aircraft as the more commercially attractive way forward, many of which made use of major components from the latest bomber types. Various single engine de Havilland (Airco) aircraft proved particularly popular while the Vickers Vimy begat the Vimy Commercial, splicing Vimy flying surfaces to a new capacious plywood cabin fuselage. Handley

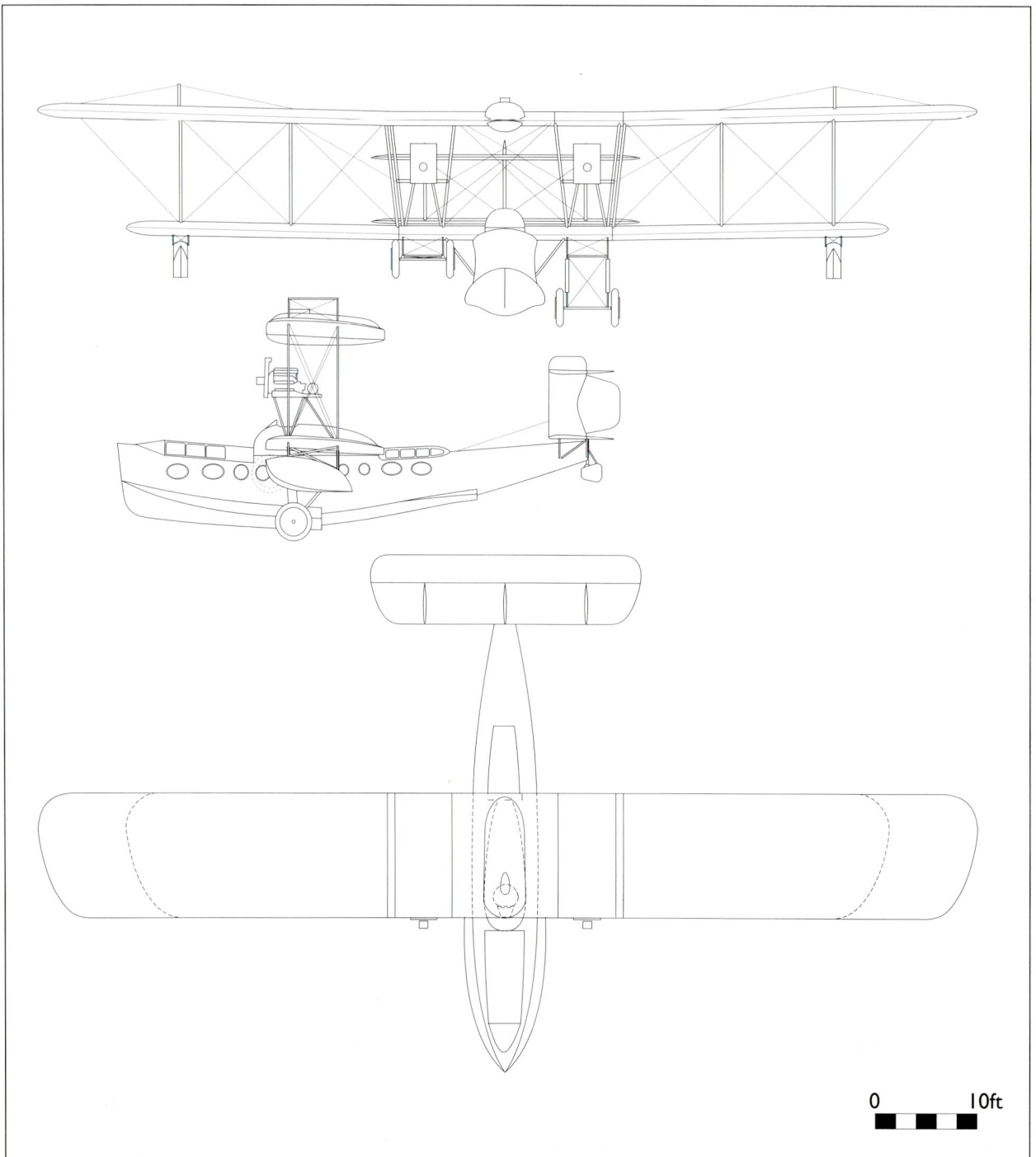

0   10ft

The large twin-engine amphibian airliner project submitted to Instone Air Line in 1921

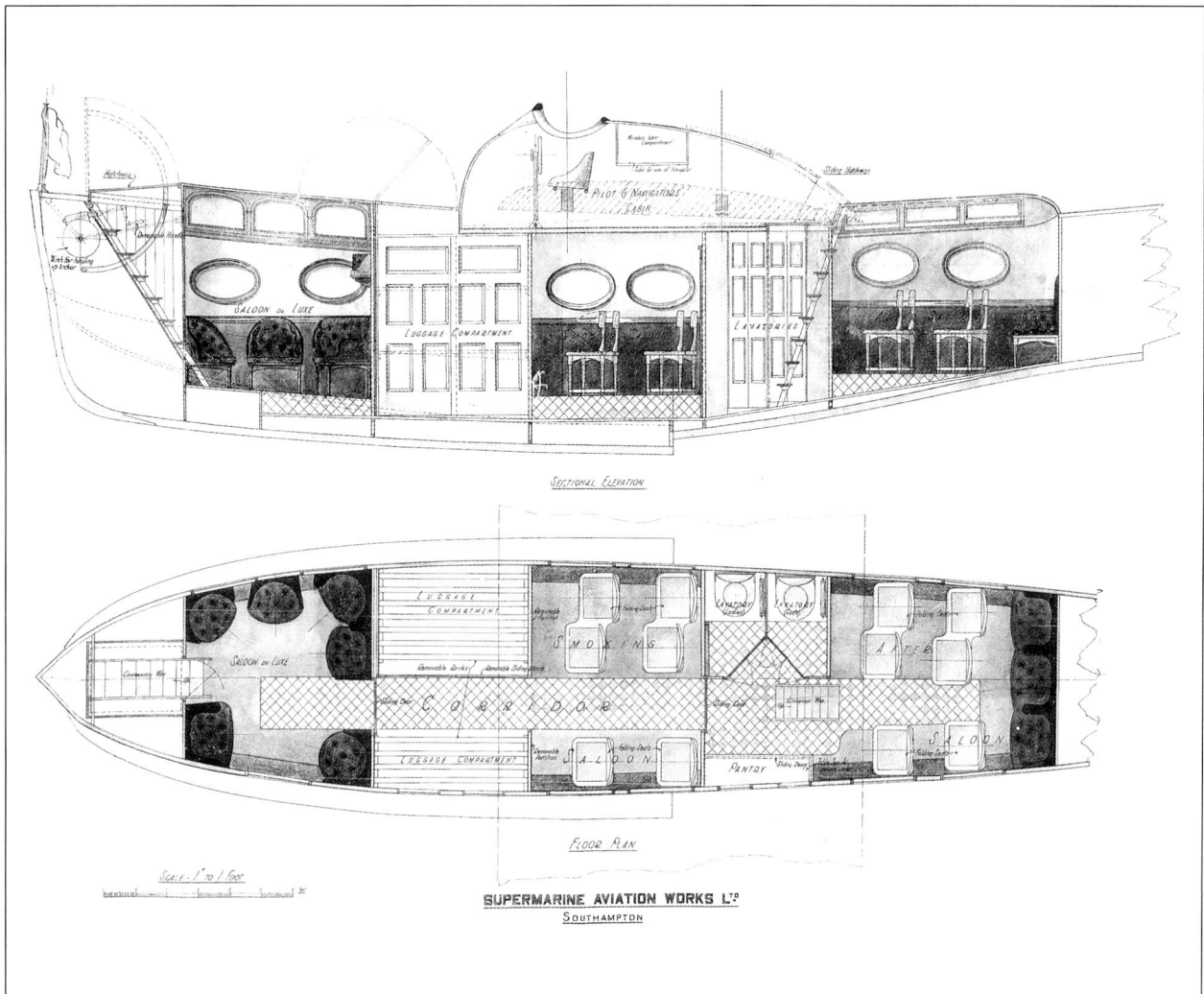

The luxurious cabins for 18 passengers in Supermarine's Instone amphibian project

Page made minimal modifications to a few HP 0/400 bombers with which to fly to Paris, initially transporting Government representatives to the Paris Peace Conference at Versailles.

One entrepreneur who was prepared to invest and try his hand at running an airline was Samuel Instone, co-owner, along with his brothers, of a cargo shipping line and coal mine in Wales. His airline company commenced operations in 1919 flying a number of aircraft, including a Vimy Commercial as the company flagship, and established services to various northern European cities. Initially these were for mail and freight but subsequently expanded to carrying passengers. They flew on the London-Paris and London-Brussels-Cologne routes with aspirations to expand.

In mid-1921 Supermarine pitched a scheme for a large twin-engine biplane amphibian flying boat to the renamed Instone Air Line, apparently in response to a specification issued by the airline as 'for S Instone & co ltd' is part of the general arrangement drawing title.

Supermarine had two seven-seat amphibian schemes under review that year, one derived directly from the Seagull and the second of similar size but with a boat-prow hull and powered by twin Rolls-Royce Eagles. This second project, suitably scaled up, was the inspiration behind the project for Instone. The new aircraft was designed to accommodate 21 passengers in three well-appointed cabins, the forward described as Saloon de Luxe with plush upholstered seats. Each cabin had large elliptical 'porthole' windows and those fore and aft also had skylights in the roof.

The cockpit for pilot and navigator was in a separate streamlined housing mounted between the wings on the top of the main hull, similar to that on Scylla. The undercarriage was of a new design. On each side, located on the lower wing centre section, a framework held an axle with two wheels that were swung forward and upwards to retract clear of the water. The engines were Napier Lions mounted mid-gap on bearers attached to the lower wing only. The unequal span two-

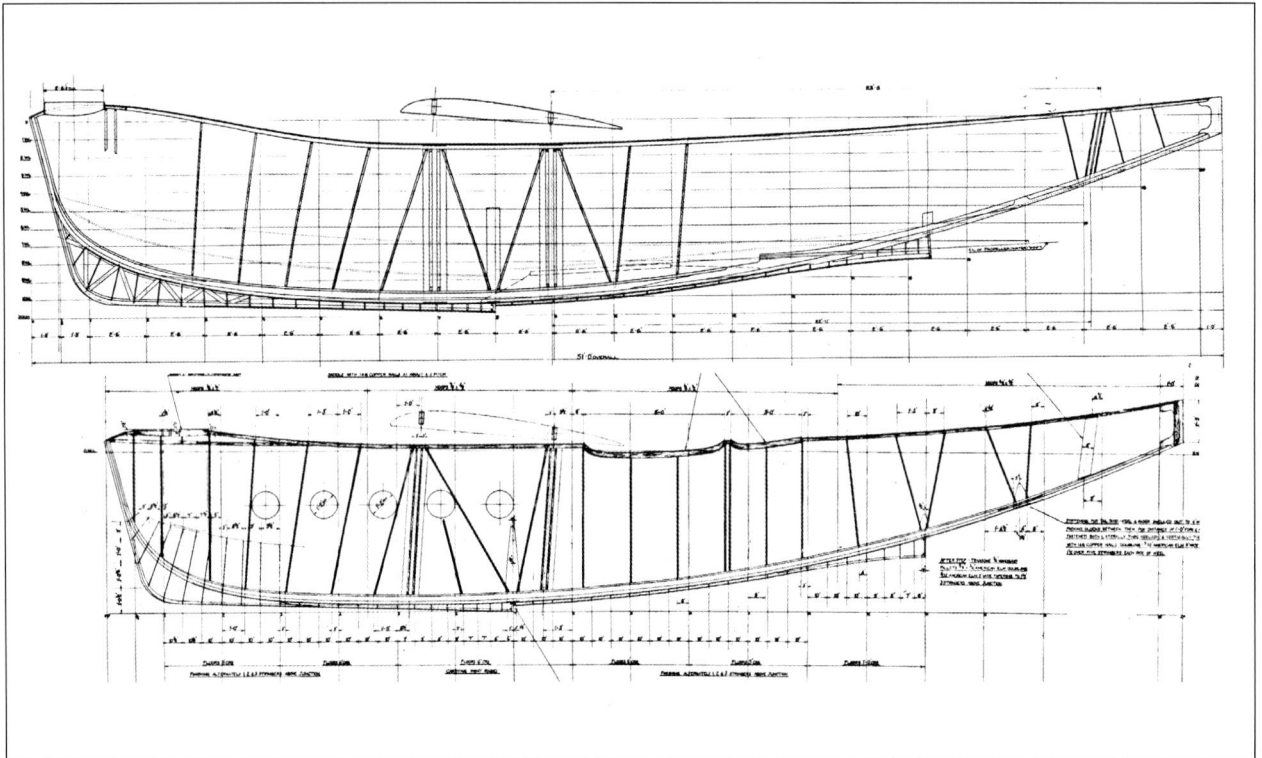

A comparison of the hull lines and internal structure for the Scylla (top) and Swan

bay biplane outer wings with kingpost bracing were reminiscent of a scaled-up Channel, as was the biplane tail with triple fins and rudders. The capacious hull was Supermarine's standard Linton Hope-type of egg-shape cross section but featuring a high boat bow, truly 'a seaworthy hull that will fly'.

All in all the design was an interesting mix of new ideas that would feature in later schemes and rather dated aspects, most especially the flying surfaces. No orders were forthcoming but the design can be considered as the forerunner for other large designs in the coming years.

By early 1922 Supermarine once again found itself desperately short of construction work. Sales of the Channel had all but dried up and there was no perceived interest in the Sea King from any quarter. Unless new orders were received in the immediate future, the company's prospects looked bleak. Bird requested an interview at the Air Ministry to discuss the situation and the imminent need to lay off some staff. He was told that an order for around 18 Seagulls was under discussion and likely to be forthcoming but could not be guaranteed. The ministry actually recommended that most, if not all, of the works should be shut pending a decision.

Meanwhile, work was under way to refine designs for aircraft of a similar size to the Scylla project. After the amphibian tendered to Instone had been declined, Mitchell and the team initiated work, on a speculative basis, for a more advanced design of large amphibian flying boat for the civilian market. The profile of the hull and planing bottom had been completed around April 1922, about the same time as that for Scylla, but progress on other aspects was slow, presumably due to the financial state of the company and the small workforce assigned to other projects. Hull structure drawings were, nevertheless, completed before the end of the year and showed the planned construction to be surprisingly different from that of the Scylla.

It was fortuitous that the Air Ministry showed interest in the concept, having seemingly gone cold over the Scylla, and Specification 21/22 was raised to cover an order for a prototype. The project was identified as the Twin Engined Commercial Amphibian Flying Boat in the final layout drawings dated September 1923 but would be christened as the Swan shortly after. At this point it had just an eight seat cabin in the forward hull with the seats facing inwards. This was considerably less than the three-cabin, 21 seat layout in the project offered to Instone.

Last of the Flying Boat Racers

A small production contract for the Seagull was finally awarded to Supermarine by the Air Ministry in September 1922, with further batches ordered in February and June 1923, after which the financial state of the company began to stabilise. Scott-Paine was engaged in talks with London and South-Western Railways Co, the Southampton Dock authorities, and Asiatic Petroleum Co with a view to initiating a commercial airline service between Southampton and the Channel Islands, and later the French coastal towns, for which Supermarine would provide the aircraft.

The joint venture was launched as British Maritime Air Navigation Co Ltd in early 1923. Design work had started at the end of 1922 on a suitable six passenger amphibian that would become the Sea Eagle; it was the endpoint of a series of similar sized single-engine pusher amphibian flying boat schemes that had commenced in mid-1921. As such it was not an outstanding design, just solidly functional – no more and no less than what it needed to be. In the true spirit of a boat that will fly, its appearance was that of a cabin cruiser to which wings had been attached. Three were ordered, supported by a government grant, the first flying in June 1923 with which a service to Guernsey commenced on 25th September.

As the RAeC began preparations for the 1923 Schneider Trophy Contest, it soon became apparent that the British aircraft industry was once again showing little interest in developing suitable racers for the national team and a plea went out for them to show a bit more enthusiasm. This fell largely on deaf ears and it was soon clear that there were no new designs on anyone's drawing boards.

Supermarine had little spare design capacity available but Scott-Paine was prevailed upon to at least try to defend the trophy that his company had won the previous year. The Sea Lion II was wheeled back into the shop and Mitchell did a

quick job designing new wings of reduced span and a number of simple measures to reduce drag

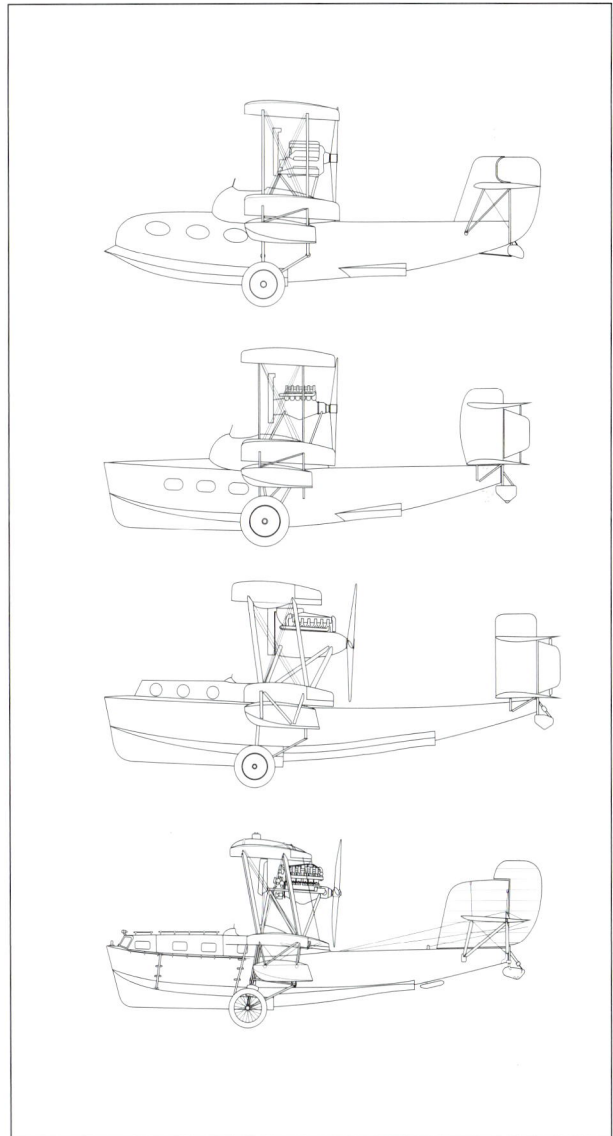

The evolution of the Sea Eagle – from top to bottom; the 'Swan' seven-seater Commercial Amphibian 1921, the seven-seater Commercial 1921, the eight-seater Commercial Amphibian 1922, the seven-seater Sea Eagle Commercial Amphibian

The Sea Eagle amphibian in service with British Maritime Air Navigation

– the most visible being a neat circular-section cowling around the engine. The revised racer, Sea Lion III, was hardly cutting-edge but did result in an aircraft that was faster than in its previous guise despite becoming rather 'lively' on the water. Whether it would prove to be competitive or not depended entirely on what the opposition would send.

The USA had indicated its intention to participate with a team run by the US Navy. For the last few years the US Navy and Army had funded racing aircraft as part of a general research programme into high speed aircraft and engines, and these had competed against each other in national air races and to vie for the air speed record. It was to be the latest versions of these aircraft, now fitted with floats, that would form the US Schneider Trophy team. Barring accidents or mechanical failures it seemed highly likely that they would win the contest with ease.

Fate did its best to favour Supermarine, with an unreasonable number of mishaps and mechanical issues plaguing all the rival foreign teams. The other British entries had similar problems however, with the Blackburn Pellet flying boat, which, like

the Sea Lion, was built around a wartime N.1B hull, being wrecked in a take-off accident. Even so, on the day the two Curtiss CR3 floatplanes with the US team flew flawlessly – pushing the Sea Lion III into a distant third place.

Construction work was now well under way on the Swan twin-engine amphibian. Although Supermarine had designed the aircraft as a civil carrier it was being built as an empty shell, no interior fittings and no porthole windows in what would have been the cabin. The engines were Rolls-Royce Eagles with the engine bearers mounted on braced inverted pyramidal frames above the lower wing, a design that Supermarine considered sufficiently novel to warrant patenting.

For reasons unknown the wings were designed to fold forwards, more a military feature than something required for an airliner. The forward retracting undercarriage that Mitchell had designed for the Instone amphibian had been discarded and replaced by a variant of Supermarine's standard outward retracting system for which the pivot point was now located on a framework outboard under the lower wing rather than the usual position on the hull side.

The Sea Lion III flanked by the Curtiss CR3 seaplane and French CAMS 36 flying boat outside the Saunders works at Cowes on the Isle of Wight prior to the 1923 Schneider Trophy contest

The wing centre section was a new design and employed a radical new form of construction as the whole structure was braced by diagonal struts to form a robust Warren truss, thereby dispensing with the usual flying and landing bracing wires and leaving just the lesser incidence wires between the fore and aft strut pairs. This was a rigid, low maintenance system.

Replacing the Felixstowe flying boats

The few aging Felixstowe flying boats that had been retained by the RAF post-war were flown only rarely, their patrol and offensive role now practically irrelevant, and there was at first no great pressure from any quarter to see them replaced. But by 1923 the RAF had finally reached the point where a replacement had to be found.

In mid-1917 the expected life of an individual Felixstowe flying boat was estimated by the Admiralty as just six months so their deficiencies were, perhaps, of little consequence. Post-war a much extended life for a flying boat would be essential. In addition to the requirement for a replacement aircraft to carry out patrol duties around the British Isles a broader role was now envisaged, with the aircraft deployed to British coastal territories around the world where they would be required to operate with limited support and to spend a fair amount of time moored rather than brought ashore. This demanded a flying boat which was far more rugged that the Felixstowe aircraft that they were to replace.

The Supermarine Swan twin-engine amphibian

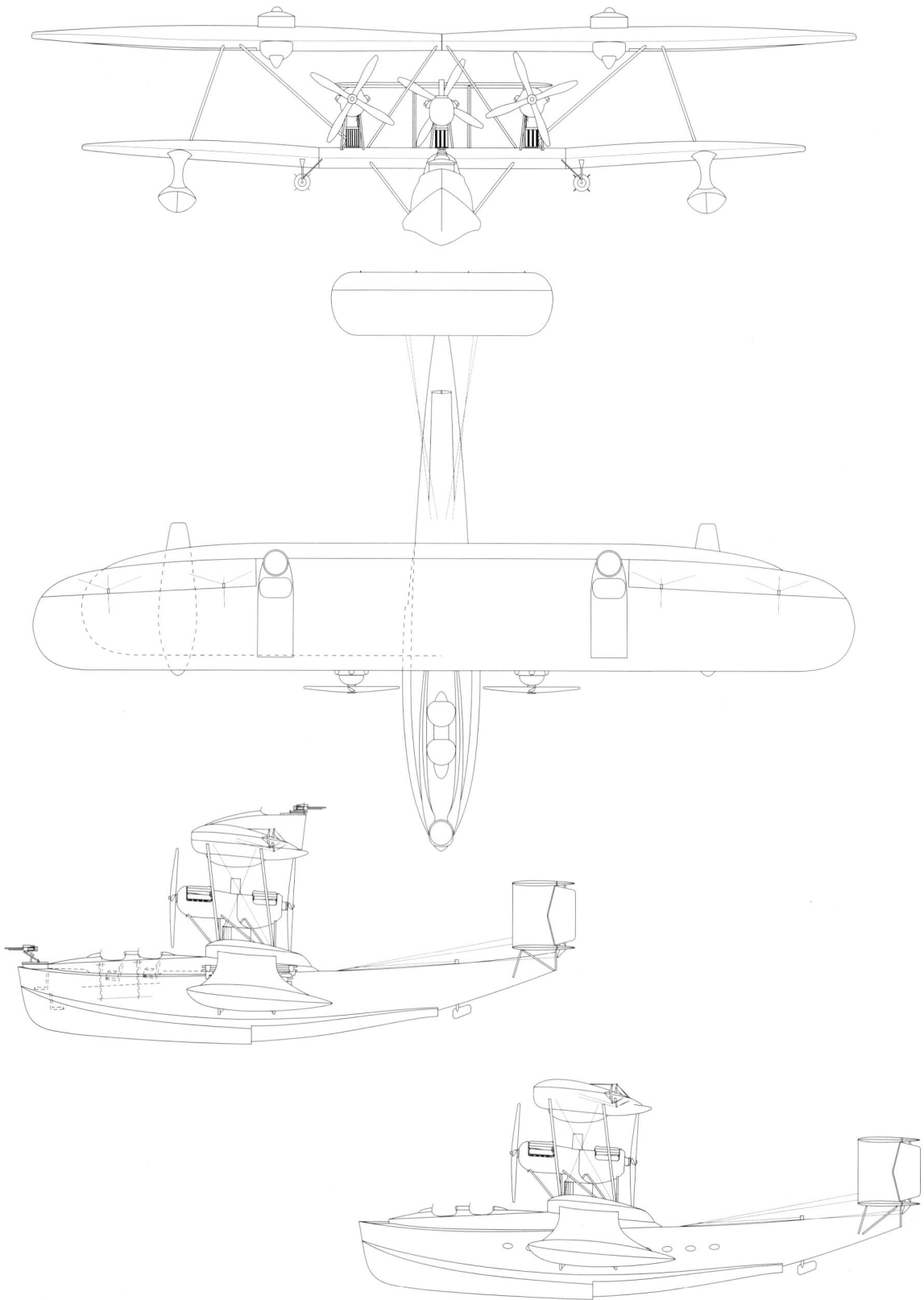

Supermarine's three-engined military flying boat to meet the requirements of Specification 9/23 and a proposal for a civil conversion

Specification 9/23 was raised for such an aircraft, calling for a three-engine design with improved offensive and defensive capability provided by placing gun positions in 'fighting tops' to provide a wide field of fire. The concept of a fighting top, a nacelle holding one or more gun positions away from the fuselage, such as a location outboard on the wings or possibly elsewhere, had recently found favour within the RAF. As an experiment, a Vickers Virginia twin-engine bomber had been modified to have two such nacelles fitted to the top wing leading edge far out beyond the arc of the propellers. A similar installation was later trialled with the nacelle on the trailing edge for comparison.

The specification attracted the interest of several companies – the brief period when Supermarine was effectively free of competition now being in the past. Vickers drew up preliminary ideas for what may have been its last flying boat proposal prior to acquiring Supermarine in 1927. And Short Bros applied for patents covering at least three different gun nacelle designs for flying boats, suggesting that it too was preparing to tender one or more projects.

One of the latter's ideas was to place the gun position within the rear of enlarged wing tip floats and to allow the gunner to move between this and the main fuselage via a crawl-way within the lower wing. This, of course, served to highlight the weakest aspect of the concept; with the fighting top located some way out from the fuselage there was no easy way for the gunner to move between the two while the aircraft was in flight, which meant that he would have to spend the entire mission in an exposed seat unable to contact his fellow crewmembers. It was far from an ideal situation but was considered worth pursuing nonetheless.

Supermarine started work on a project to meet the specification in late 1923, resulting in yet another completely new large flying boat design from Mitchell, quite different in almost all respects from the concurrent Scylla and Swan. The final layout drawings are dated November 1923 and show a large flying boat powered by three Napier Lions, two outboard as tractors, and the central one as a pusher. Twin fighting tops, with their gun positions to the rear, were placed on the top wing.

Prior to the start of this project all of Supermarine's larger Linton Hope hull designs had been fairly broad in the beam, in excess of 6ft in width and height, a little over 40ft long, with a separate faired cockpit structure built on top. This provided a voluminous interior entirely appropriate for a commercial carrier or, in the case of the Scylla, an

aircraft designed for protracted periods spent at sea with the fleet.

For the 9/23 flying boat, however, the emphasis was more on aerodynamic refinement. Although the hull was of similar cross section, it was now considerably longer with the tandem cockpit relocated to the nose, eliminating the need for the large drag-inducing turret fairing. While the now-familiar boat prow had been retained it was of much lower profile and devoid of the flared spray-deflecting lip that had characterised the earlier designs. To the rear of the second planing bottom step there was a small water rudder. The wing tip floats were also of a new streamlined design, a simple flattened teardrop shape with the attachment struts enclosed in a fairing.

Expanding upon the system introduced for the Swan the entire wing structure was now in the form of a Warren truss. Although this structure left a considerable unbraced overhang on the outer upper planes it facilitated rigging and maintenance. The wing section of the upper plane thickened outwards to the point where the struts were attached and then reduced again outboard, while the thickness of the lower wing was constant throughout. The fighting tops, with the gun ring located to the rear, were positioned just inboard of the strut attachment point and immediately above the fuel tanks, the fillers for which were within the windshield shroud, a basic shelter for the gunner, ahead of the gun ring. The biplane tailplane was mounted on struts above the stern of the hull and fitted with quadruple fins and rudders.

The bearers for the three Napier Lion engines were held on sharply slanted 'N' struts secured to the lower planes and were partially enclosed in aerodynamic fairings that covered the bearers and crankcase but left the cylinder heads exposed to aid cooling. A radiator was positioned under each engine along with the oil tank, both enclosed in a downward extension of the engine fairing which had controllable shutters at the front.

In addition to the two machine guns in the fighting tops there was a third in the extreme nose of the hull. The bomb racks were attached under the lower wings outboard of the engine mounts and were each capable of holding one 500lb and one 250lb bomb in tandem.

Also included with the project was a version configured for use as a civil carrier for 20 passengers.

At some point in early 1924, and probably before any tenders had been submitted, the Air Ministry withdrew the specification, this aircraft type possibly considered too large for the role it was intended to fulfil. After a review of the operational requirements, new specifications for flying boats were soon produced – one for a smaller two-engine type as a more direct replacement for the Felixstowe aircraft and others for larger two- and three-engine aircraft. The requirement for any of these to include fighting tops was shelved, although tests continued with the Virginia and later with a Southampton flying boat.

Under new management

An argument between Scott-Paine and Bird at the end of 1923 boiled over and came to an abrupt end when Scott-Paine accepted Bird's cash offer for his share of the business and left. The cause of

the argument has never been explained so we can only speculate as to what this may have been; was it Scott-Paine's pursuit of interests in airlines? Maybe. A difference of opinion as to the direction of the firm, military or civil? Possibly. However, it all remains conjecture. On this change at the top a visible shift in direction may have been expected, but business continued largely unchanged. Very mysterious.

The last of the racing flying boats

The 1924 Schneider Trophy contest was scheduled to be held in the US in the autumn. After the lack of interest shown by the British aircraft industry to provide competitors for the 1923 contest, and the

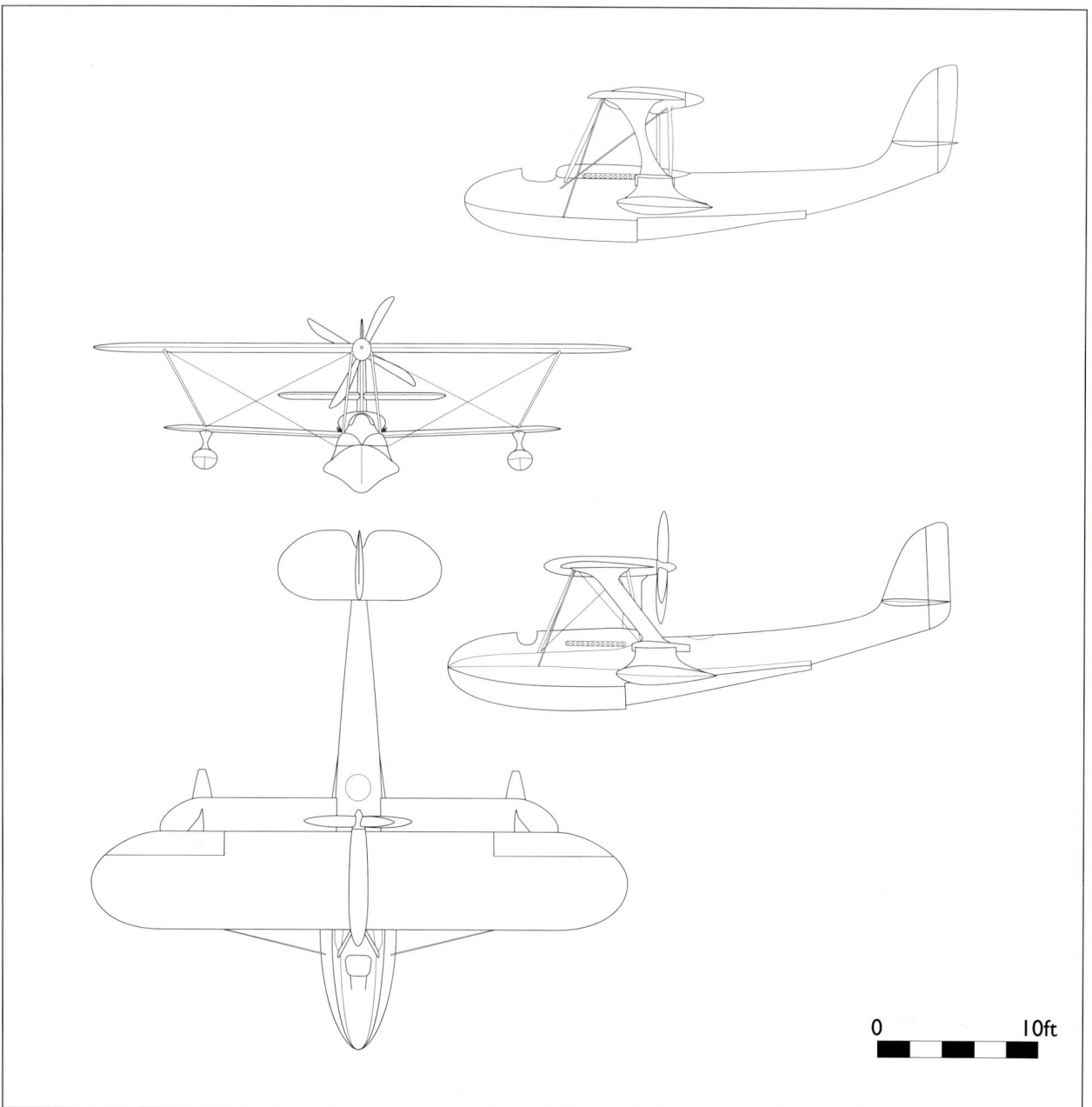

0   10ft

The Sea Urchin racer was designed to compete in the Schneider Trophy contest scheduled for 1924 – preliminary design at the top and final configuration below

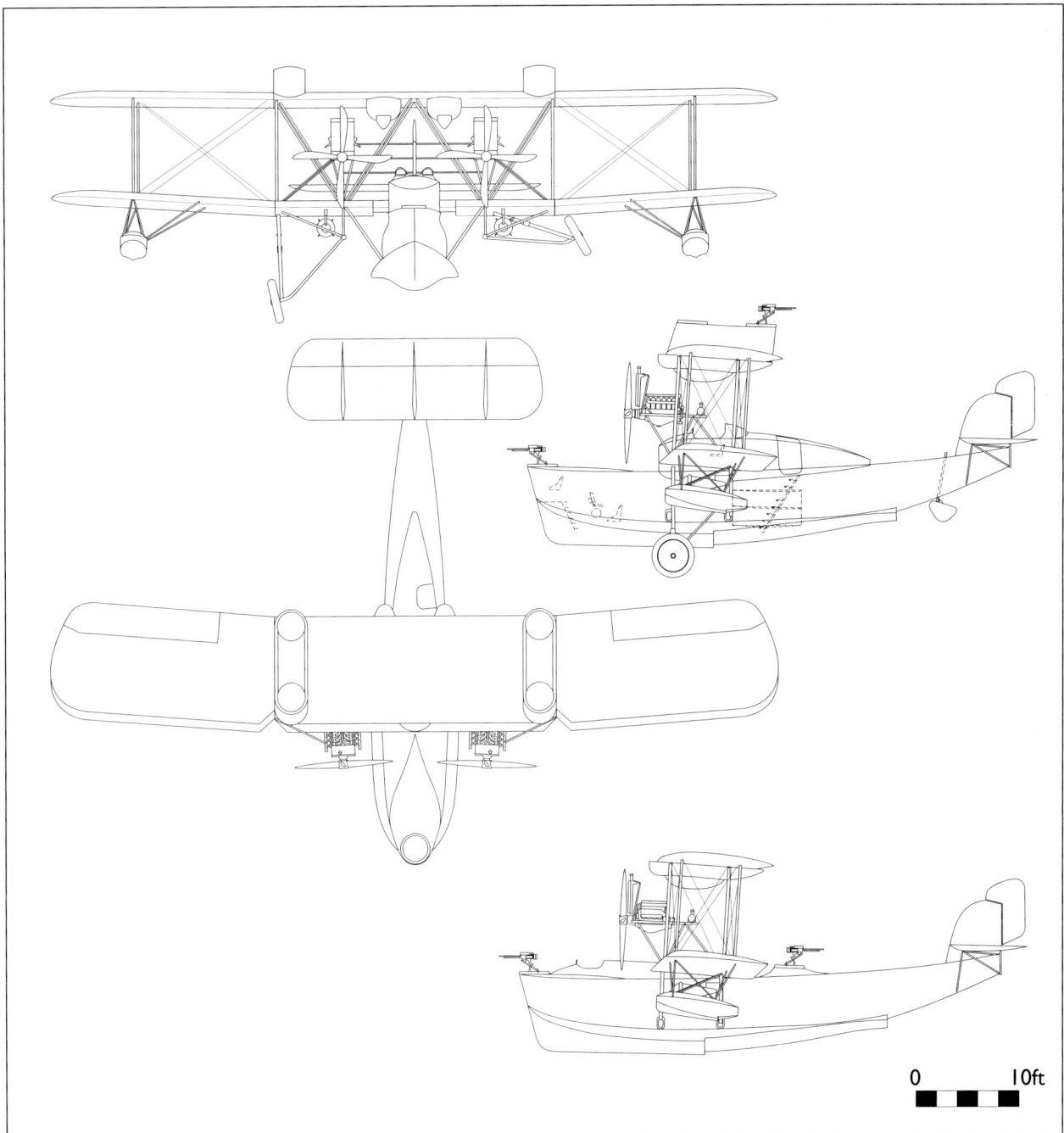

A proposal to convert the Swan for military use. The lower profile shows amendments made in pencil to the blueprin

subsequent easy defeat of the Sea Lion III, there was even less sign of enthusiasm for 1924.

It was readily apparent that without substantial funding from government it would not be possible to design, construct and develop an aircraft capable of putting up a credible performance against the Navy-funded US team. The government was reluctant but was prevailed upon to provide part-finance, raising Specification 39/23 for the Gloucestershire Aircraft Company to convert one of its land racers by fitting floats, as the Gloster II, while 40/23 went to Supermarine who elected to design an all-new aircraft.

Not wishing to stray too far from the company's area of expertise, and not yet convinced that seaplanes such as the Curtiss CR3 were a better way forward, Mitchell decided that the new racer should be another biplane flying boat. After discussion with Rolls-Royce, it was agreed that it would be powered by a race-rated Rolls-Royce Condor VII. This would be installed within the hull, driving a pusher propeller on the trailing edge of the upper wing via two right-angle gearboxes.

The Single Seat High Performance Flying Boat commenced as a project towards the end of 1923 and basic layout drawings had been produced by

December. The aircraft would soon bear the name Sea Urchin. The hull generally followed standard Linton Hope practice but with the innovation of a graceful upturned stern, a feature also being developed for the Southampton flying boat, which on the racer terminated in an integral fin.

The cockpit was set low in the bow with the Condor installed immediately behind, the engine bearers supported by strong bulkhead hull frames fore and aft to form the engine bay. From the engine a right angle gearbox at the rear drove a vertical shaft to a second right angle gearbox on the top wing which took the drive to a pusher propeller. The upper gearbox and fuel tank were housed in a long bullet-shaped fairing around the wing centre section. The biplane wings were of extreme sesquiplane form with the lower serving mainly as a mount for the wing tip floats and the interplane bracing struts.

The top wing was of greater span and over twice the chord of the lower. It was supported above the hull by a single hollow central strut at the rear, which also served to house the vertical drive shaft from the engine, and at the front by inverted 'V' struts secured on the forward bulkhead frame of the engine bay. Outboard, the wings were supported by single 'I' struts on either side to the lower planes and braced by lift wires extending from the top of the 'I' struts to the forward hull bulkhead. The tailplane was set around halfway up the fin, well clear of the water. In principal the layout appeared sound.

As design progressed a number of tricky issues raised their ugly heads and proved extremely difficult to resolve. The heavy engine had to be installed in the hull between the bulkheads and the position of the upper wing was then dictated by the geometry of the drive shaft and gearbox system. This in turn determined the position of the propeller at the wing trailing edge. Alignment of the aircraft's centre of gravity and centre of lift further constrained the wing position.

The final position turned out to be some six inches or so forward of the location initially planned. Ideally, the lower wing would then have been located below the upper with a small amount of stagger, but structural strength considerations meant that the front spars had to be secured to the rear bulkhead of the engine bay, necessitating a rearward shift of more than a foot. The 'I' struts between the wings were now set at quite an acute angle and the wingtip floats set back in a potentially unstable position to the rear of the main hull step. Presumably this could all have been solved given more time.

Mitchell had been able to view the low profile corrugated copper surface water radiators on the wings of the Curtiss CR3 racers in 1923. These followed the contours of the wing and created very little drag. Some kind of surface radiator was intended for the Sea Urchin but by April 1924 he was having misgivings as to whether a viable radiator could be produced in time and sought advice from the experts at the Royal Aircraft Establishment (RAE) regarding alternative low-drag systems. It was suggested that conventional honeycomb tube radiators of semi-circular shape could be installed below the upper wings, and fitted with controllable shutters.

Late in the year some thought was given to the use of ethylene glycol as coolant, but this may well have been after the project had been abandoned. The calculations included with the RAE report show that the race-boosted Condor was anticipated to produce 800hp and that Supermarine's estimate for the Sea Urchin's top speed was 215mph with a sustained race speed of 210mph. It has also been suggested that Rolls-Royce was having difficulties designing the small right-angle gearboxes required to take the 800hp drive of the engine to the propeller, which is distinctly possible.

The mounting problems and associated delays resulted in the Sea Urchin being withdrawn as a competitor, and when the Gloster II suffered serious damage on landing after a test flight the whole British team withdrew from the contest. As they were to be the only challengers to the US team, the National Aeronautic Association of the USA chose to reschedule the contest for 1925 rather than to fly unopposed.

The evolution of the Swan

The Swan made its maiden flight in March 1924. No issues were reported publicly but within a few days the aircraft was taken back to the works. The Eagle engines changed for more powerful Napier Lions, and both the undercarriage and wing folding were removed. There appears to be nothing to suggest that the Swan had ever taken-off or landed on its undercarriage. In this revised form it was tested by the Marine Aircraft Experimental Establishment (MAEE) at Felixstowe where the reports were all favourable.

In March 1924 Supermarine investigated ways of converting the Swan to an armed reconnaissance machine. On the project drawings bomb racks for a 500lb bomb were added under each inner wing and fighting tops placed on top of the wings. It was a short lived concept, with pencilled amendments (by Mitchell?) showing the first steps on the way to the final design of the Southampton.

The Southampton and Beyond

6

CHAPTER

Although a little out of the scope of this book, as it was produced in large numbers, it is important to have a brief review of the Southampton because of the impact it was to have on the development of Supermarine as a company and also for its influence on the design of future flying boats.

After the Swan amphibian had been reconfigured as a flying boat and re-engined with Napier Lions it received favourable reports for its handling both on the water and in the air. However, the government had just completed the forced merger of several British airlines to form Imperial Airways, including British Maritime Air Navigation Co Ltd, the company part owned by Supermarine, and this new company was not yet in a position to order additional aircraft for its fleet.

There was, therefore, no immediate prospect for Supermarine to obtain orders for a civil Swan. But a military derivative, capitalising on the design's key strengths of a hull planing bottom and Warren truss wing structure with simple engine mounts,

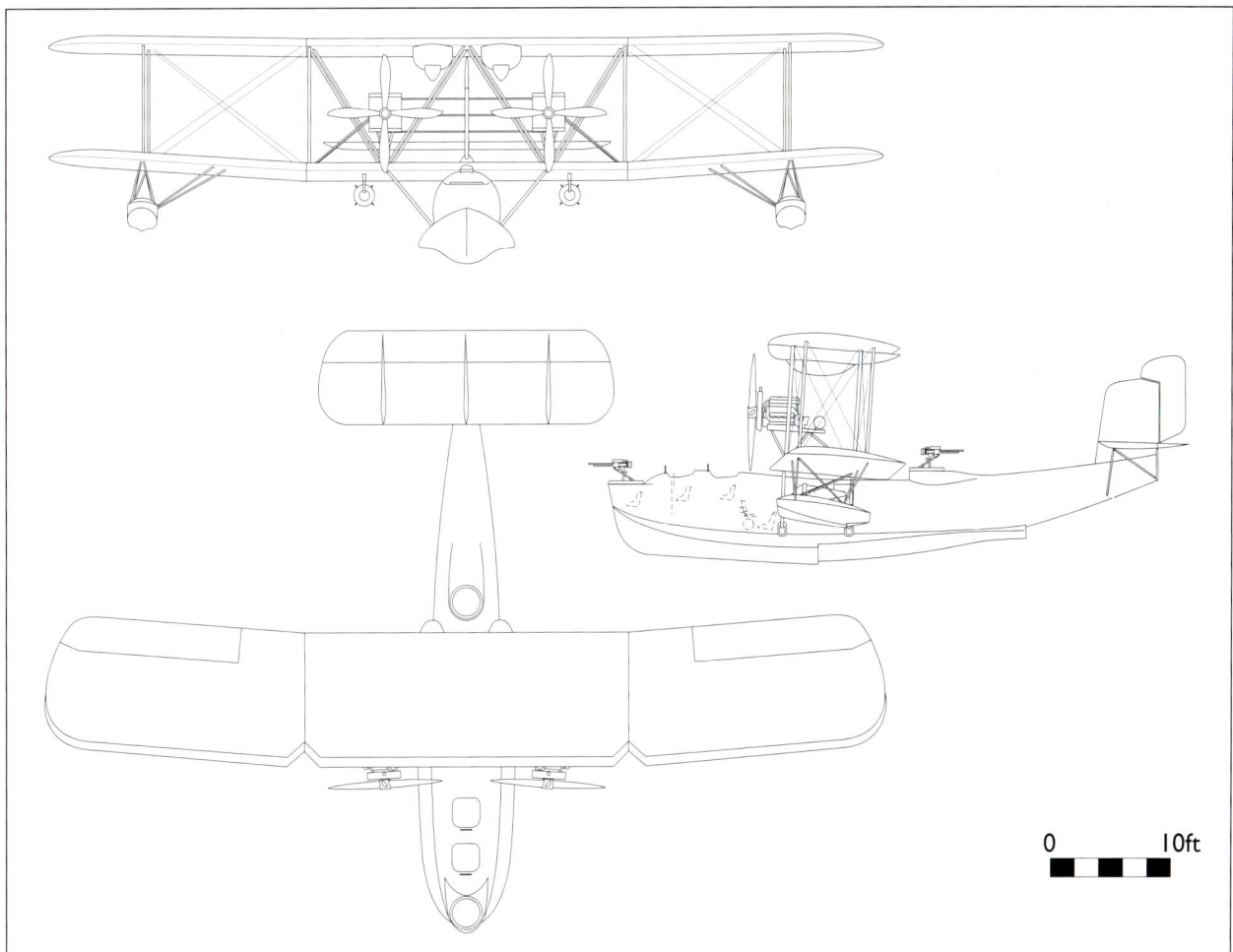

The Service Type Twin Engine Flying Boat project – the immediate precursor to the Southampton

The wooden hulls for the first six Southamptons were constructed in adjacent jigs at the Woolston Works

was ordered by the Air Ministry and Specification 18/24 was written around it.

Supermarine had moved ahead with development ideas derived from the military Swan concept and now looked to the aborted 9/23 project for further inspiration. A new longer, slender hull was designed with a stern which swept upwards into a short pillar of aerodynamic cross section (on all previous flying boats the stern terminated at a vertical rudder post). The flat top of the pillar then provided a firm broad mounting surface for the tailplane, positioning it in the slipstream from the propellers and well clear of the water without the need for a deepened or angled rear hull profile.

This layout also meant that the tailplane could be stabilised by lighter bracing struts and the control activation cables could be run internally within the hull. The gun position in the nose of the hull was lowered slightly to improve the forward view from the tandem cockpits, within which the seats were offset to port. Rear defence was provided by two gun positions in the hull behind the wings,

offset to the left and right and staggered fore and aft. Supermarine considered the design of the hull layout and tail surfaces to be sufficiently novel to justify the application for a patent.

As most of the design elements were well proven, no prototype was deemed necessary by the Air Ministry and a full production order was placed for six aircraft, followed shortly after by a second contract, this time for one fitted with an experimental metal hull. Specifications for more experimental flying boat prototypes were also now issued; 13/24 for a larger twin-engine flying boat with a metal hull, to Short Bros for the S.5 Singapore, and 14/24 for an even larger three-engine flying boat, for which prototype contracts went to Blackburn for the R.B.1 Iris and Saunders for the A.5 Valkyrie, the latter amended to Specification 22/24.

The initial production contract, and likelihood of more to come, was sufficient to warrant investment in an extension of the Woolston Works. The old tidal mudflats immediately upstream from the current works were filled in, the wharf front extended and

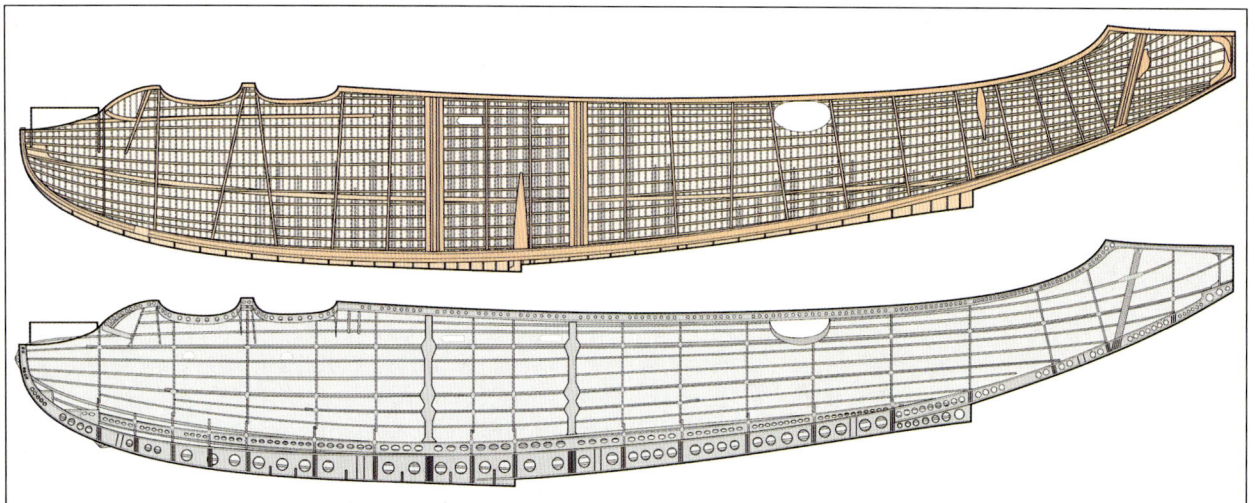

A comparison of the internal structures of wooden and metal Southampton hulls

The metal centre section of a Southampton hull

construction commenced of a large new hanger with riverside sliding doors.

A metal-working department was assembled through 1925 and into 1926 which involved investment in new workshop tools, metal annealing tanks, analytical laboratory and trained staff, all working under the supervision of Arthur Black, a qualified metallurgist. The prototype Southampton metal hull was completed at the end of 1926 and flown, as N218, in early 1927. To mitigate any risk that the merits of the Southampton could be compromised by introducing a completely new hull design, Mitchell chose to make no changes to the basic Southampton hull shape and simply reproduced it in metal. The planing bottom was now an integral part of the primary hull structure rather than a separate unit – but otherwise the layout remained unchanged.

The Southampton, as with the Seagull before it, cast a long shadow with many of the design concepts in the following years drawn from that basic layout. First a proposal was put forward for the aircraft to be re-engined with Rolls-Royce Condors, a project for which the name Shark was resurrected. Then there were various ideas for a civil version; including in an amphibian in early 1925 which combined Swan and Southampton features and was named as the Swan Mk II. Later

in the year there was another idea for a more direct civil conversion of the Southampton.

Work had started on three-engine derivatives of the Southampton as early as the end of 1924 following an enquiry from Denmark for a large flying boat to be used as a torpedo bomber. This was a slow-burning project that developed over more than two years. Retaining a Southampton hull, but with just a single gun position in the rear, it eventually emerged with new wings of greater area and deeper aerofoil sections plus a revised tail. In order to accommodate three engines, the Southampton's characteristic Warren truss wing centre section had to be discarded and replaced by a new structure where the engine mounts themselves formed part of the primary wing centre section support. The Danish aircraft, flown in 1927, was named Nanok. For other markets it was given the name Solent.

Supermarine made considerable effort, with Air Ministry support, to test the torpedo dropping capabilities of the Southampton. This included devising a patented torpedo rack, and one of the first batch of aircraft, refitted with a metal hull, was adapted to carry out trial drops. These were not considered particularly successful however, the aircraft lacking the necessary manoeuvrability, and for similar reasons the Danish Navy declined to purchase the Nanok as it performance did not

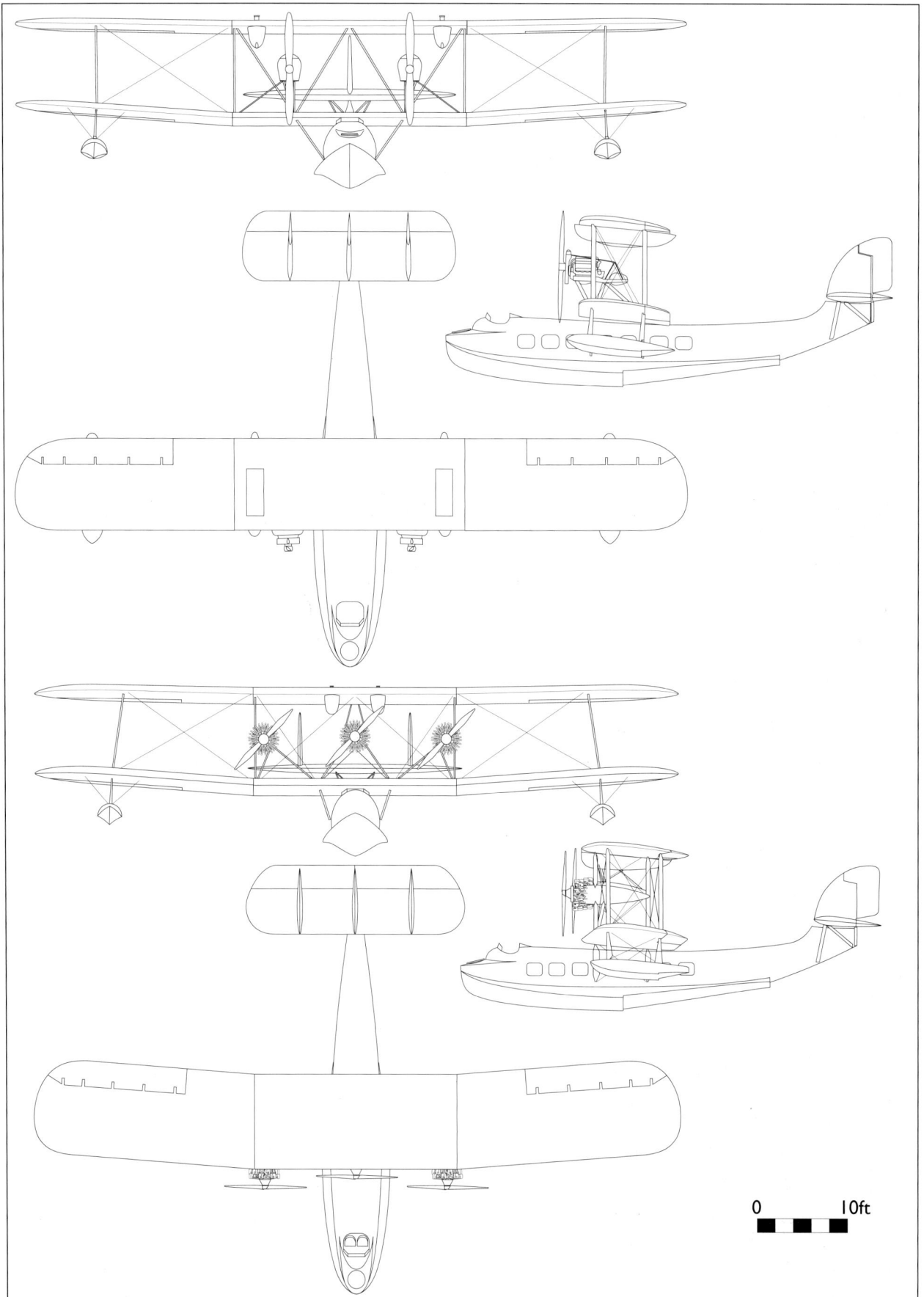

Supermarine offered civil variants of most of their flying boats. These were two projects based on the Southampton and Solent

The centre section of the biplane wings constructed for the Nanok, showing the engine mounts and wing support struts

meet specifications. The aircraft was retained by the company, converted for civil use as an air yacht and sold to A.E. Guinness. A fully civilianised version was also planned but not built.

A further three-engine Southampton derivative appeared on the drawing board in mid-1926, referred to as Southampton Development and featuring a completely new form of metal hull, the significance of which would be demonstrated soon after.

Production of the Southampton was in full swing by 1927 with both wooden and metal hulled versions passing through the works. Three of the metal-hulled aircraft, formed as the RAF Far East Flight, would set out to fly to the Far East and around Australia, a mission that was a great success both for the crews and the aircraft. The ability of flying boats to operate from remote locations with minimal support had been proven.

The Short S.5 Singapore prototype had also flown successfully and was about to embark on an extended route-proving and survey tour around Africa, again demonstrating the capabilities of flying boats. Blackburn's R.B.1 Iris had taken to the air equally successfully and was now back at the factory to have its hull replaced with a metal one. A number of Short S.8 Calcuttas, a three-engine civil flying boat that built on the company's experience with the Singapore, had been ordered by Imperial Airways.

Three-engined flying boats

With these capable flying boats all in service or under construction it may therefore appear a little perverse that in the early part of 1927 the Air Ministry issued Specification R.4/27 for a three-engine military flying boat to supplement or replace the Southampton. This move is very likely to have been prompted, at least in part, by Short Bros actively pursuing a market for a military version of the Calcutta, the company chasing orders from foreign buyers with one secured from France. The Air Ministry was positive about the prospects for such a flying boat and decided to review alternative designs from other manufacturers.

It appears that the initial approach to industry may have indicated a desire to see innovative designs, since the tenders put forward were quite diverse. Most of the projects were approved for funding and an individual tailored specification was raised for each – a clear sign that at this stage they were considered as experimental. R.4/27 went to Saunders for the A.7 Severn, featuring a novel hull of corrugated metal plating. R.5/27 was issued to Blackburn for the RB.2 Sydney, a braced parasol monoplane, and R.6/27 went to Supermarine for the Southampton Mark X.

Supermarine's response to Specification R.4/27 has tended to be underplayed or ignored in most

The Solent air yacht, a conversion of the Nanok torpedo bomber that had been rejected by the Danish military

histories of the company, yet the designs put forward and the subsequent construction of two aircraft were hugely important over the following three or four years for their influence on the fortunes of the company as a builder of flying boats.

Supermarine actually chose to tender two distinct designs to the Air Ministry for consideration, one a fairly conventional biplane and the other a monoplane with lateral stub stabilisers instead of wing floats. Sponsons, stabilisers, pontoons or stubs, various names were used, were wing-like floats of short span attached to the hull sides to provide lateral stability in place of the more usual wingtip floats. Their use had been pioneered, with considerable success, by the German designer Claus

Dornier, and the Dornier Wal family of civil flying boats had found a decent market. One example, on the British civil register having been purchased to make an attempt at a crossing of the Atlantic, made a brief visit to the RAF base at Calshot, downstream from the Woolston Works, where curious Supermarine staff had the opportunity to view it.

Mitchell had made the pragmatic decision to retain the tried and tested shape of the Southampton's wooden hull when moving to metal construction for the MkII in order to avoid the possibility of introducing new handling problems. It also simplified the replacement of interior fittings between the two types and indeed the eventual

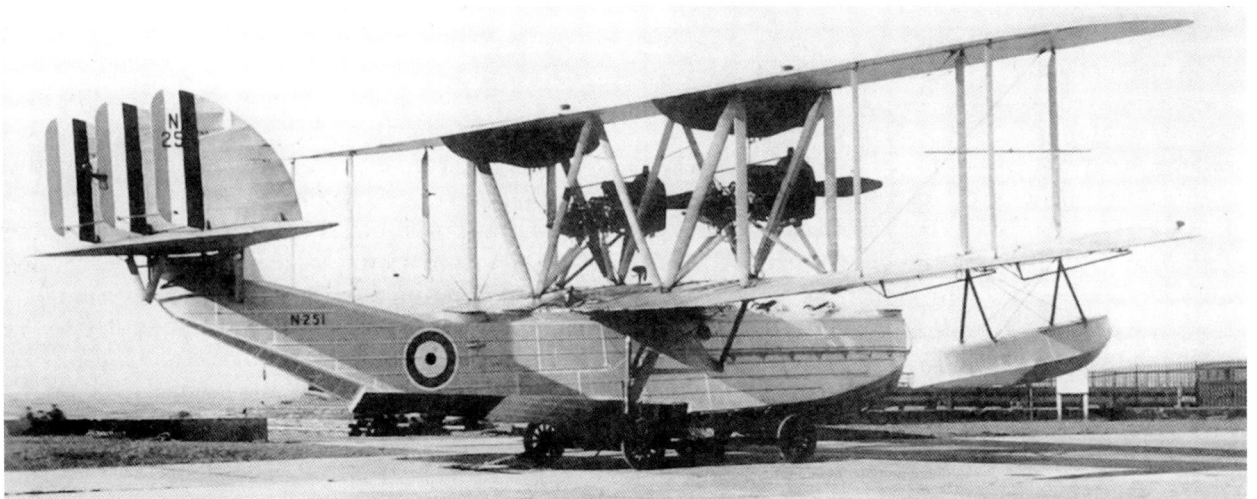

The experimental Saunders A10 metal hull with corrugated plating was fitted with Southampton wings and tail surfaces

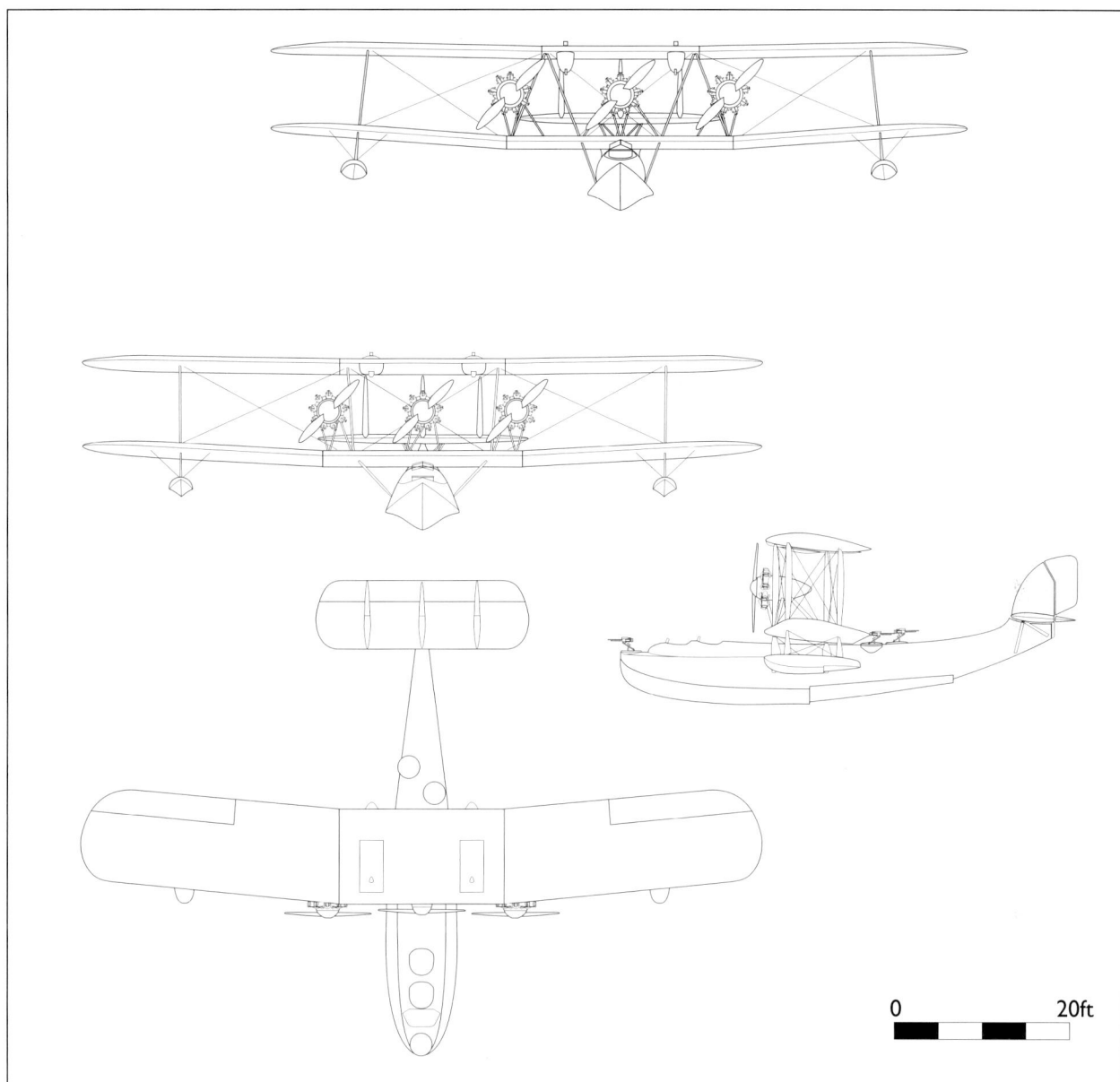

The three-engine Southampton Development project, from March and May 1926

replacement of life-expired wooden hulls with metal ones.

The down side was that the wooden hulls featured complex three dimensional curves – relatively easy to produce in wood but considerably hard to form using larger duralumin plates on the metal-shaping English Wheel. It was clear that a significantly simpler and cheaper style of design would be required for future projects.

Supermarine was far from alone in the quest for simplicity and cost saving; it had been the same driver behind Saunders' introduction of corrugated plates to provide hull stiffening without the need to rivet stringers to them. This innovation appealed to the Air Ministry at the time and as a first step Saunders was contracted to produce an experimental hull fitted with Southampton flying

surfaces for evaluation. This experiment was not entirely successful as several of the plates buckled, but it did provide Saunders with a wealth of hull design data for other projects. It was also a wake-up call to Supermarine that Saunders was rapidly shaping up to be a significant competitor.

Supermarine's biplane 4/27 project was the safe option, a project derived directly from the Southampton Development project of May 1926 which itself was based on a scheme from March that year to install three Jupiter engines in the wooden-hulled Southampton, a variation on the Nanok/Solent theme.

The simplified flat sided metal hull of the Southampton Development scheme was deepened and the fore part widened at the top to allow for a side-by-side cockpit arrangement. A lip was added, running from the nose to just under the wing, which acted as a combination of spray suppresser and hull plate stiffener.

The engine mounts and wing centre section bracing struts had been simplified further, 'Y' configuration for the outer engines and inverted 'Y' for the central. In addition to the Southampton-style nose and twin staggered rear gun positions, one more was added firing through the floor of the hull stern. Nevertheless the Southampton ancestry was still self-evident.

The 14/27 monoplane was an untried departure from the design norm by Mitchell and his team. Their construction and flight experience with monoplanes was limited, as, indeed, it was for most of their competitors, and restricted to small aircraft: the S.4 and Sparrow II. The ill-fated S.4 racer had taken the British airspeed record on 13th September, 1925, but had crashed prior to that year's Schneider Trophy contest due to suspected aileron flutter. The diminutive Sparrow II parasol wing ultra-light had been rebuilt from the biplane Sparrow I so it could take part in the 1926 Light Aircraft Competition at Lympne. By now, however, Mitchell's team were within weeks of seeing their stunning S.5 Schneider racer start its test flights.

The new flying boat design had a superficial resemblance to one of the Dornier Wal types, the decision to make it a monoplane with sponson stabilisers placing distinct limitations on possible layouts. The parasol wing centre section was supported above the hull on a pair of inverted 'V' struts, fore and aft, braced by cross wires, while the outer wings were each supported by twin struts running at an angle down to the outer edge of the stabilisers.

The position of the engines relative to the wing was the subject of experimentation in the Vickers wind tunnel to assess whether they would better sit above the wing or in front of the leading edge. The hull itself was of the same basic type as that designed for the biplane but lengthened by about 10ft. The stabilisers were of symmetrical aerofoil section and tapered sharply in both plan and thickness.

The award of a contract, under Specification 6/27, for the biplane design rather than the monoplane does appear counterintuitive. Given that all of the three-engine flying boats designs awarded contracts were experimental in one way or another, this might have been an ideal opportunity to evaluate one with sponson stabilisers. But apparently that was not the way the Air Ministry was thinking. None of the projects were given high priority, a case of déjà vu mirroring the attitude towards the flying boat prototypes under construction at the end of the war, and none would fly before 1930.

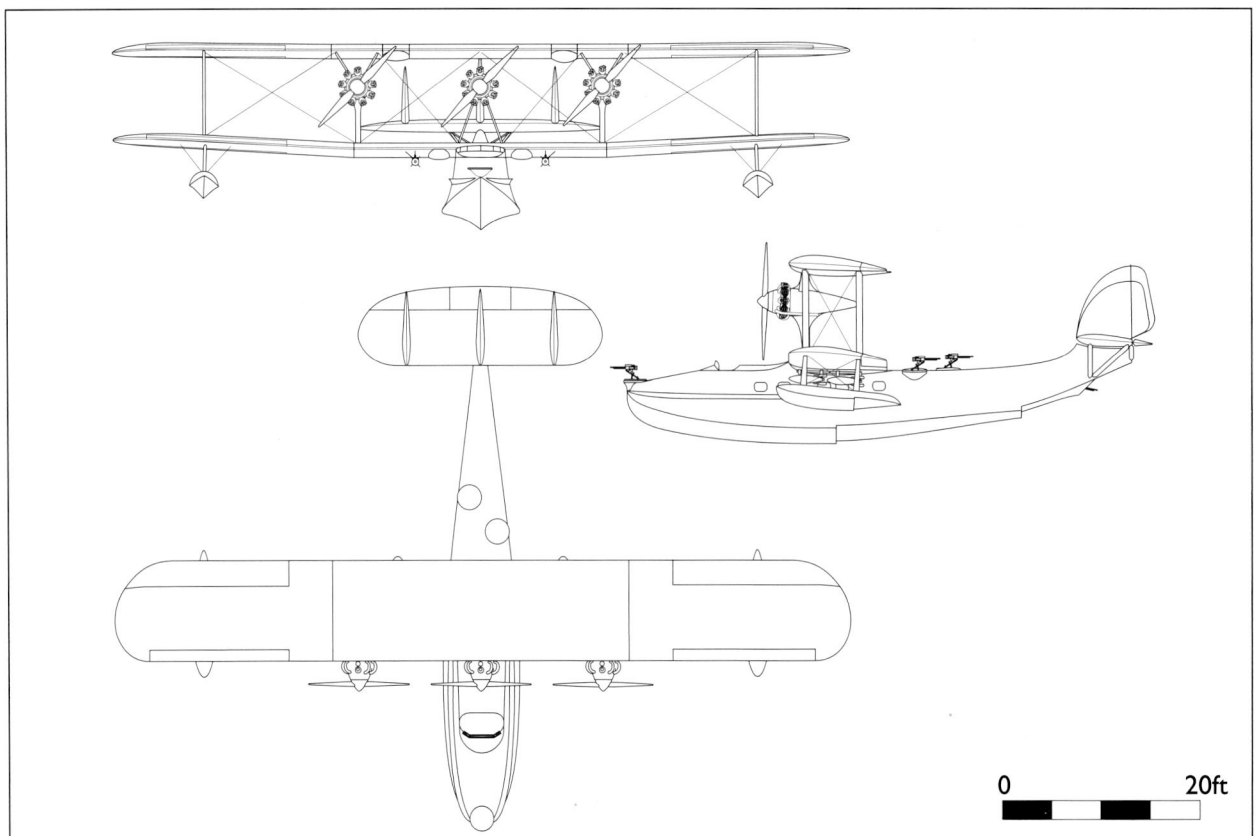

Supermarine's biplane project to meet Specification 4/27

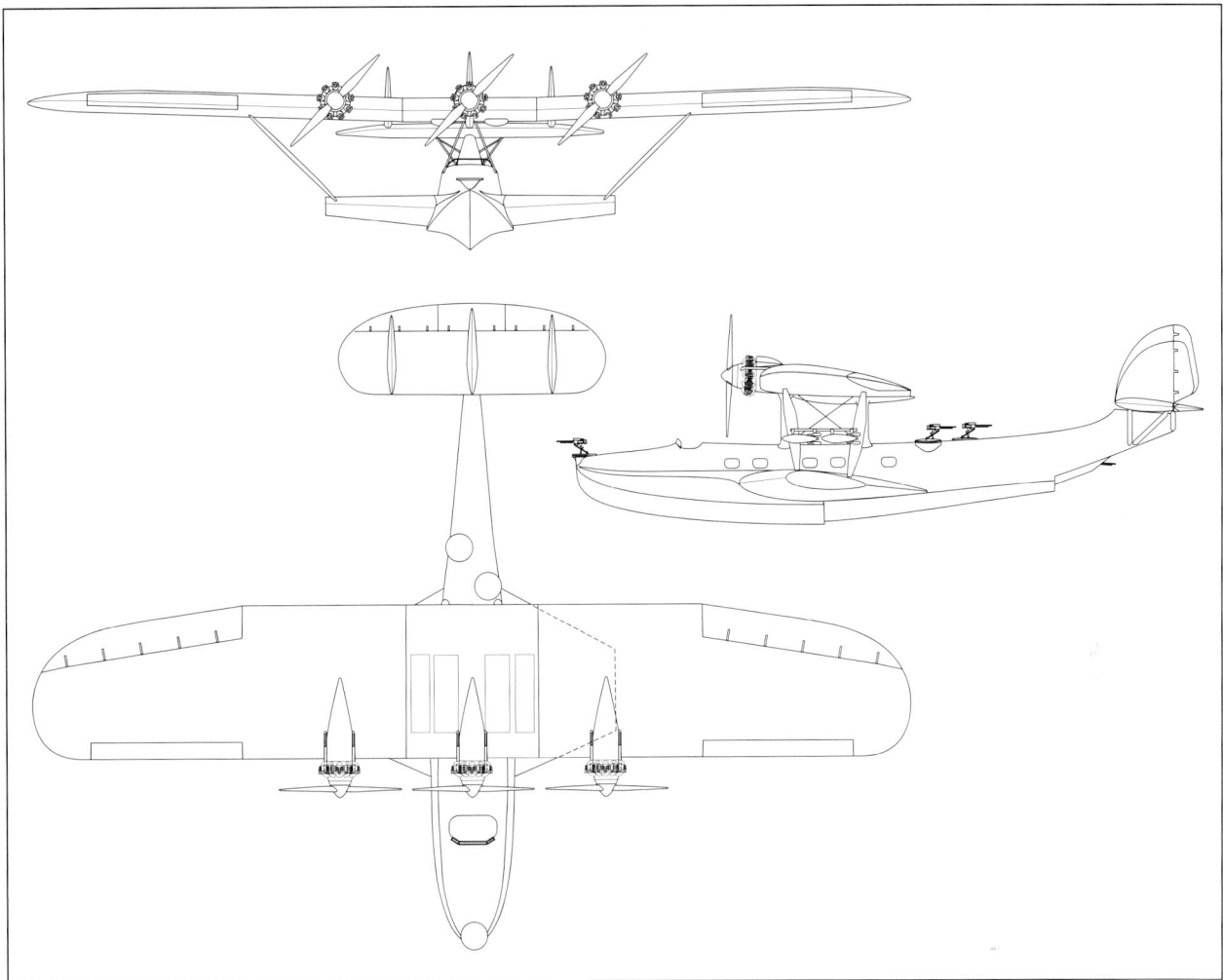

Supermarine's sponson-stabilised monoplane project to meet Specification 4/27

As it turned out, neither of the Supermarine projects were destined to proceed as originally designed. Both underwent a thorough review and re-emerged as fundamentally different aircraft. This change has to be, at least in part, the result of Vickers Aviation having purchased the entire share capital of Supermarine Aviation Works Ltd at the end of 1927.

Bird became a director of Vickers Aviation but all major decisions were now to be made by the new owners and many of Vickers' work practices were imposed on Supermarine, despite design independence being maintained. One director on the board of the now renamed Supermarine Aviation Works (Vickers) Ltd was Reginald Mitchell. In 1923, around the time that Bird had ousted Scott-Paine, he had renegotiated his contract and had inserted a clause whereby he would be offered a directorship at the end of 1927, although these were clearly not the circumstances under which he expected it to happen.

In the design department, Mitchell introduced a new scheme of alphanumeric project naming to replace the frankly shambolic document naming

and drawing numbering that dated back to the Pemberton-Billing years. This may have been an attempt to stave off Vickers introducing their own system which, within a year, they had.

In order to take both three-engine flying boat projects forward, Mitchell was already planning structural simplifications. The biplane, of which a prototype had been ordered, moved yet further away from its Southampton heritage although it was given the somewhat spurious Southampton Mark X name and under the new alphanumerical system received the project designation 'A'. Why the name 'Mark X' was chosen is far from obvious as there are precious few design features in common with those of the Southampton II.

The monoplane became project 'B' but will be described first as it was completed slightly ahead of the Southampton Mark X and was an isolated project with no derivatives.

Construction work on both aircraft appears to have commenced somewhere late in the second half of 1929, just prior to the Wall Street Crash and the worldwide slide into depression.

7
CHAPTER

The Air Yacht

Although the 4/27 monoplane had not received ministry funding, Supermarine decided to proceed with it as a private venture and it was revised as a civil project; not a commercial airliner but an air yacht for the super-rich. The hull of what was now named as the 3-Engined Monoplane Air Yacht, with project designation 'B', followed that of the Southampton Mark X onto the design team's drawing boards. It was broadly similar in form but 64ft in length compared to 50ft for the Mark X. It also went through the same simplification process by maximising the use of flat plates stiffened by external stringers. The wing was now of simple rectangular plan with square tips and constructed in metal on two spars with fabric covering. The aerofoil was Clark Y.

The design of the sponson stabilisers gave Supermarine a great deal of trouble. As part of the simplification process, Mitchell had chosen to eliminate all taper, both in plan and thickness, as a starting point. He then contemplated two alternative designs, both based on a deep aerofoil section. The first was set at a relatively small angle of incidence and had a step built into the lower surface, aligned with the main step of the hull. The second had no step but incorporated progressive droop of the rear two thirds of the aerofoil so that the trailing edge dipped downwards outboard.

Both of these alternatives plus a few other designs were evaluated in model form in Vickers' water tank at St Albans, a facility constructed to evaluate the hulls of ships but now a valuable resource made available to Supermarine as a result of the Vickers takeover. The tank measured 410ft in length, 21ft in

width, and depth varied between 10ft 6in and 12ft. The model to be tested was held in a towed cradle which restricted lateral movement, roll and yaw but allowed free movement in the vertical plane and in pitch. Mitchell was already making great use of the tank while designing the floats for the Supermarine Rolls-Royce S.6 racer, destined for the British team defending the Schneider Trophy in the contest scheduled for September 1929.

There proved to be considerable variation in the performance of the various models tested and a lot of experimentation was required given the number of variables in play; position fore and aft, angle of incidence, span, taper, type of step. Particular problems were encountered with the stabilisers, which interacted adversely with the hull bow wave, especially when simulating overload conditions. In

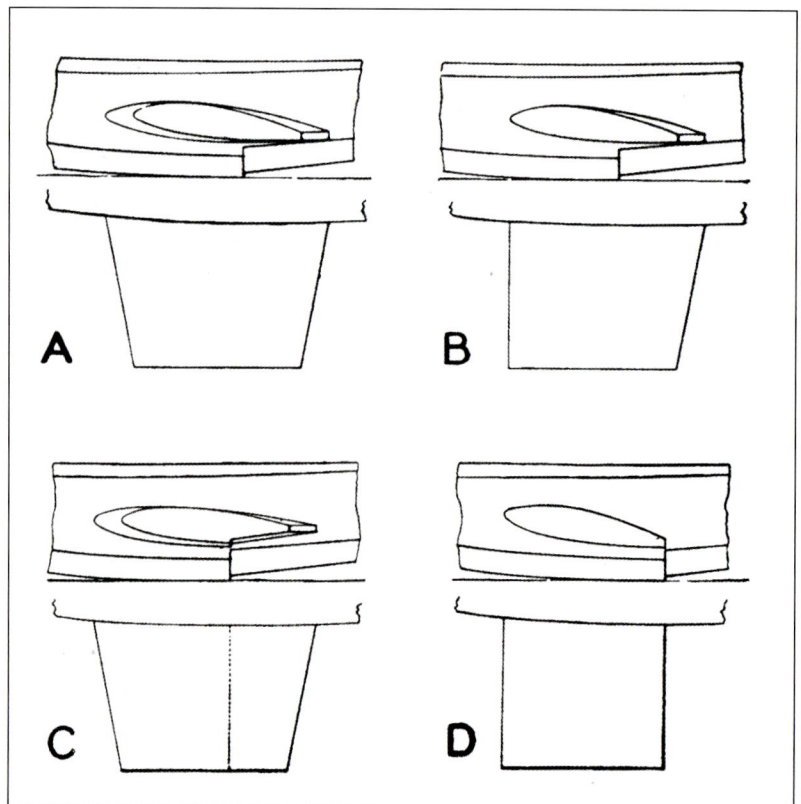

A selection of the sponson stabiliser models that were evaluated in the Vickers water tank

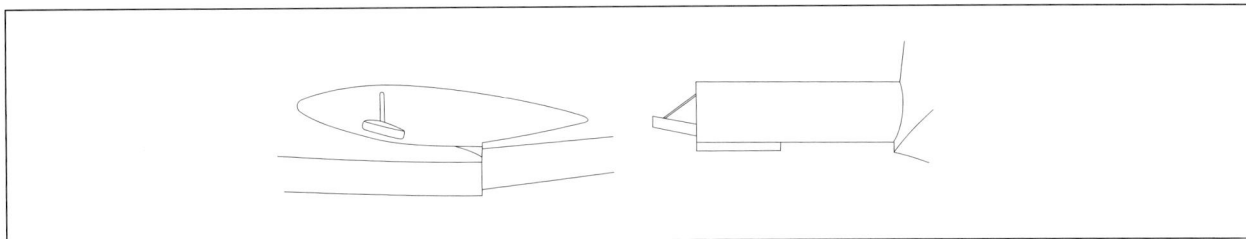

When the sponson stabilisers on the Air Yacht proved to be inadequate a quick solution was sought by attaching a vane and wedge to their outer edges. Model tested in the Vickers water tank

the end, one of the simplest layouts gave the best balance of performance characteristics overall: no taper, full-span step and low angle of incidence.

Both the Air Yacht and Southampton Mark X were finally ready for their first flights by early 1930. The Air Yacht was shown to the press in mid-February 1930, both on the forecourt of the works at Woolston and resting on the water.

At this point it became known that A. E. Guinness, the brewery magnate and noted investor in aviation, had commissioned the Air Yacht to replace his Supermarine Solent. The radical change in Supermarine design style since then was readily apparent. The wing was of constant chord with simple square-cut tips and the engine nacelles were mounted with their engine thrust line just above the mean chord line of the wing. The Armstrong Siddeley Jaguar engines were enclosed in drag-reducing Townend rings. The tailplane, triple fins and rudders, all elegantly curved on the Southampton flying boats, were reduced down to basic rectangular shapes. Overall the aircraft appeared functional rather than graceful, but appearances can deceive.

Once the Air Yacht had been run down to the water for initial taxiing trials it soon became clear that the water tank tests had neglected one important factor; the movement constraints of the towing carriage had not allowed for transverse, or roll, movement. Static model tests had suggested that there would be ample roll stability, which corresponded with the calculated values, but experience with the aircraft when taxiing soon showed that very different conditions were encountered in the real world and even a few degrees of roll brought about by side winds or engine torque would render the stabilisers' ability to restore upright balance ineffective.

Checks with the aircraft stationary corresponded with calculated and model results. Fitting extensions to the outer edges of the stabilisers that doubled their static stability proved totally ineffective when under way.

As a result of this experience, the Vickers test tank's towing carriage was modified to allow freedom of movement in roll and also for the model to be towed with the application of varying amounts of heeling moment. When model testing

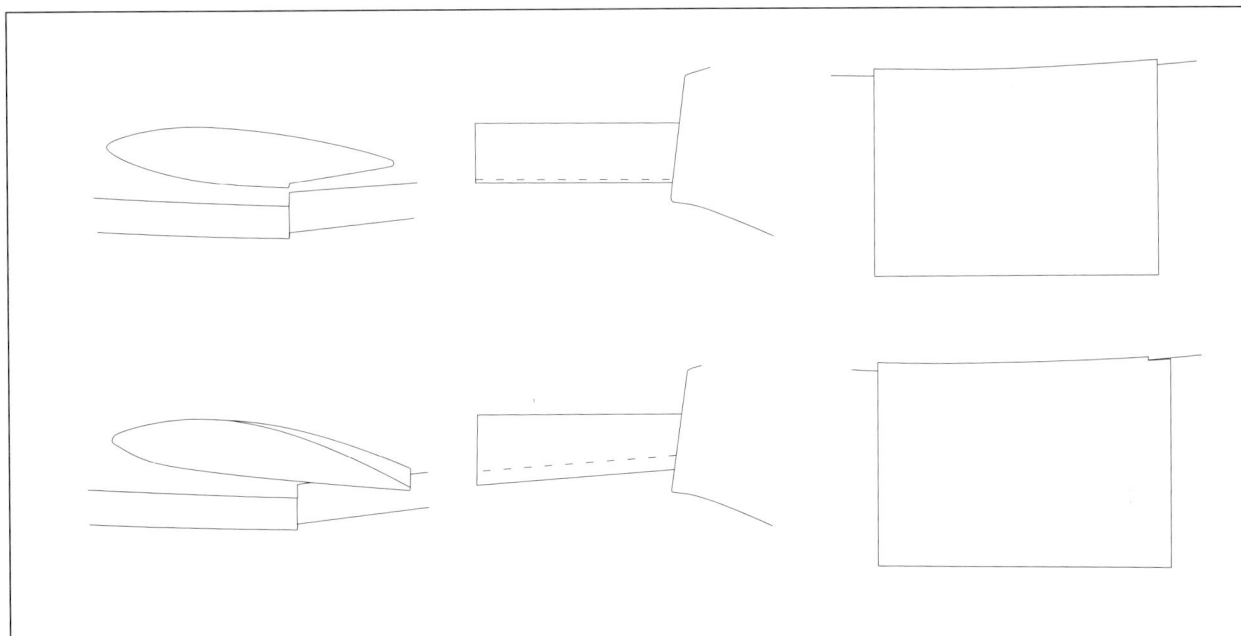

The original and final form of the sponson stabilisers on the Air Yacht

resumed, it was soon found that there was a critical spot at the scale equivalent of 10 knots and so most tests were then run at this speed. In the worst case, a heeling moment that only produced a 1 degree list when stationary caused the model to capsize and roll right-over at 11 knots. Thankfully this situation had not been encountered while testing the aircraft.

Raising the stabiliser nose slightly to prevent water passing over them showed little improvement and actually reduced stability. The final fix, very much a compromise, was to fit a small wedge to the outer step and a hydrovane on the tip. Mitchell's narrative regarding these tests, which he presented at a conference in September 1930, is clear about this modification and Supermarine drawings of the model show the configuration. However, there do not appear to be any photographs showing that either the wedge or hydrovane were ever fitted to the aircraft.

When the aircraft was first shown to the press in February 1930, photographs show that it was fitted with the original design of stabilisers that had a step on the lower surface. All later photographs show that the aircraft had been refitted with stabilisers with a flat rear lower surface and no step, possibly with the concept of rear edge droop reinstated, much as Mitchell had originally intended. The revised stabiliser design was worked up over the summer and three-view general arrangement

drawings of the aircraft dated October 1930 also show this profile.

All this delay in dealing with the water handling problems and consequent return trips to the works for modification had seriously delayed full testing of the aircraft and it was only in May 1931 that it was sent to the MAEE for its Certificate of Airworthiness (CofA) trials, now powered by 525hp Armstrong Siddeley Panthers.

Halfway through the trials, the structure of the starboard stabiliser failed and inspection showed the port stabiliser to be similarly fatigued. Supermarine carried out repairs, strengthened the affected parts and added an additional bracing strut between the wing and the rear outer corner of the stabiliser.

After all the modifications, the Air Yacht handled adequately on the water but swung to starboard on take-off. It was also found that the aircraft could not maintain height on two engines. Overall performance in the air was judged as inferior compared to other flying boats, largely due to the drag of the stabilisers. The CofA was issued on 22nd December 1931.

Whether Guinness accepted the aircraft or not is unclear, some say he did, some not. The aircraft was undoubtedly significantly overweight and well down on the pre-flight estimates of performance so he was probably well within his rights to turn it down if he so wished. What is clear, however, is

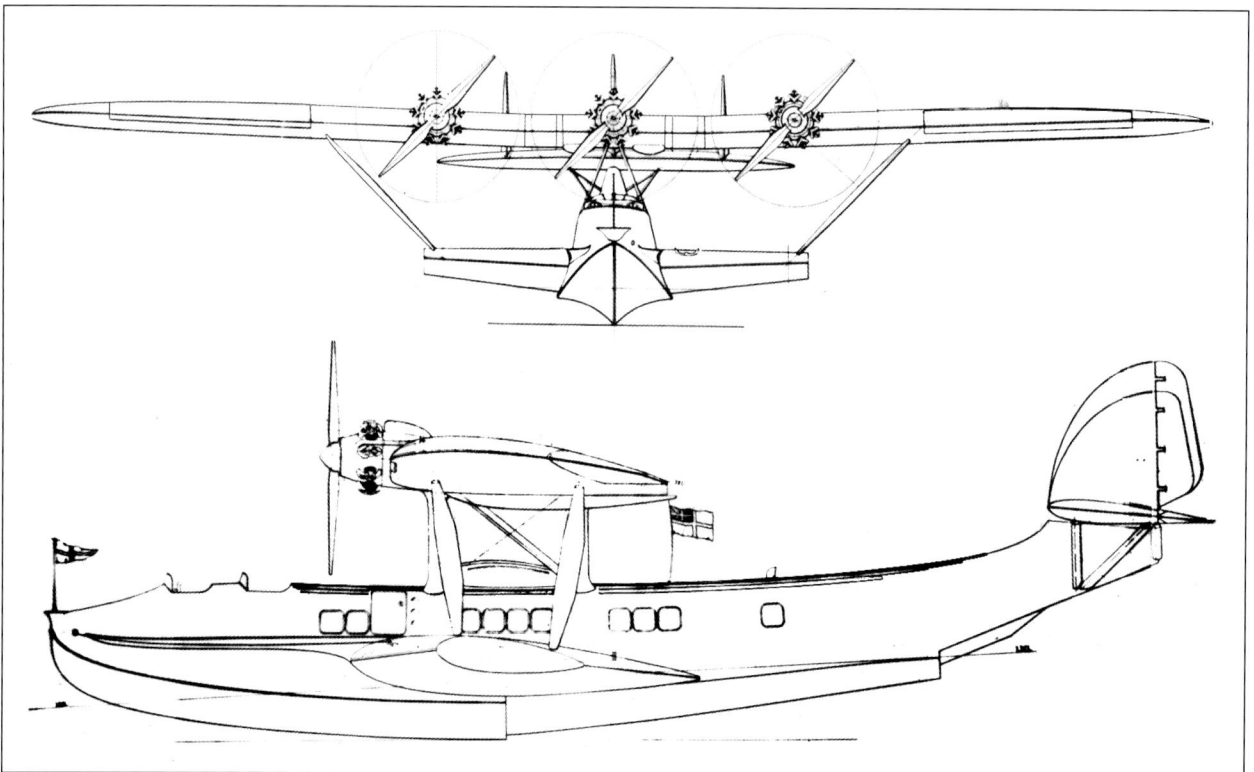

The Air Yacht as advertised in late 1929 – a reversion to the original 1927 design

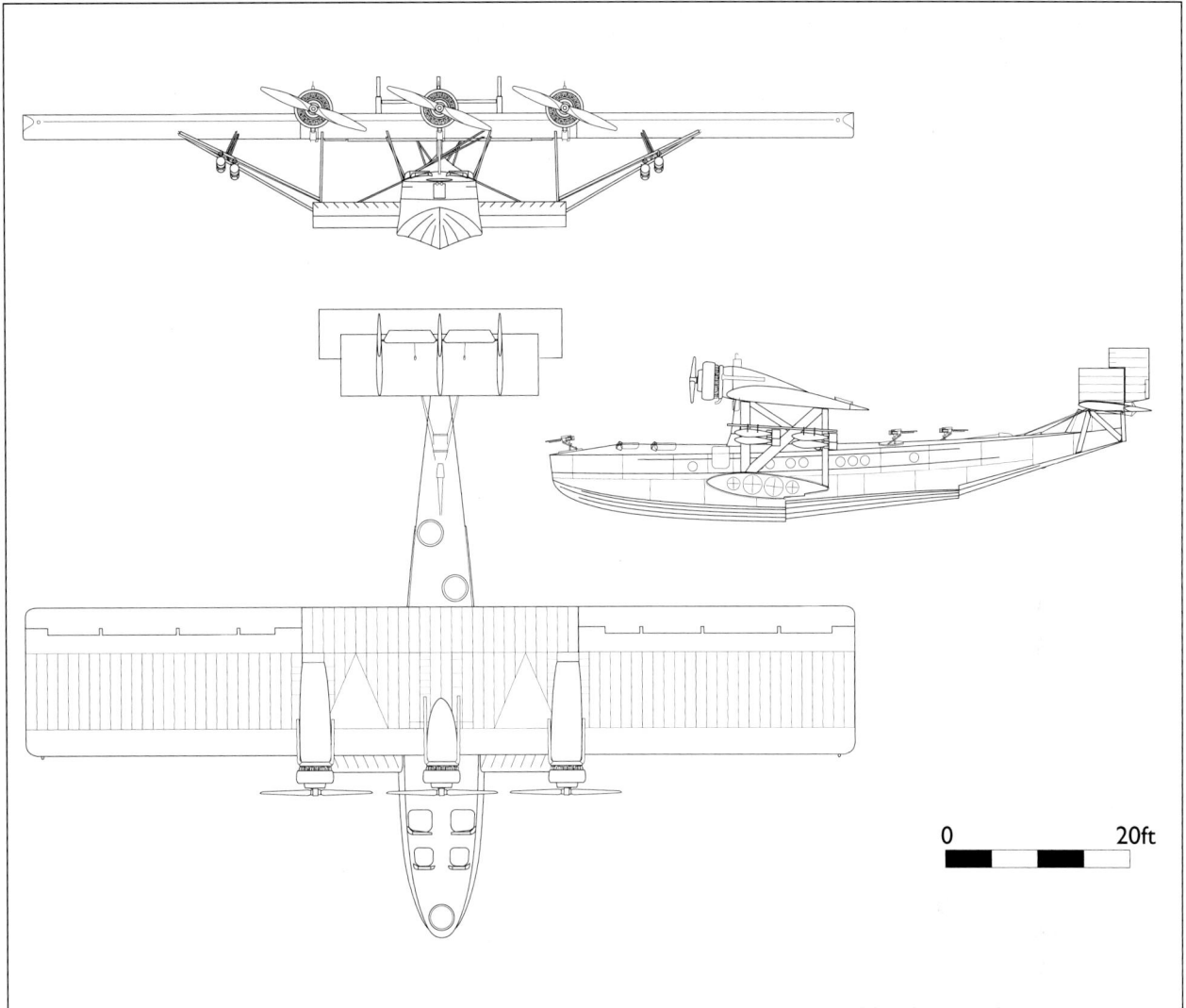

A military scheme for the Air Yacht dating from 1931

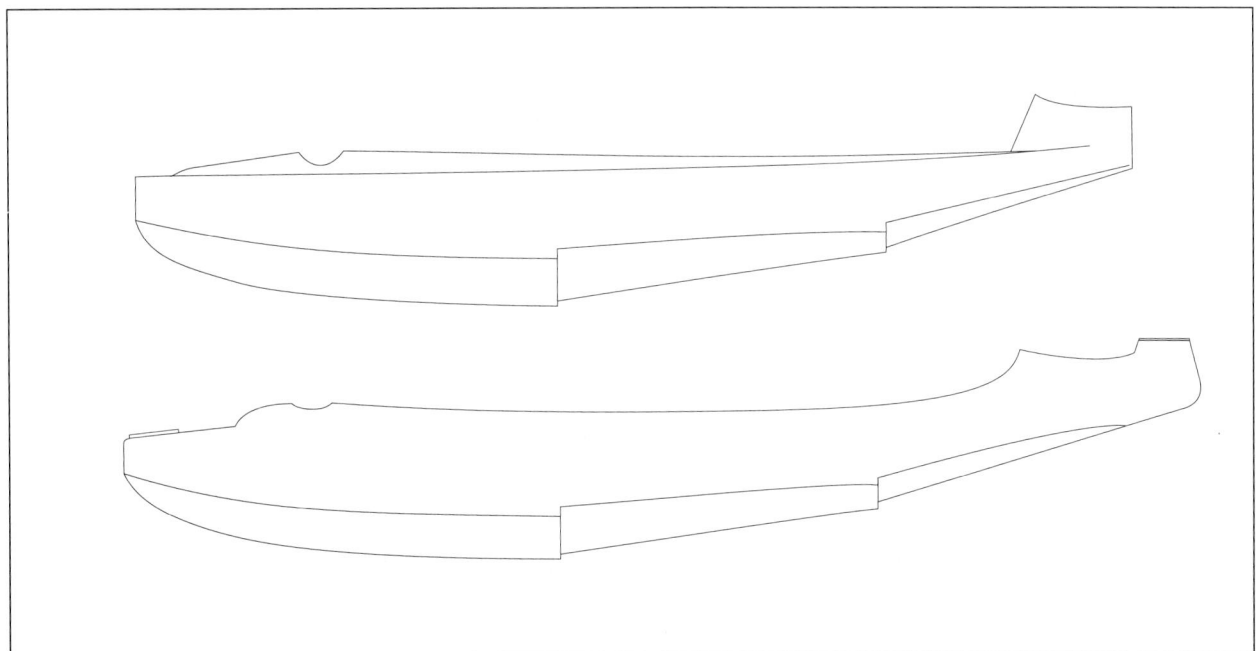

The form of the hulls for the Southampton Mark X – as Project A and Type 171

that the civil registration documents do not list him as an owner. The Air Yacht had been flown from the start with civil registration G-AASE but it is not until 8th October 1932 that the records show the aircraft to be registered officially, the owner being Mrs June Jewett James.

It appears more likely that she purchased the Air Yacht directly from Supermarine. On 25th January 1933, while touring around the Mediterranean, the Air Yacht stalled while landing in the Gulf of Salerno, the wing structure collapsed and the aircraft was wrecked beyond economic repair.

In late 1929 Supermarine's sales material and details for the Air Yacht included drawings of a civilianised version of the 4/27 monoplane design powered by three Bristol Jupiter engines, rather than the simplified Jaguar-powered aircraft that was then nearing completion in the works. Make of that what you will.

Finally, in February 1932 the company prepared a schematic showing the Air Yacht converted for military service, with gun rings, Southampton-style, in the hull and bomb racks on the wing support struts, and so the design had come full circle and returned to its original purpose as defined under Specification 4/27.

Southampton Mark X and offspring

Even though it was a more conventional design than the Air Yacht, the Southampton Mark X was to prove almost equally problematic.

Project work started on a thorough redesign of the hull in early 1928, and this they had completed in detail by mid-year. The plates of the hull sides and bottom were now to be stiffened by riveting on long external strakes/stringers of 12 or 14 gauge extruded duralumin in place of the usual internal stringers, which would have required

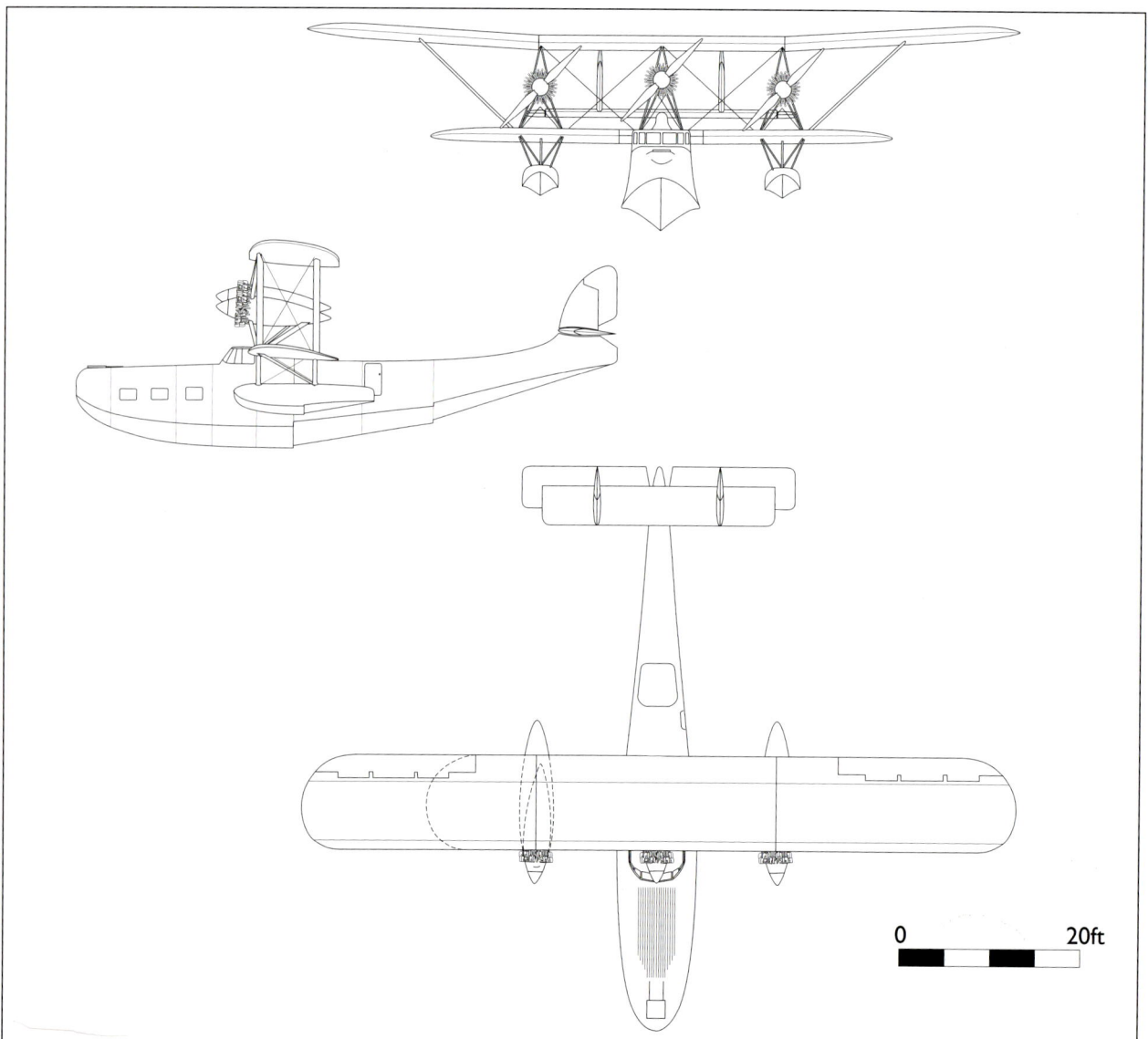

The Civil Southampton Mark X project – mid-1929

either notching the bulkheads to allow them to pass through or applying them in short lengths.

The planing bottom was to be fabricated in stainless steel, another first for Supermarine. However no work was undertaken at this stage on the design of the wings, which were also to be of metal construction. Supermarine had plans in hand to produce metal wings for the Southampton II but design work on these was still at a relatively early stage, while Vickers had experience producing large metal wings for the Virginia bomber and other projects.

After reviewing both options, the management decided that the wings for the Southampton Mark X would be designed and produced by Vickers, and the Vickers project designation Type 171 was assigned to the work. Not only was this seen as a pragmatic solution to a potential design bottleneck for Supermarine but it would also get the two design teams learning to work together. However, from the dates on drawings it would seem that no work was done on these wings until mid-1929, by which time

Supermarine had produced its own metal wings for the Southampton II and presumably could have handled the Mark X wings in house, other work in hand permitting.

Also in mid-1929, Supermarine engaged once again in the process of redesigning the Project Type 171 hull shape. This time the bow and stern reverted to a look more akin to the Southampton Development scheme. The construction method for the hull was as previously described.

While Supermarine was revising the hull, Vickers was designing and constructing the wings. The joint team had agreed that they would be of sesquiplane form, although it is not clear what benefit was thought to come from this, neither team having used that layout for any of their previously built aircraft. The internal construction of the metal wings followed the Vickers practice of twin spars and fabricated ribs. The centre section of the lower wing bolted directly to the hull top and the outer panels, unlike on previous Supermarine flying boats, were not braced to the hull by struts.

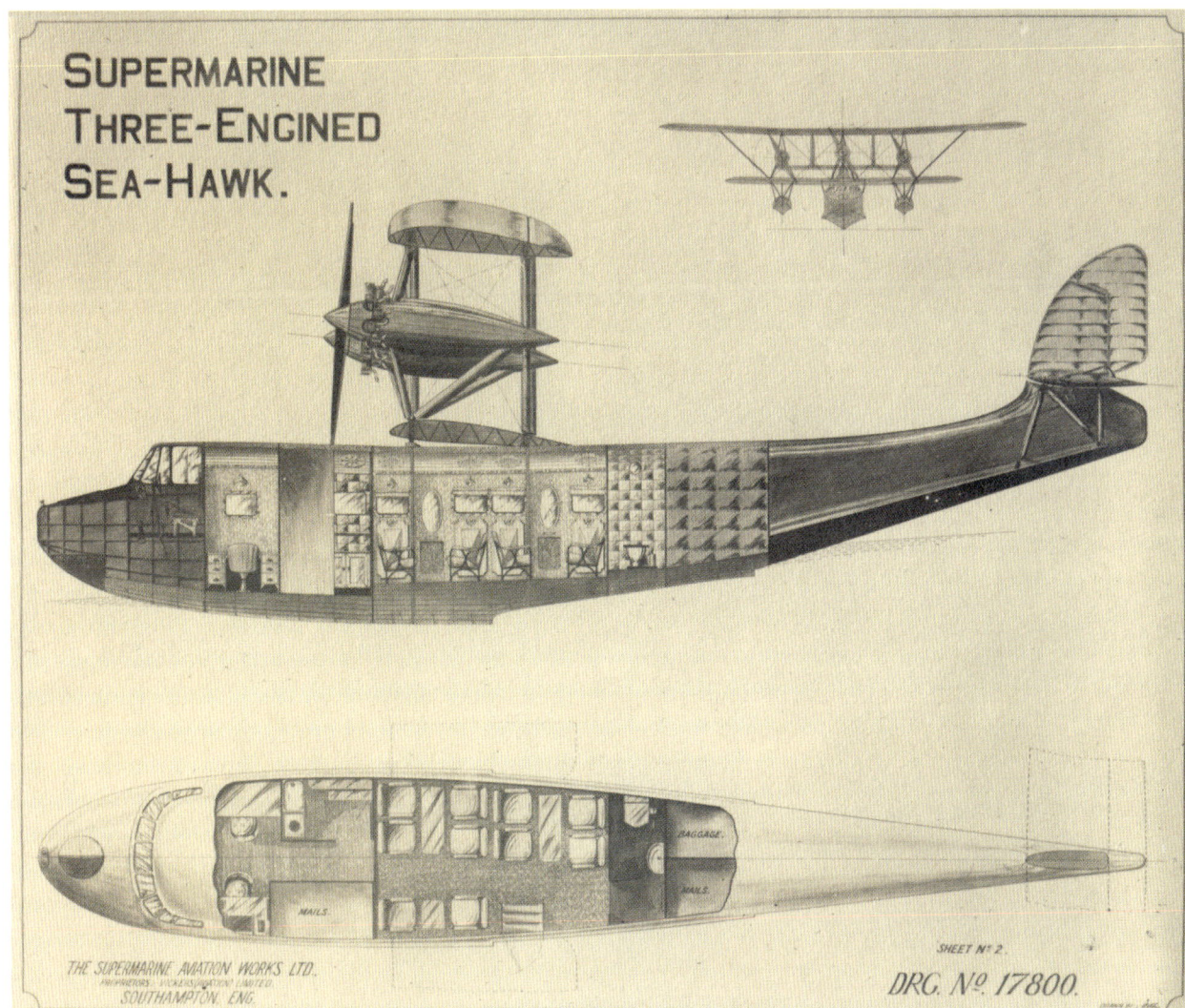

Supermarine Sea-Hawk MkII – October 192

The Supermarine Type 180 four-engine civil flying boat was proposed in various forms, all scaled-up from the Southampton Mk X and Sea-Hawk

The centre section of the top wing was supported by the frameworks of vertical and inverted 'V' struts that formed the mounts for the three engine nacelles. The long span outer panels were then supported by large sloping struts running up from the base of the outer engine frames. As these struts were of considerable length they were themselves stabilised by additional small sloping struts running from mid-strut back to the top wing. It was not a particularly tidy arrangement.

Wing floats of a larger volume than would be considered normal for a flying boat of this size were positioned below the outer engine mounts and contained the fuel tanks. The engines were 430hp Armstrong Siddeley Jaguar VICs.

Of the two 4/27-based projects, Supermarine considered that the Southampton Mark X had greater potential and derivatives of the design were soon under consideration. An early sketch for a civil version, unnamed and undated, shows the wings and tail surfaces of Mark X mated to a new deep fuselage with the enclosed cockpit on top, ahead of the lower wing. This was almost certainly from the early-mid 1929 period and by June it had been superseded, as Type 178 00, by a basic civil conversion of the Mark X with an open cockpit. This received the name Sea-Hawk.

By October this new project had acquired a proper civil airliner hull, which Supermarine said conformed to Imperial Airways standards, with the enclosed cockpit located at the front. In this form it was named Sea-Hawk II and publicised with articles and the issue of sales brochures. It was, in effect, a direct competitor to the Short Calcutta.

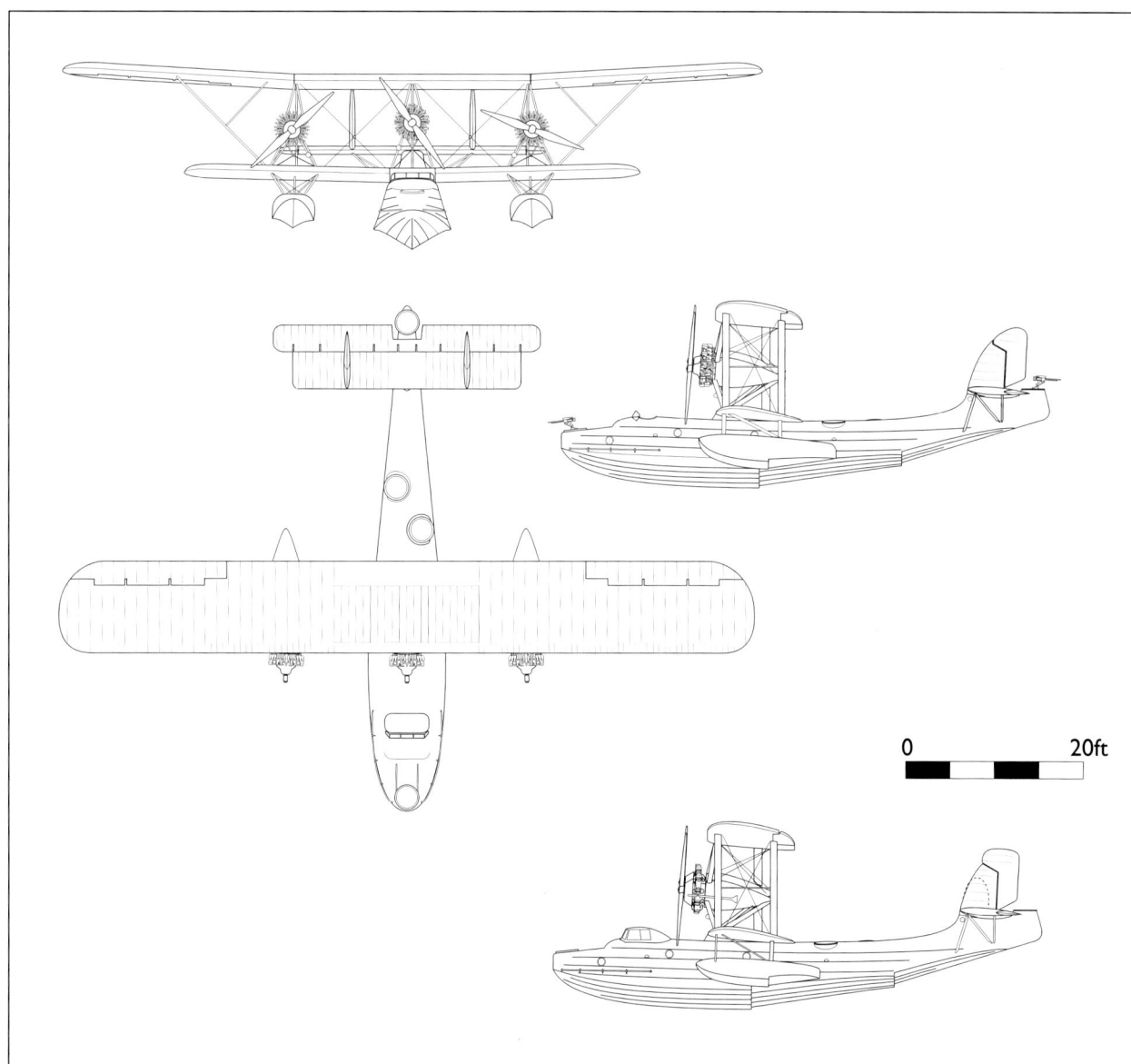

0   20ft

Southampton Mark X – main drawing, as first flown, extra sideview with enclosed cabin, revised tail, small wing floats and Jupiter engines (not all modifications were applied at the same time)

The Sea-Hawk II was designed to carry between 10 and 20 passengers depending on internal configuration, the smaller number for when half the interior space was allocated for the carriage of mail. The specification changed over time but the initial offering, in late 1929, was for the aircraft to be powered by three 500hp Armstrong Siddeley Jaguar engines giving a top speed of 130mph, cruising speed of 105mph and a range of 300 miles.

The project was modified over the coming months to incorporate some of the changes trialled on the Southampton Mark X and was still included in model form among the projects on Vickers' exhibition stands through to at least the end of 1930.

Under the Vickers project numbering system, the Sea-Hawk was logged as Type 178. This Type number became a sort of catch-all designation used for a variety of Supermarine schemes and projects in the early stage of design around this period. A few would eventually gain their own unique project number and more detailed design would proceed. The Sea-Hawk was not to be one of them.

Other schemes based directly on the Mark X included an amphibian and a version powered by Rolls-Royce Kestrels.

The design style and layout of the Mark X was also used as the basis for a much larger four-engine flying boat developed in October 1929 as Type 180. If the Sea-Hawk can be considered Supermarine's response to the Short Calcutta, then the Type 180 was to meet a new requirement from Imperial Airways for a four-engined flying boat, circulated in September.

Supermarine submitted a design that was, in most respects, an enlargement of the Sea-Hawk. The engines were Armstrong-Siddeley Jaguar Mayor radials installed in individual egg-shape nacelles mounted in fore and aft pairs. All were tractors with the propellers of the rear engines of lesser diameter than those of the front engines, since they would be operating in their slipstream. Two layouts were offered, one as in the original Civil Mark X with the cockpit on top of the hull and the other as in the Sea-Hawk II.

Capacity in both cases was for up to 22 passengers in a cabin three times the volume of the Sea-Hawk II's, plus hold space for mail and freight. Range was to be 450 miles in standard mode at a leisurely cruising speed of 90mph. Both Blackburn and Short also produced designs for the Imperial Airways specification and the latter won the order with the Short S.17 Kent.

The first flight of the Mark X took place just as these civil projects were being offered to the airlines, in March 1930, shortly after that of the Air Yacht.

Its performance was far from impressive, certainly disappointing for a design that Supermarine intended to form the basis for a family of flying boats, and an urgent and extensive programme of modifications and upgrades commenced.

The engines were first changed to more powerful Armstrong Siddeley Panthers and then to Bristol Jupiters. Townend rings were added and then discarded. The large floats were removed and replaced by smaller ones positioned further outboard with the fuel tanks now suspended under the lower wing. The outer panels of the lower wing were increased in span, eliminating the sesquiplane layout, with consequent modifications to the bracing to the top wing. Finally, an enclosed cockpit was installed. Modest improvements in performance were achieved, but insufficient to revive the project.

In attempting to explain the lacklustre performance of the aircraft it has been said that it had proven to be significantly overweight compared to pre-flight estimates, with some reports indicating that this was as much as 30% and to which the Supermarine hull and Vickers wings contributed equally.

However, comparing Supermarine's pre-build estimates from 1929 and the post-flight figures published in 1932 no such discrepancy is apparent. Furthermore, the weights are all quite similar to those of the Saunders Severn and Blackburn Sydney – both of which were built to the same basic specification. With no prospect of a military order, the Mark X line was effectively dead.

It was not entirely bad news as the rivals to the Mark X fared no better, their performance broadly comparable. Both the Saunders Severn and Blackburn Sydney disappointed and no orders were received for either. Neither were any sales achieved for Blackburn's civil version of the Sydney, the Nile. On the other hand, the Short Calcutta had entered service with Imperial Airways in late 1928 and its proven success encouraged the Air Ministry to order a military version, the Rangoon, which flew in September 1930 and entered service shortly after.

The proven capability of Short's Singapore, Calcutta and Rangoon placed the company at the forefront for larger flying boat designs and the Air Ministry then commissioned a new four-engine prototype as the Singapore II, which flew in March 1930. That in turn led to a further development as the Singapore III, of which 37 were ordered for the RAF in the mid-1930s. Supermarine, Blackburn and Saunders, now Saunders-Roe, had a lot of ground to make up.

Giants

Oswald Short, chairman of Short Bros, had approached the Air Ministry at the end of 1927 with a proposal to build a really large six-engine flying boat. It is unlikely, as has been so often suggested, that this was a direct response to the Dornier Do X, an aircraft which had yet to commence construction. Dornier's project had been initiated in 1926 and rumours about it began to circulate in 1927, but reliable information was lacking as to its size, form and potential and could not have influenced Short. Brigadier-General Groves of the Air League of the British Empire claimed to have obtained data in March 1928, but as an editorial in *Flight* demonstrated these appeared to be flawed, although the magazine's own assumptions were equally poor.

The first official information, although still questionable in part, was presented as general figures and graphs prepared by Dornier himself in a lecture before the RAeS in May 1928. It was very different from Short's proposal.

At the point when Oswald Short visited the Ministry, the Singapore II was on his company's drawing board and his suggestion was to take this design as the starting point, basically just scaling it up. The proposal was that this would be an experimental aircraft which, if successful, could have a role as a large transport and reconnaissance

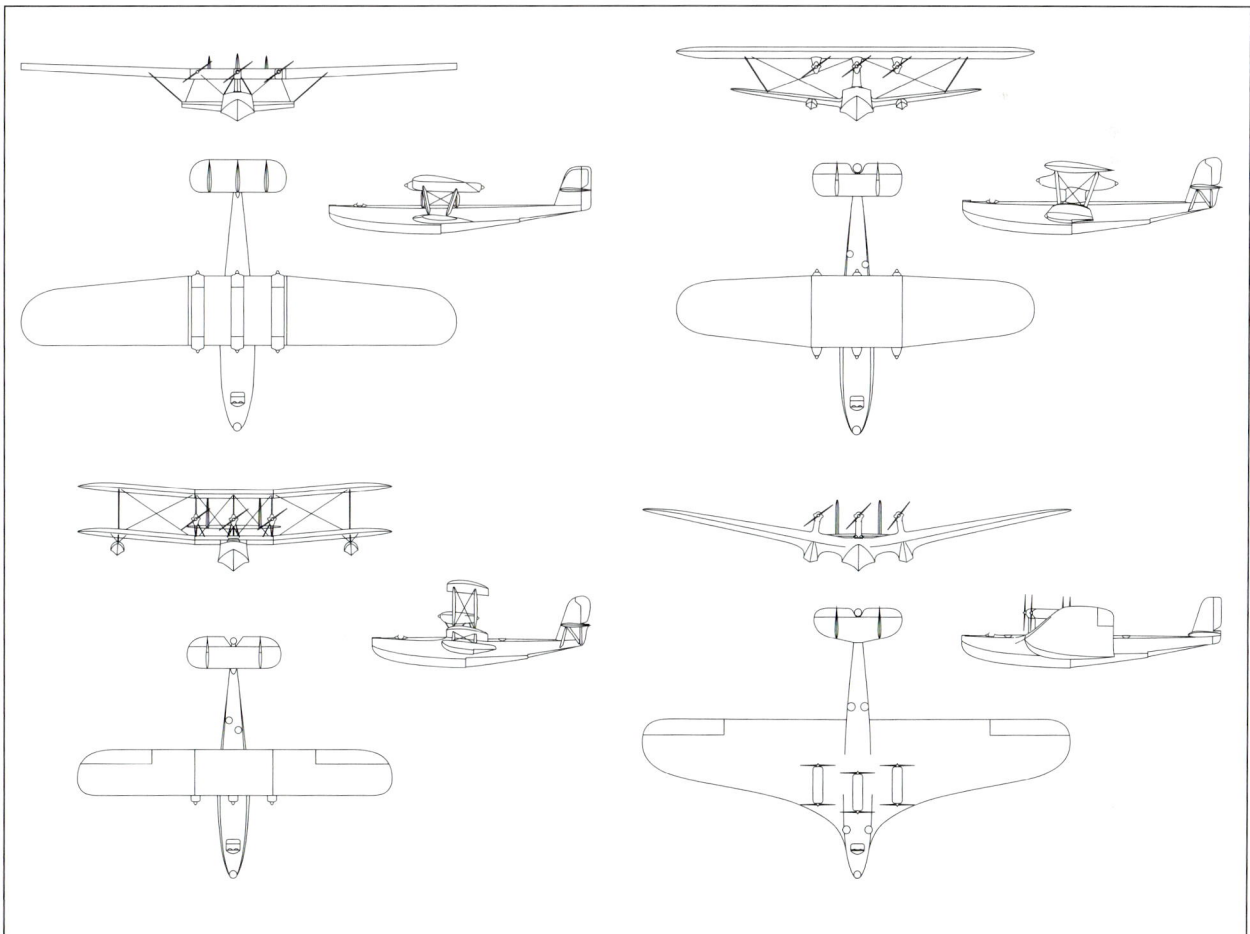

The Supermarine design team sketched a number of alternative schemes for six-engine flying boats in early 1928

aircraft or a sort of 'mother ship' to support flights of flying boats in remote locations. After some initial reluctance, the Ministry did accept the project and wrote Specification R.6/28 around it. The aircraft would emerge in 1932 as the S.14 Sarafand.

Although a contract for a prototype would most likely be awarded to Short Bros – indeed, it may already have been awarded to Shorts – the specification was still circulated to the other flying boat manufacturers, Supermarine receiving a copy in November 1928. Yet Mitchell must have been aware of its contents much earlier since his design team was already engaged in devising alternative schemes for a very large military six-engine flying boat.

This is one of only a few examples that have survived where we can see how the design department worked to develop new ideas. Sketch drawings of four of their initial schemes have been preserved, all as simple general arrangements with handwritten drawing numbers added, which would place them in the Supermarine list as having been produced in the first two months of 1928.

Two of the schemes clearly drew inspiration directly from the two flying boat projects the company had only recently tendered to R.4/27, the third was a sesquiplane with the lower wing set

low on the hull, while the fourth was quite radical – a monoplane with a massive wing set at a large dihedral angle that blended into the hull at the root. The engines were mounted on tall pylons.

In all cases the aircraft were to be powered by six Napier Lion XI engines. It is likely that further schemes had been considered but no further work appears to have been done for many months.

Under Mitchell's new designation system, project 'D' was initiated at the end of 1928 soon after Specification R.6/28 had been received. This project followed the Supermarine Rolls-Royce S.6 Schneider racer, allocated 'C', in the new catalogue. Layout drawings produced in January 1928 show a 'Six Engined Flying Boat to A.M spec. 6/28' that was unlike any of the known earlier schemes.

It was a large cantilever monoplane with a thick wing of elliptical plan shoulder-mounted on a slab-sided fuselage. The deep wing floats attached directly to the outer edge of the wing centre section.

The six engines were installed as tractor and pusher pairs within long nacelles. These were held on strut framework pylons mounted on the wing centre section. The engine type is not specified on the drawings but is clearly a water-cooled type

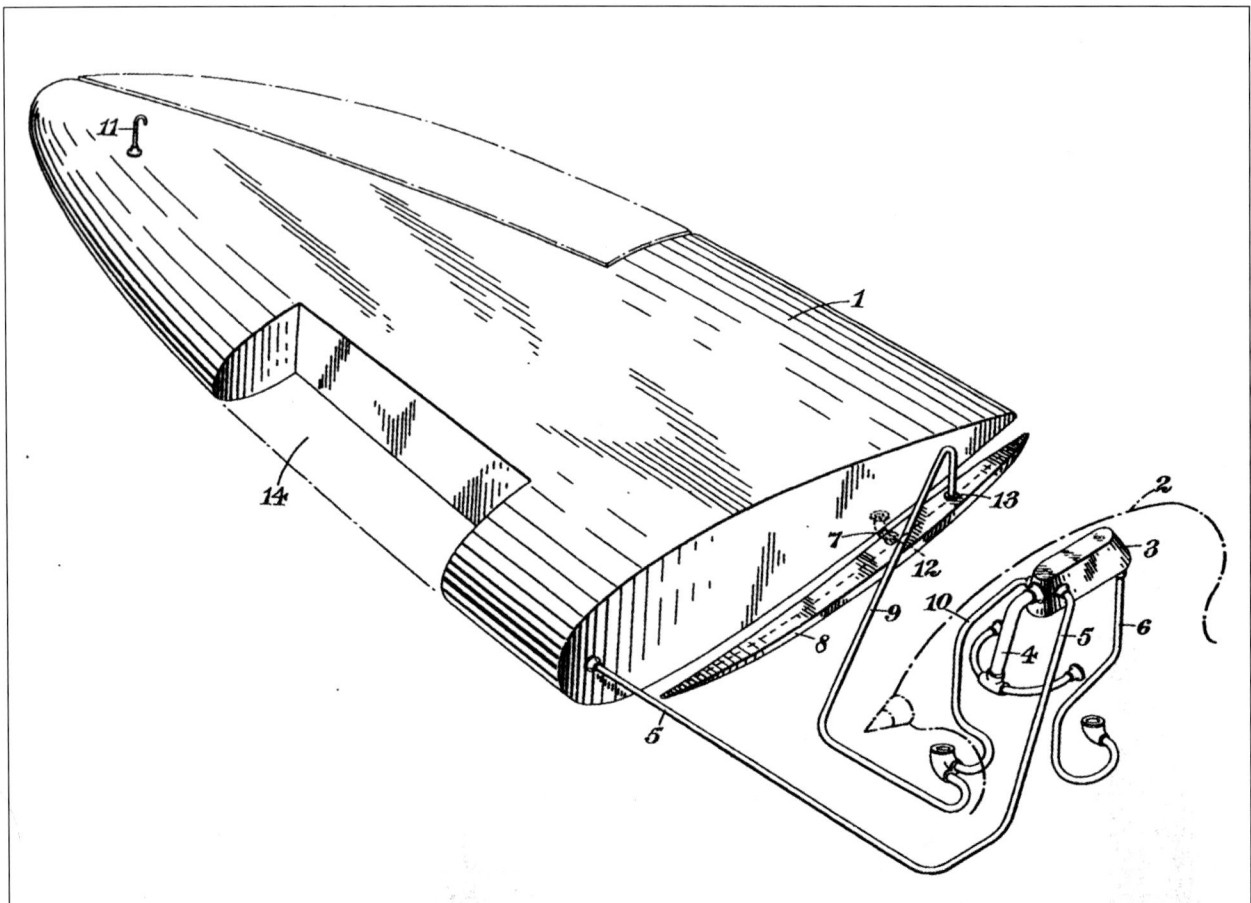

An illustration from patent GB329411 showing the interior of a wing utilised as a steam condenser

The large Supermarine six-engine flying boat to meet Specification R.6/28

and not a Napier Lion, as had been selected for the early schemes.

There are no indications of radiators, the reason for which became apparent in February 1929 when Supermarine submitted a patent application for 'Improvements in the Cooling System of Engines for Automotive Vehicles'. This was described as a "…cooling system for automotive vehicle engines wherein the steam formed in the water-jackets is condensed on some part of the vehicle and then returned to the engine". The patent illustration shows the interior of an aircraft wing forming the steam condenser, and this is evidently the system intended for the flying boat; the elliptical wing and pylon-mounted engine are quite distinctive.

It is highly likely that the engines were intended to be Rolls-Royce 'H' types, an engine under development for use in flying boats and other large aircraft. Supermarine had built a very close and mutually beneficial relationship with the experimental design department at Rolls-Royce while collaborating on the development of the S.6 and its Rolls-Royce 'R' racing engine, itself based on the 'H'. Rolls-Royce was also in discussion regarding the potential benefits of an evaporative cooling system for water cooled engines and had interested the Air Ministry in testing the concept on a Rolls-Royce 'F' engine, soon to be renamed as the Kestrel.

These modified engines were destined to be installed in a Southampton flying boat currently serving with one of the RAF units, the metal-hulled S-1122. In 1929, Rolls-Royce applied for the first of several patents associated with the engine ancillaries required for an evaporatively cooled engine and would continue to do so for several years. In Mitchell's patent the entire interior of the outer wing panels was designed to act as the steam condenser and would therefore have been skinned with metal, suitably sealed. This form of cooling was not an essential part of the flying boat design however and a more conventional radiator could easily have been substituted.

Whether rival tenders for R.6/28 were still under considerations at this date does seem a little unlikely but either way no contract was forthcoming. While work on R.6/28 was under way, the Air Ministry was also considering funding a civil flying boat of comparable size and circulated Specification 20/28 for such an aircraft – although there is no indication that Imperial Airways had expressed any interest in a flying boat of this type. Supermarine received a formal copy of the specification in May 1929.

Supermarine took the layout of the R.6/28 project and simply scaled it up and adapted it for civil use. The project was initiated in the summer of 1929 and was given the designation Type 179, the Vickers project naming convention finally having been adopted by, of more likely imposed on, Supermarine. Mitchell must have decided that an evaporative cooling system could be too experimental for an airliner and changed the

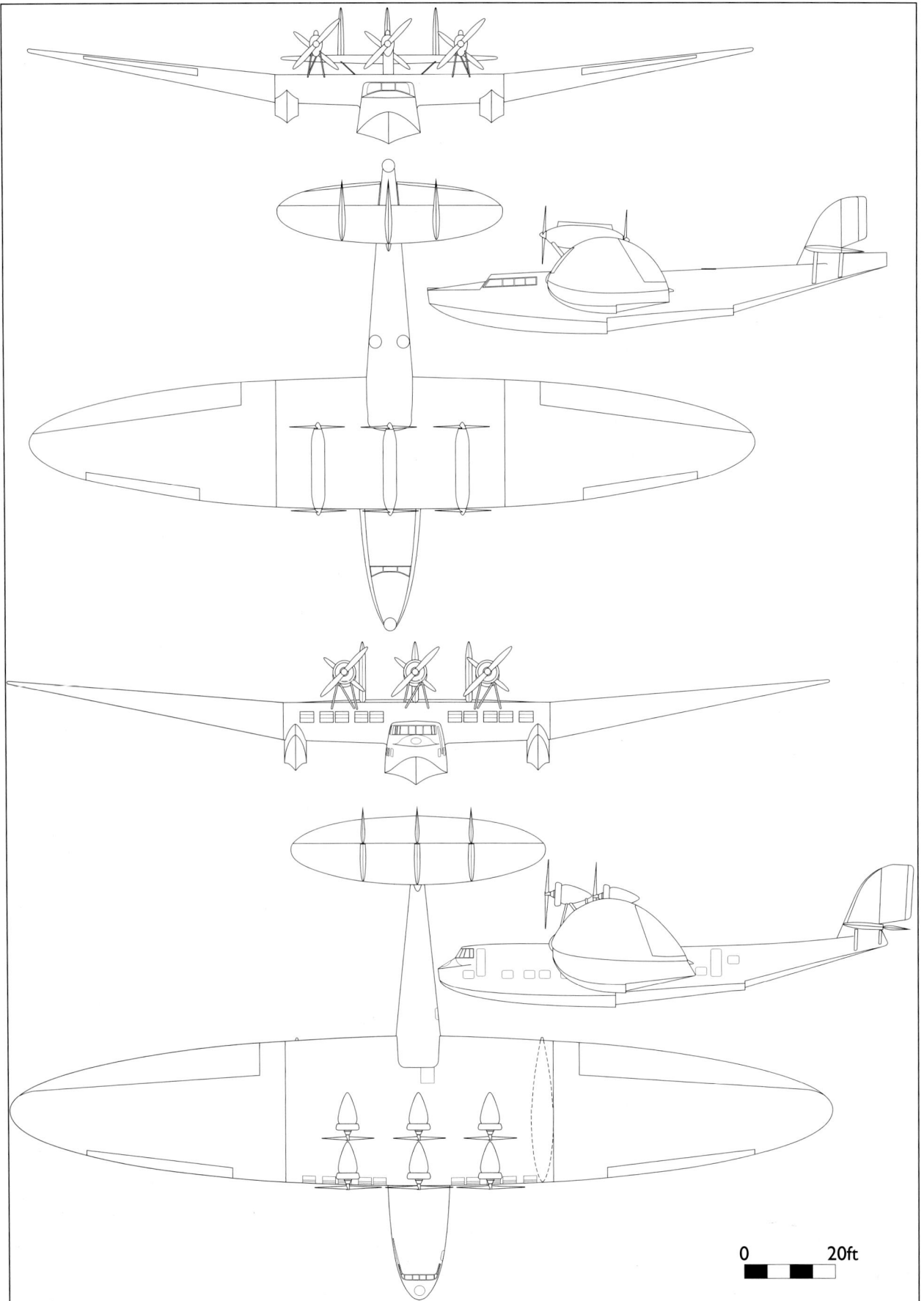

The Supermarine project for R.6/28 (top) provided the basis for the company's six-engine civil flying boat submission to Specification 20/28 (bottom)

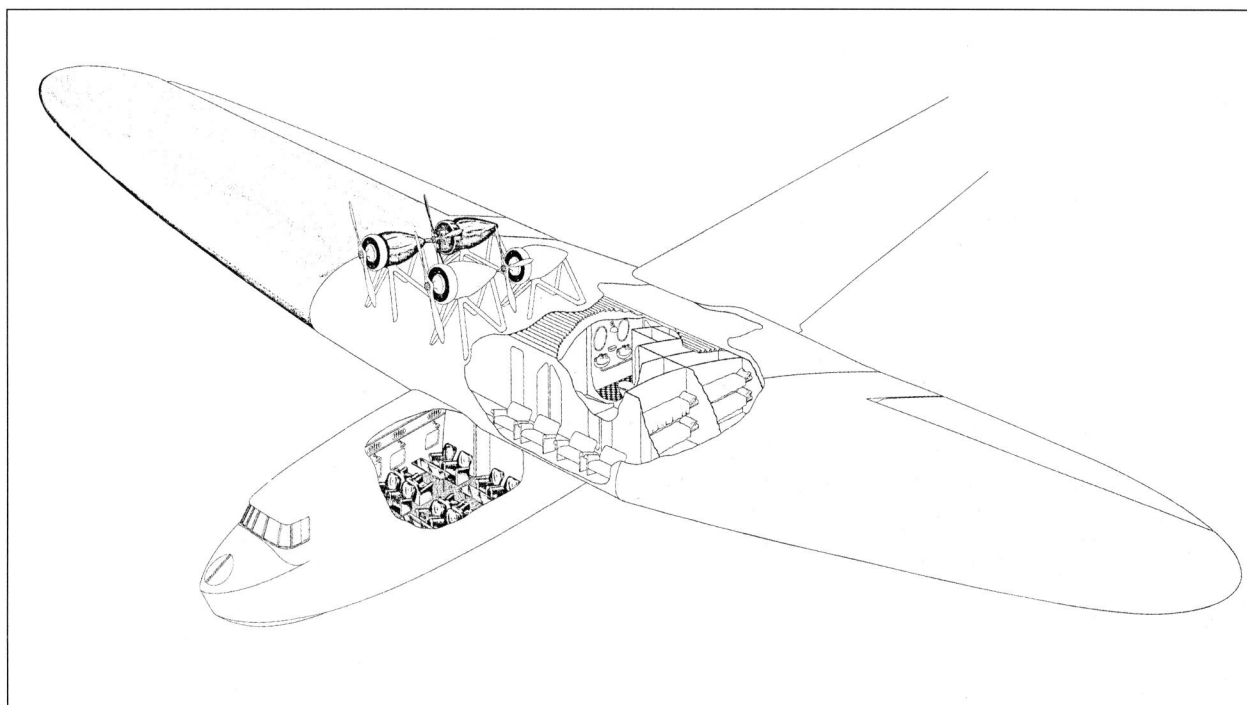

The interior of the Type 179 civil flying boat included cabins and an observation lounge within the wing centre section

engines to Bristol Jupiters, still in tandem pairs but each as a tractor unit in its own nacelle.

The cockpit was moved to the nose of the hull to increase space in the passenger cabins, which were to be configured for four abreast seating with a central aisle. In a bold move the interior of the wing centre section was to be used for additional seating or, for longer range routes, for sleeping cabins with bunk bed, washing facilities and, in the leading edge, an observation lounge provided with large forward-facing windows.

Later in 1929 Mitchell concluded that the Jupiter was insufficiently powerful for the aircraft and changed the choice of engine to 850hp Armstrong Siddeley Leopard radials. The laden weight was 75,000lb, giving the flying boat a cruising speed of 110mph and a top speed of 132mph at sea level. The payload varied depending on the range required, the fuel tanks capable of holding up to 2,500 gals, sufficient for 1,250 miles carrying 40 passengers or 660 miles with 100 passengers.

Blackburn also prepared a design, the C.B.5 Oceanic, a flying boat sharing its basic layout with the company's military 5/27 RB2 Sydney and the aborted CB2 Nile civil flying boat project. The Oceanic was also a monoplane carrying up to 80 passengers and powered by six 800hp Rolls-Royce 'H' (Buzzards), installed as four tractors and two pushers.

It was directly comparable with Supermarine's Type 179 in all regards; weight, accommodation, speed and range, but curiously the drawings included in the tender document are dated February 1929 and no mention is made in the text of an Air Ministry Specification, yet it is hard to imagine that it was not aimed at meeting 20/28 or, indeed, may have influenced the writing of the specification. As with R.6/28, it is likely that the broad requirement had been discussed with industry prior to the issue of the final specification.

The Air Ministry responded to the tenders at a leisurely pace and it was not until early 1930 that Supermarine was awarded a contract for a prototype. Prior to this award however, the whole design concept had been abandoned and replaced by an entirely new one prepared to the same specification. The new design first appears in drawings dated July 1930.

The hull was now considerably taller with a more refined aerodynamic shape and the large cockpit and glazed observation deck ahead of the wing. The elliptical wing plan had been discarded in favour of one of simple straight taper and the centre section was of reduced span and depth, but the outboard dihedral was retained.

No passenger accommodation was provided in the new wing, although artwork produced towards the end of the year appears to suggest that at an intermediate stage in the evolution of the aircraft it had been considered while the wing was still the elliptical type – a halfway house between the original design and the new one.

The wing floats were now of conventional form, supported by struts and moved further outboard.

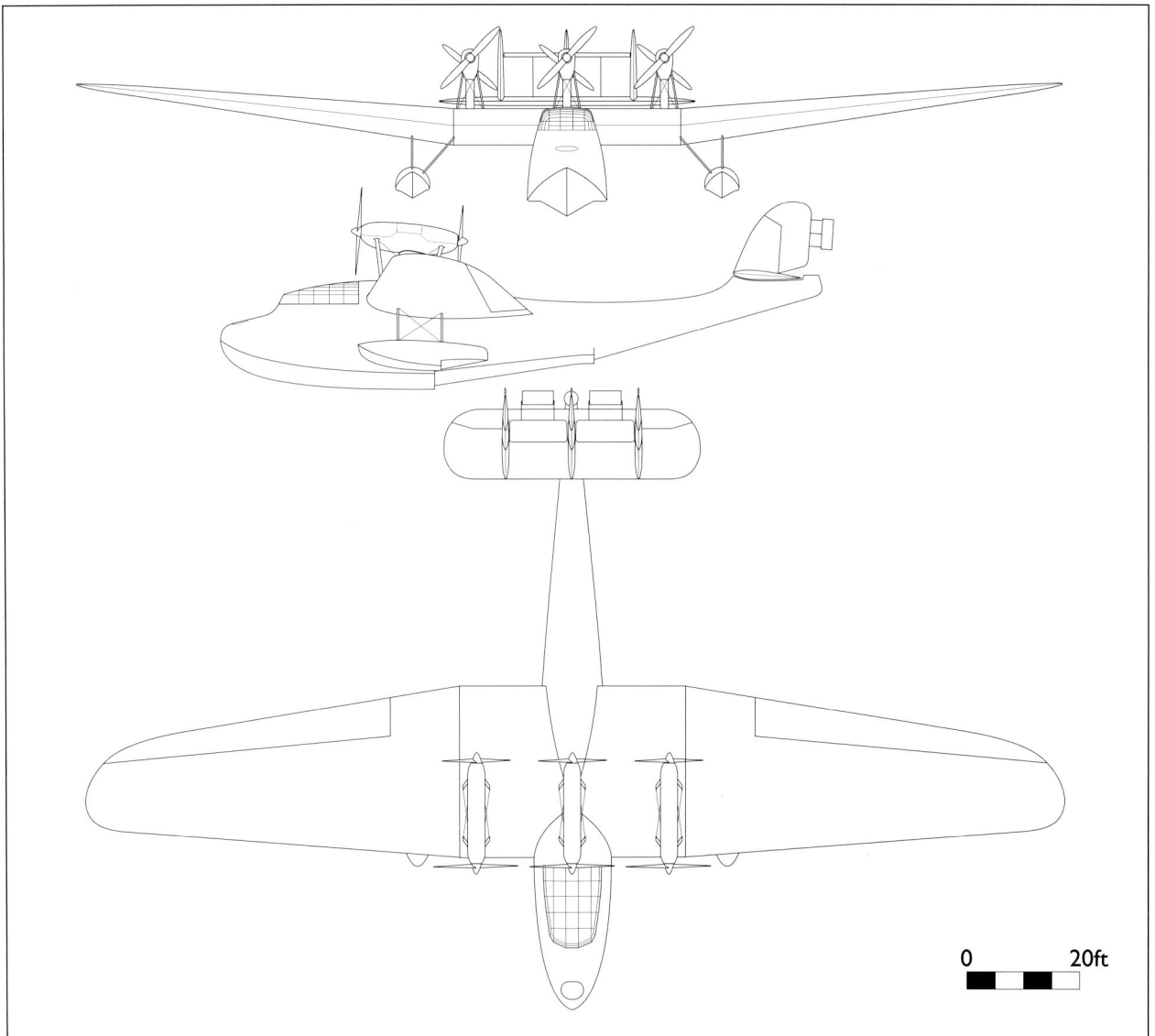

The Supermarine Type 179 project as it appeared in July 1930 after a thorough redesign

The tail, with triple fins and rudders, reverted to the familiar Supermarine style from the days of the Southampton. The favoured engines had been changed again, now reverting to 900hp Rolls-Royce 'H' Buzzard with evaporative cooling. Mitchell had conceived of an improvement to his previous wing steam condenser that also introduced a new form of single-spar wing structure, for which a patent application was submitted in March 1931.

A single spar and the fore part of the wing including the leading edge were to be constructed as a robust 'D' section metal torsion box that also doubled, suitably sealed, as the steam condenser, leaving the aft part of the wing free. The skin of this torsion box would likely to have been corrugated to increase the area available for cooling. Though he did not know it at the time this form of wing construction would prove a major factor in the future success of the company.

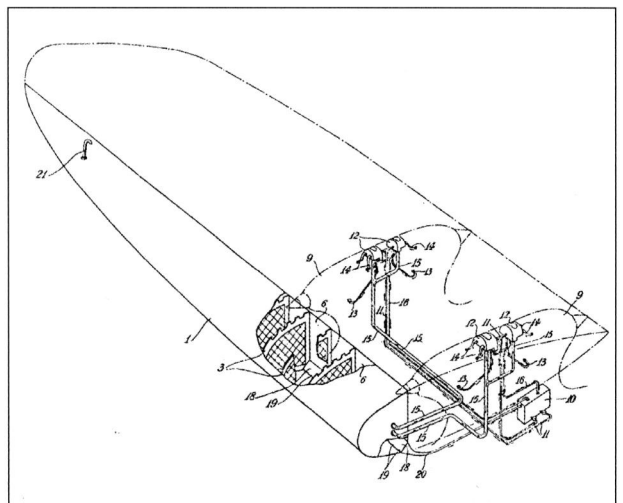

An illustration from patent GB370610 showing a wing constructed on a single spar and leading edge torsion box that also functions as a steam condenser for the engine cooling system

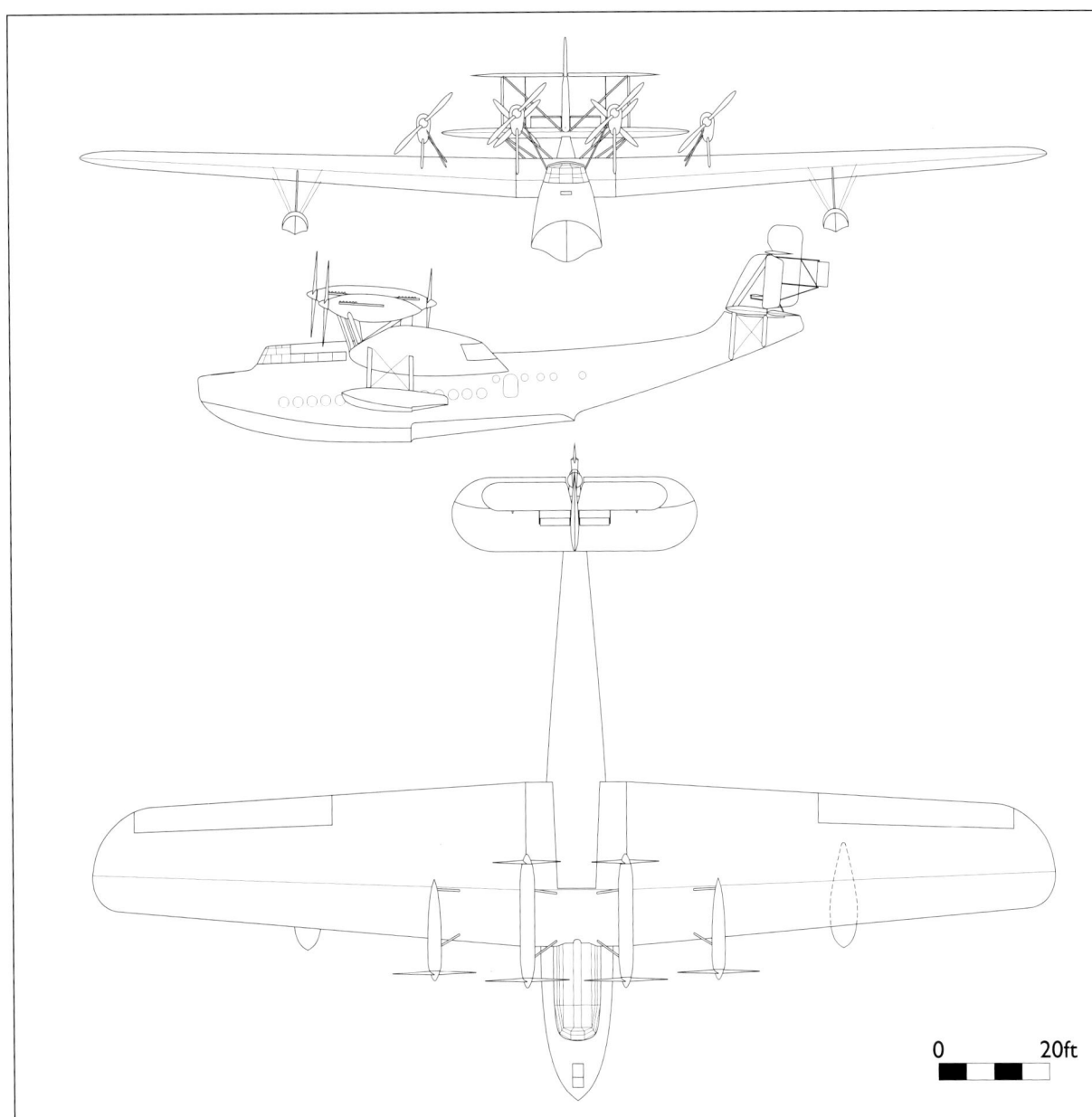

The final form of the Type 179 in late January 1932, just prior to the cancellation of the project

A model of the Type 179 in this revised form was displayed at the Olympia show in November 1930. The laden weight remained essentially unchanged at 75,090lb but maximum speed had risen to 145mph. The range with 20 passengers and the cabin configured for sleeping berths was 1,300 miles and with 40 day passengers it was 700 miles. A scale model of the aircraft was then sent to the RAE for evaluation in the wind tunnel while Supermarine ran tests on the evaporative cooling system.

Yet more changes were introduced to the design in 1931. The wing had undergone another complete redesign with a reduction in chord, slight thickening for the centre section, less dihedral and simplified taper in plan for the outer wings. The wing section at the tip was also much thinner with a consequent greater rate of decrease in thickness outboard. The wing floats were positioned much further out on the wings, thereby almost doubling their spacing.

The configuration of the engine nacelles was subject to an equally major change. Previously in tractor and pusher pairs in three nacelles, one central and the other two on the outer edge of the wing centre section, there were now two tractor and pusher pairs on the centre section and two tractors on the outer wings. The glazed area to the rear of the cockpit was removed. A significant number of revisions to the tail surfaces included enlarged rudders and the addition of an all-flying secondary tail surface, similar to that which had been flown on the Nanok to improve the effectiveness of the tail.

The hull was to be constructed with a frame and

skin of duralumin except for the planing bottom which would be stainless steel. The wing structure was also metal: duralumin ribs and the spars fabricated from stainless steel. The wing surface ahead of the spar, the 'D' torsion box, was also skinned in duralumin while aft of the spar it was fabric covered. The centre section was modified RAF34 and the outer panels RAF34.

Construction of the aircraft commenced in 1931 and registration G-ABLE was assigned on 7th April. The frame structure of the hull was well under way by the first days of 1932 when the Air Ministry abruptly cancelled the contract. There were a lot of complaints about this in the press, and it did result in quite a number of redundancies in Supermarine, but the aircraft was still a long way from completion, looking increasingly dated in concept and unwanted

by Imperial Airways. Cancellation on the grounds of economy was eminently sensible. Construction of the Short Sarafand was also ongoing at this time and nearing completion, so it was allowed to continue. That aircraft flew in June 1932 and was found to be equally dated, with the RAF having no operational role for it.

A fair amount of research work associated with the project was still under way at the National Physical Laboratory at the point when construction was cancelled. It was the intent to publish some of the incomplete wind tunnel test results on the model of the full aircraft but this does not appear to have occurred. One part of the programme that was near complete was published in 1934. This was an evaluation of the resistance to twist of the single-spar wing under torsion forces caused by

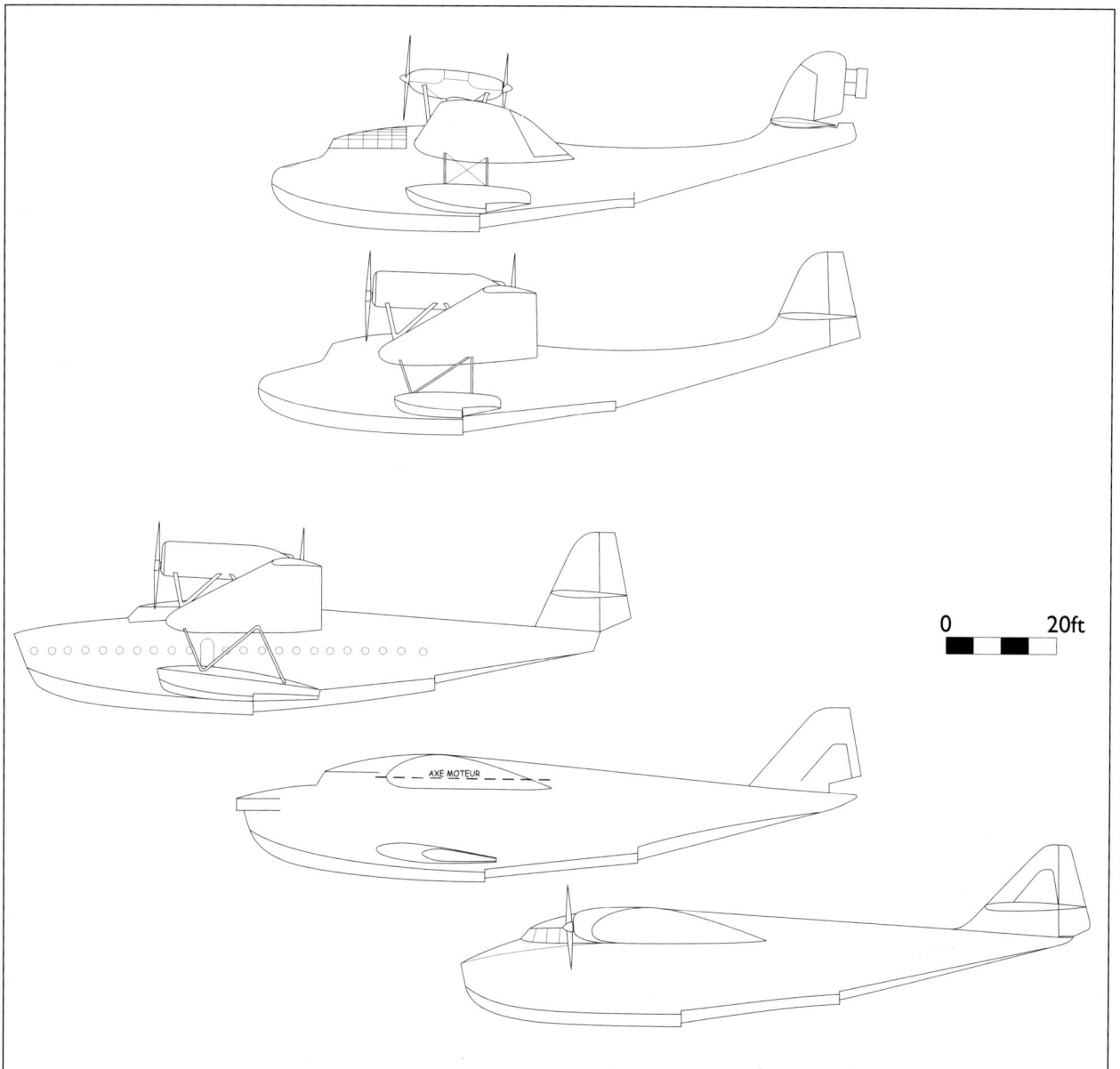

AXE MOTEUR

0   20ft

Wibault large flying boat projects from the 1930s – top side view is of the Supermarine Type 179 for comparison

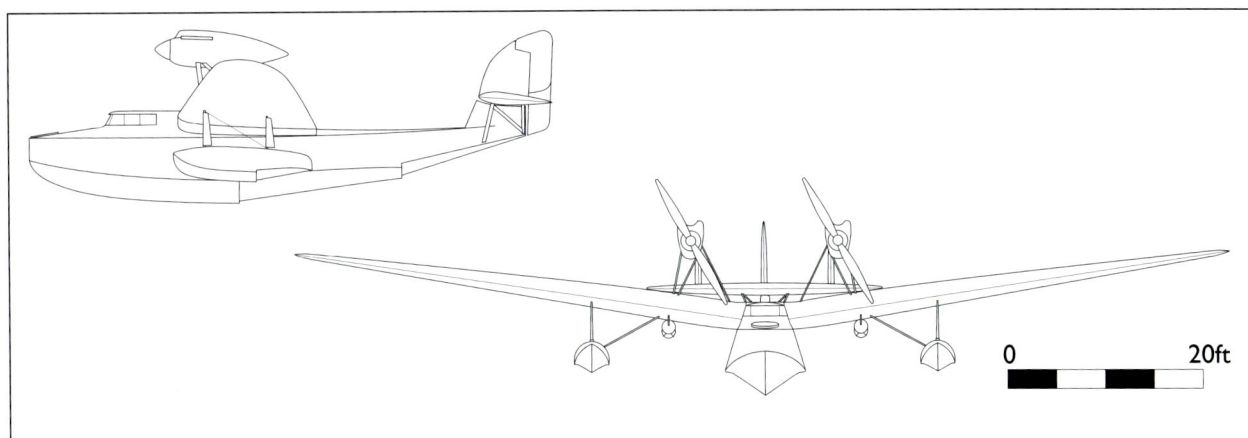

One of three military patrol flying boat projects powered by two Hispano-Suiza engines, presumably targeted at a foreign buyer

aileron movement. A 1:24 scale model of the full span wing had been constructed with pressure sensors embedded across the span and chord. The research was of great value to Supermarine for future monoplane designs.

The Type 179 aircraft is frequently referred to now as the Supermarine 'Giant', although that name does not appear to have been used at the time, neither formally nor informally.

Wibault projects

Before moving on there are four additional projects for large flying boats to which Supermarine contributed, all associated with or designed by the French company Société des Avions Michel Wibault. Very little is currently known about these and hence there are more questions than answers.

In mid-1930, Supermarine appears to have been requested by Vickers management to comment on elements of flying boat studies made by Wibault. Vickers had negotiated a patent licence, sales and consultancy business partnership with Wibault in 1925 regarding the application of that company's patented metal construction methods, which included corrugated wing skinning. The metal construction system had then been used with some success in the Vickers Vellore, Jockey, Viastra and others.

The exact nature of Supermarine's involvement with Wibault's plans is not known and the small number of annotated drawings archived are mostly undated. The first, however, was produced while Supermarine was working on the redesigned Rolls-Royce 'H'-powered iteration of the Type 179. A side view drawing, tracing dated 31st July 1930, appears to be a proposal prepared by Wibault for a 70,000lb monoplane flying boat that had been retraced onto Supermarine blueprint stock. The drawing was then annotated in red ink with comments on the wing incidence and planing bottom geometry, and a copy

then returned to Wibault. This work took place just two weeks after Supermarine had produced the latest general arrangement drawings of the Type 179, and the hull lines of the two are remarkably similar. No more is known regarding this scheme.

Three more flying boat hull drawings produced by Wibault appear to be plans for wind tunnel models. All are undated but from the drawing numbers added by Supermarine for their files they are certainly no earlier than late 1931 and from their style probably significantly later. They are include here in the hope that someone may be able to make use of the information and relate them to other project work in France.

Flying boats for export

Three more Supermarine layout drawings are also dated to July 1930, with drawing numbers adjacent to that of the earliest of the Wibault drawings. These are all for a Southampton-sized military flying boat powered by two Hispano-Suiza engines, and therefore almost certainly prepared for an overseas customer. All three feature the same slab-sided metal hull with gun positions in the nose and staggered in the rear hull, as on the Southampton.

The first is a simple re-hulled Southampton, the second has wings similar to a scaled-down Southampton Mark X, while the third is a cantilever monoplane with wings of marked dihedral and the engines on pylons. Around this time Supermarine was deep in discussion with Turkish military authorities regarding their requirement for a number of patrol flying boats. Eventually Turkey would opt to purchase six standard metal-hulled Southamptons powered by Hispano-Suiza engines, so it would appear most likely that these three schemes had been presented to them as alternatives during early negotiations.

9
CHAPTER

The Seamew

After the first Southampton production contracts had been secured and construction work was under way, Mitchell looked at options to replace the Seagull. The company had achieved some small success with sales of Seagull and Scarab single-engine military amphibians in the early 1920s and Supermarine was keen to continue producing flying boats in this class, a market where it appeared to have a lead or at least no strong competitor. The company's enthusiasm does not appear to have been dampened by the fact that the Seagull was deemed inferior to the Fairey III floatplane for service with the carrier force and was already in the process of being phased out from 1925. On the civil side, sales of single-engine types had been negligible, just three Sea Eagles, and those had been sold to an airline in which Supermarine was a major stakeholder.

Notwithstanding the all too apparent limited market, Supermarine pressed ahead. Both single engine and twin-engine schemes were considered with the greater effort placed in the latter, but work on this was to prove somewhat protracted as a result of higher priority being placed on other projects, especially the Southampton and its derivatives, and the Schneider racer programme.

The new type receiving most attention was conceived as a direct replacement for the Seagull. Its dimensions were much the same since it had to meet the restrictions imposed by the size of carrier lifts. The design could be considered almost as a scaled down Southampton with the one notable change that the wooden hull was to be constructed as a single unit with an integral planing bottom as part of the main structure, as in the incomplete large hull Supermarine had built alongside that for the Scylla. The project was conceived in late 1924 and was of sufficient interest for the Air Ministry to issue a contract and place an order for two prototypes the following year, but detailed design did not commence until February 1926 because of the aforementioned priorities. This design work included a rather basic six-passenger civil version.

Supermarine Seamew

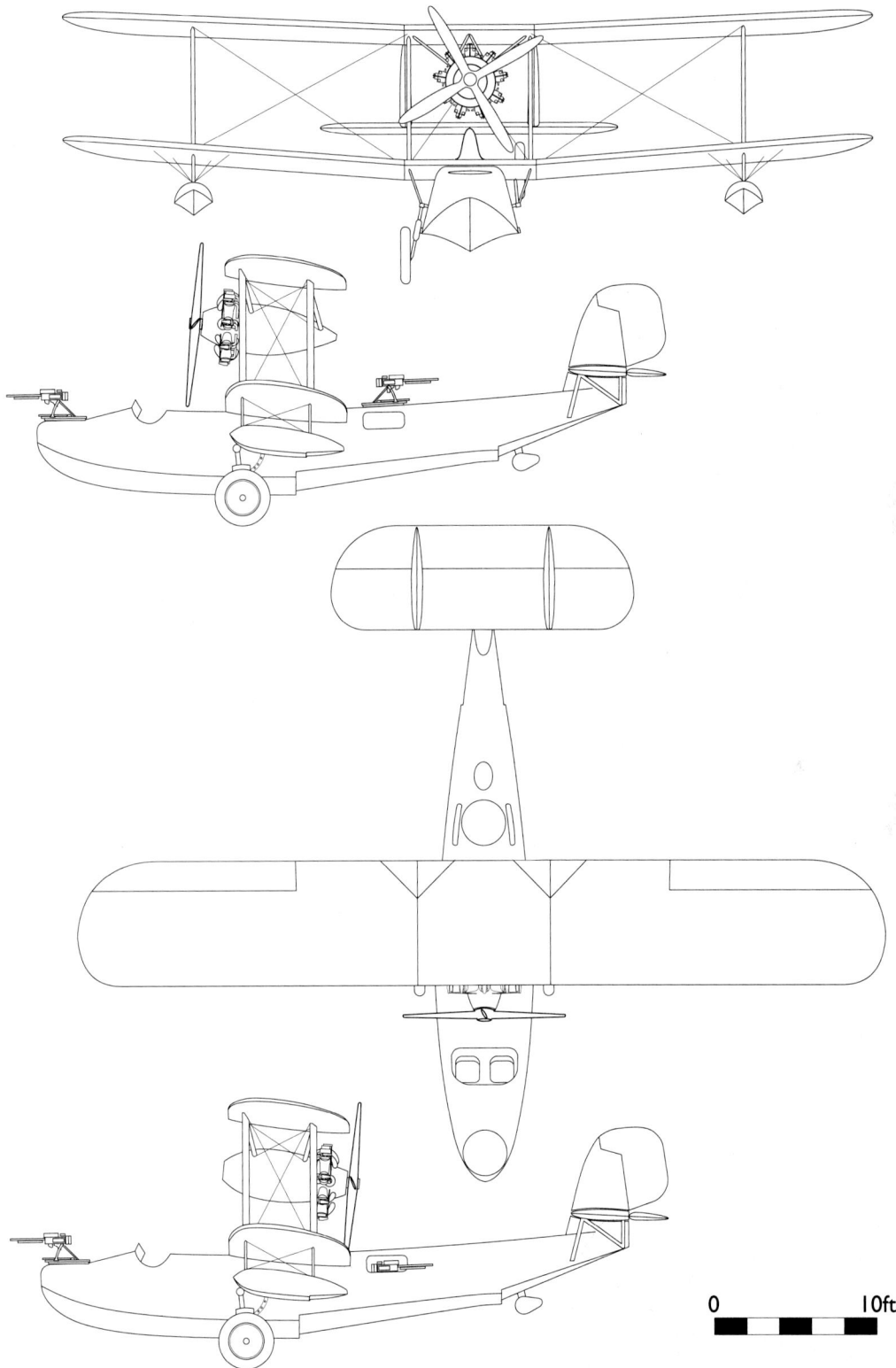

Type 181 – a single engine flying boat in either tractor or pusher configuration to meet a requirement issued by the RAAF

Construction of the two prototypes started in 1927 and the aircraft, named Seamew, was flown on 9th January 1928. It was already somewhat dated.

When evaluated by the MAEE, the Seamew soon proved disappointing for a variety of reasons including a lack of power, spray ingestion by the engines, and nose heaviness. Nevertheless the civil version, now offered with a metal hull, was still being advertised for sale in mid-1929. The failure of metal components in the mixed wood and metal wings of the Seamew prototype effectively put paid to any sales prospects.

No doubt the metal fatigue issue and nose heaviness could have been addressed in any future production aircraft but water ingestion and damage was a fundamental design flaw. Service experience with the Southampton had shown that spray from the nose of the hull could impact on the large two-blade propellers and limited their life, but the RAF accepted this as the price that had to be paid for what was otherwise a valuable service machine. The Seamew's propellers were closer to the water surface and the damage was far worse – which was completely unacceptable.

The fitment of four-bladed smaller diameter propellers to try to keep the blades clear of spray had a detrimental impact on climb rate, which had not been stellar in the first place. As a consequence the company reverted to designs for single-engine types where the engine and propeller were shielded against the worst ravages of spray by the hull itself. Initial ideas involved straightforward revisions to the Seamew with the option for it to be powered by a single Bristol Jupiter or Napier Lion engine, in either tractor or pusher form. Basic general arrangement drawings for these were produced in March 1928 but the schemes were not taken further.

With the design team now engaged in serious and detailed design work on large, larger, and very large civil flying boats – Sea-Hawk, Type 180 and Type 179 'Giant' respectively – some of the design team were also tasked with addressing, once again, the potential market for smaller flying boats and amphibians

Replacing the Seagull – part 1

The one customer that had expressed satisfaction with the Seagull was the Royal Australian Air Force (RAAF), and its initial purchase of six Seagull III aircraft for surveying work had been supplemented by the later purchase of three RAF Seagull IIs that had seen little use and been deemed surplus to requirements. Their purchase was intended to provide a source of spares for the Seagull IIIs but the

flying boats turned out to be in such good condition that they were simply added to the flight line.

The RAAF then expressed an interest in a replacement type for when their flight of aircraft reached the end of their lives. A crew of three was specified along with four hour endurance and to be catapult-capable at maximum weight, which should not exceed 8050lbs. The aircraft had to be able to operate in the open sea with wave heights of up to 6ft. Supermarine looked at options towards the end of 1929.

A new project, Type 181, was initiated for this work and Mitchell chose not to stray too far from the path well-trodden. As a consequence, the layout followed closely that of the Seagull III. Drawing upon experience with the designs of the civil Seamew and an experimental Seagull that had been built with wing leading edge slots, flaps and a twin-fin tail for research purposes, the Type 181 was to have a duralumin and stainless steel hull, duralumin wing structure, twin fins and an all-new form of retractable undercarriage.

It was offered in either tractor or pusher form with the engine nacelle suspended on struts from the top wing centre section with no support from below other than bracing wires down to the hull. The undercarriage featured a rearwards-rotating retraction system that was very similar to that devised for the Vickers Viking family and may well have been a direct development of that type given that Vickers was now the parent of Supermarine. When retracting, the wheels passed upwards through slots on the lower wing, protruding above and below. There was provision for a gun in the nose with a side-by-side cockpit immediately behind. A second gun ring could be installed in the rear hull in the tractor version of the aircraft, and for the pusher there were ports on either side through which a gun could be fired.

A civil version of the Type 181 amphibian had been planned from the outset but in mid-1929, before this was ready to be advertised, Supermarine would receive an unexpected wake-up call when it was rather wrong-footed by the arrival on the scene of the Saunders-Roe Cutty Sark. Saunders-Roe had taken great delight in flying the small civil amphibian around the Solent during the preparations for the Schneider Trophy contest that year, an event that Supermarine was most keen to use to promote its products. Obviously the Supermarine Rolls-Royce S.6 racer held centre stage but they could have done without the distraction of a neat, closed cockpit, twin-engine monoplane, metal-hulled amphibian drawing appreciative comments all around.

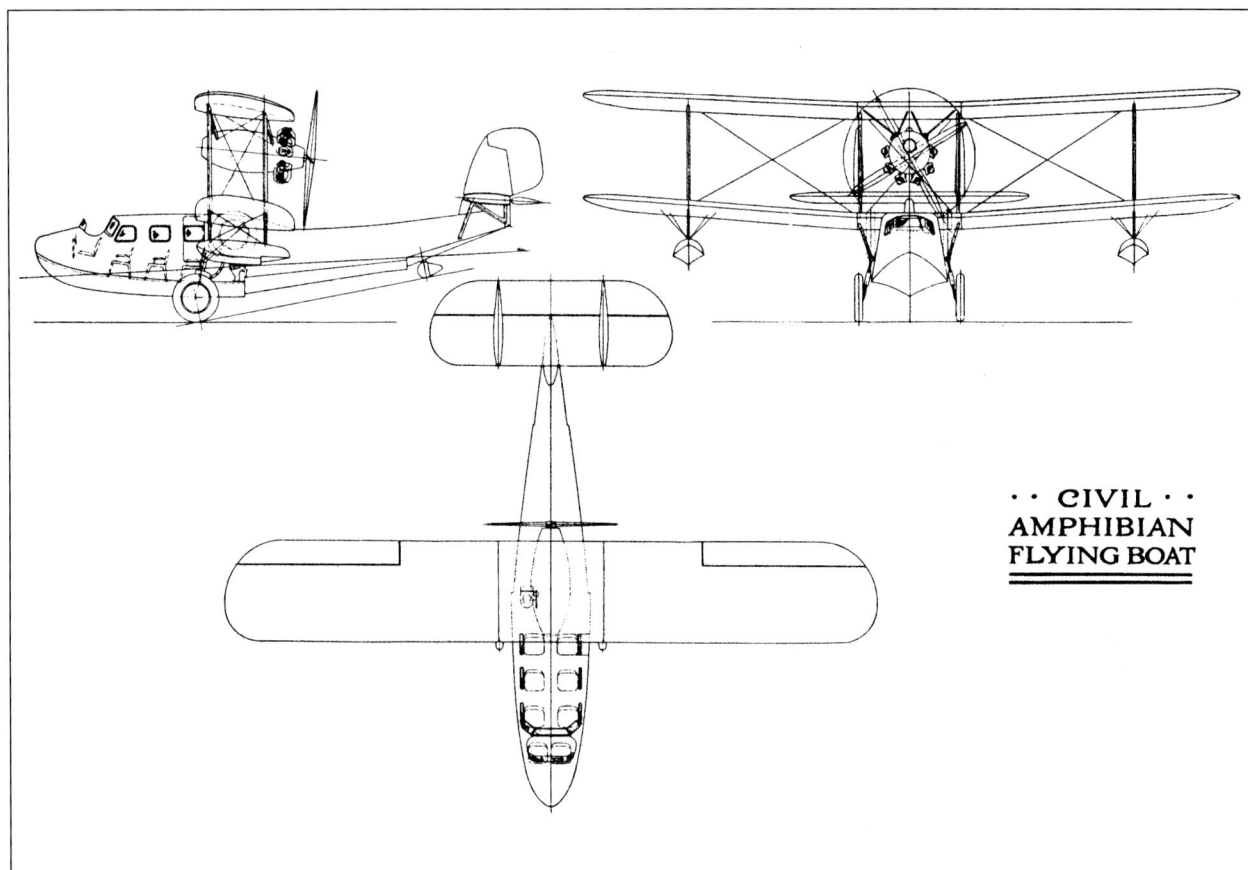

· · CIVIL · ·
AMPHIBIAN
FLYING BOAT

The civil version of the Type 181 for six passengers

It did not help that Saunders-Roe let it be known that it had under construction a larger flying boat of similar layout, and the Cloud would fly the following July. There was nothing even remotely like the Cutty Sark or the Cloud on Mitchell's drawing board.

The Type 181 Civil Amphibian Flying Boat was offered for sale from April 1930 when brochures were sent to prospective customers, including Imperial Airways. As with the civil Seamew project of the previous year, the Type 181 carried six passengers and a crew of two. The passenger cabin was enclosed and placed ahead of the wings, with the side-by-side open cockpit in the nose, although there was an option for this to be enclosed too.

After the adverse experience with spray damage to the propellers and engines on the Seamew, Supermarine was at pains to highlight the benefits of a pusher installation shielded by the hull. There was a choice of engine, either a 570hp Bristol Mercury VI or a 580hp Armstrong Siddeley Panther II. With a fuel tank capacity of 175 gals the range was 400 miles at a cruising speed of 95mph.

It probably comes as no surprise that there were no sales; the target market was very small and the Type 181 was looking out of step with the latest aircraft and projects. Twin engine monoplanes had the edge. However, it was not to be the last formal single-engine biplane civil flying boat project to come from Supermarine.

10 CHAPTER Replacing the Southampton

While the R.4/27 three-engine reconnaissance flying boats were still in the design stage, neither the Air Ministry nor Supermarine had neglected further work on twin-engine types; the programme of Southampton development had continued.

Commercial realities often necessitate a progressive evolution of an existing design rather than the introduction of a completely new concept, regardless of the capabilities of the design team. Similarly, for many customers a type that requires no great change in operational procedures or support can prove to be the pragmatic choice. So when the RAF began to contemplate a direct replacement for the Southampton, it was really looking for a 'better Southampton', and Supermarine was able to offer exactly that.

The Southampton itself, of course, had grown out of the Swan flying boat, a design having its roots in 1923, and various schemes for improved or enlarged versions had been under review even as the first batch of aircraft were nearing completion. It had then seen considerable modification and upgrade through experience gained while in service, adding new wing floats, a metal hull, more powerful engines, and sweep-back on the wings. Some had enclosed cockpits, metal wings had been built in 1929, and trials had taken place with the Napier Lions replaced by Bristol Jupiter or Rolls-Royce Kestrel engines. The route to produce a Southampton replacement appeared clear enough and the process by which the later Scapa and Stranraer flying boats came to be developed is an interesting story of design evolution in action.

The most successful aspect of the Southampton was without a doubt its clean performance on the water, a low bow wave that produced limited spray, and minimal tendency to porpoise, all key strengths that Mitchell wished to carry forward into later designs. As a result the planing bottom of the Southampton was retained with minimal change in the schemes that followed, even as everything else was revised.

Mitchell's close association with the development engineers at Rolls-Royce nudged him increasingly to favour their 'F', Kestrel, and 'H', Buzzard, V12 water or evaporatively-cooled engines over air-cooled types. The installation of evaporatively cooled Kestrels in modified Southampton II S-1122 in 1930 had proven entirely successful and a second experimental Southampton aircraft, registration N253, would also use these engines. It was somewhat inevitable that the first proposal for a Southampton replacement would use these engine too.

The first Kestrel-powered Southampton development, however, would not be a military aircraft but a tender to meet a version of the long-delayed Imperial Airways requirement for a dedicated mail plane, formalised as Air Ministry Specification 21/28.

In the late 1920s responsibility for carrying mail overseas to distant territories had been transferred from the RAF to Imperial Airways. While volume and weight remained relatively low there was little problem to include it along with passengers on existing airliners, even though this meant that the mail travelled at the sedate pace appropriate for the passengers. As volume increased and new routes were added, Imperial Airways and the Air Ministry considered following the model that was becoming increasingly popular in the USA where dedicated fast mail planes were being developed – a sort of flying 'pony express'.

Specification 21/28 had proven of great interest to the aircraft industry but had been put on hold for a few years, most probably deemed low priority when the great depression hit. When the requirement was revitalised in 1931 it appears that Supermarine may have been approached directly for the design of a mail-carrying twin-engine flying boat to meet Imperial Airways' needs. In its tender Supermarine quotes an aircraft capable of carrying a 1,000lb load over a 550 mile route with a cruising speed of at least 110mph. Apparently this was considered an immediate requirement so Mitchell decided that a quick adaptation of the Southampton looked to be the most logical response. Specification 21/28 may well have been partially rewritten in 1931, or the requirement received by Supermarine could have been a special case since the full requirement of the specification, to which the winning Boulton-Paul P.64 was built, was stated to be a 1,000lb load, range 1,000mph and cruising speed 145mph.

Supermarine's Mail Plane project, one of the Type 178 series, took the metal planing bottom, rear and lower hull of the Southampton II and grafted a new design of topside and nose onto them. This resulted in a hull which was deeper than the standard type in order to provide more headroom and an enclosed cockpit. There was a crew of three, the pilot in the glazed cockpit and wireless operator and navigator immediately behind.

The new upper hull incorporated an integral wing root for the cantilever lower wing, which would be built with the same type of structure which Supermarine said had been developed on the Air Yacht and had proven satisfactory. The biplane wings, of unequal span and with a new single-bay design, made use of the metal spars and ribs system developed for the Southampton. The span of the top wing was 58ft and chord 9ft. The tail surfaces were standard Southampton types.

The two engines were evaporatively-cooled 650hp Rolls-Royce Kestrel II.MS fitted within monocoque metal nacelles that were constructed along the same lines as the fuselage and cantilever engine mounts of the S.6 Schneider racers. These nacelles were supported by the outward-splayed inner wing struts and sat a little above mid gap, with the engines canted at the same angle as the struts. The steam condensers were tall units of ogival shape, a type patented by Rolls-Royce, placed on top of the nacelles. These gave the Mail Plane a top speed of 148mph and a cruising speed of 120mph. An alternative engine choice was the Bristol Jupiter XI.F, with which top speed was reduced to 135mph and cruise 110mph, just barely meeting the specification.

The first of the true Southampton replacement projects was derived directly from the Mail Plane and was also included under Type 178. The familiar open tandem cockpit layout, nose gun and staggered rear fuselage guns had returned. The engines were still Kestrel MS but their nacelles were now mounted a little higher and with the engines upright, no longer at the angle of the supporting struts. The radiator had been moved to the rear of the nacelle with air intake ducts on either side and it is not clear whether the intent was for evaporative or conventional water cooling. A second version had wings of greater span with a suggestion of finely curved tips. In this case the engine nacelles had been raised to a position on the underside of the top wing. The height of the rudders had been increased.

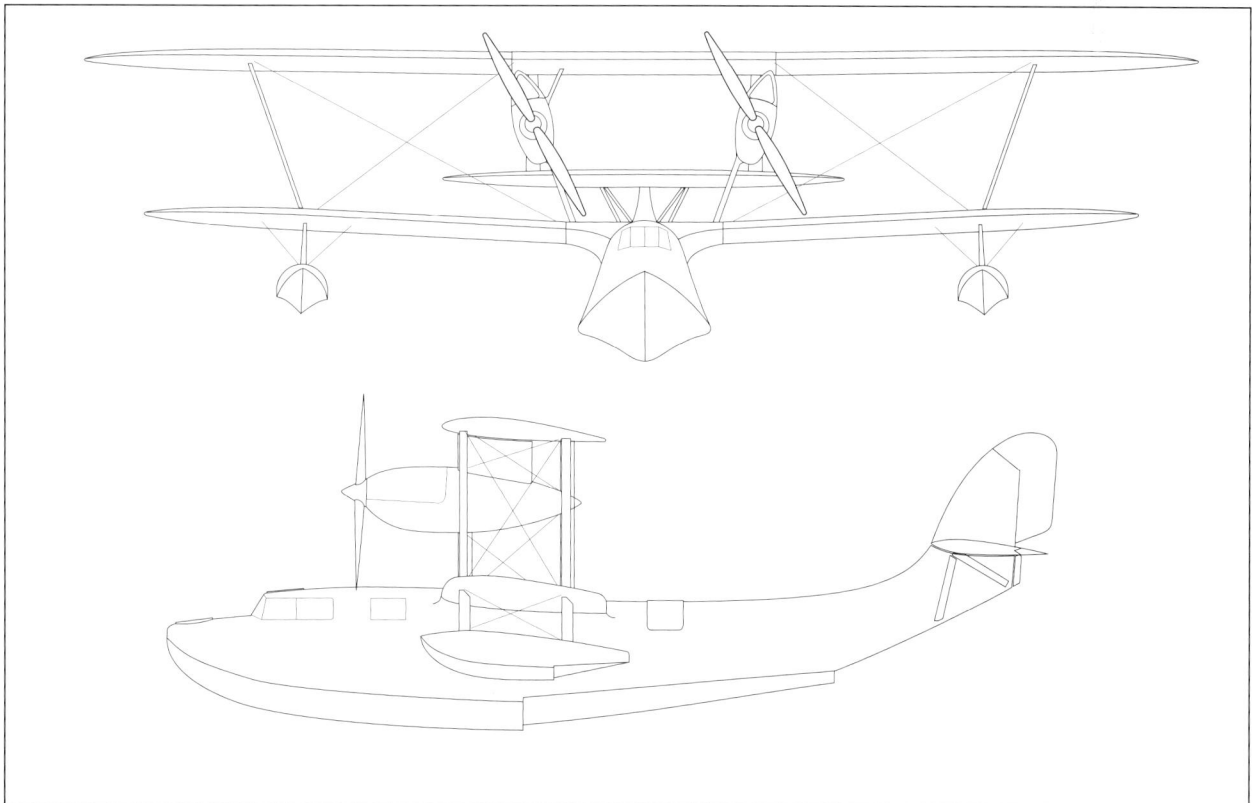

A flying boat Mail Plane submitted in response to a requirement of Imperial Airways

In mid-1931, one final project under Type 178 is the first to be named as Southampton IV. This was a 10-passenger civil flying boat based on the long span project noted above. The pilot had an enclosed cockpit that appears to be based on that trialled on the Southampton Mark X during one of its later modifications. The Southampton IV was then approved for further work and formalised as a full project for military use, being allocated Type 221. Detailed design commenced.

This begs the question: what was the Southampton III? Various suggestions have been made; the metal-hull prototype N218 when fitted with Bristol Jupiter engines? The all-metal Kestrel-powered experimental aircraft N253? The answer remains uncertain since the designation does not seem to appear on any Supermarine drawing. Like the Seal II with no Seal I and the Southampton Mark X it may just be a quirk of Supermarine's management and sales policy to suggest the production of rather more aircraft types than actually existed.

Supermarine ran increasingly low on work through 1930 and 1931. The Type 179 was progressing, slowly, and the last batches of Southamptons and replacement metal hulls were making their way through the works. Other than that there was just piecemeal modification work on the Southampton Mark X and the Air Yacht, and construction of the two S6b Schneider racers.

Nothing substantial was on the horizon so Vickers management transferred a little construction work from Weybridge to Woolston to keep the works active. Sir Robert McLean, chairman of Supermarine Aviation Works (Vickers) Ltd and their parents Vickers (Aviation) Ltd, is overlooked far too often for the shrewd business decisions he made to support both companies, most especially in these difficult years. An engineer by background, he had an inherent ability to know when a design idea was worthy of investment, and in this tough period his support proved to be invaluable.

It was McLean who was responsible for funding the Vickers Wellesley as a private venture for Vickers, a move that saw Barnes Wallis' geodetic structures come to the fore and enabled the design and development of the Wellington bomber. He did the same for Supermarine when he underwrote the building of the Seagull V prototype, forerunner of the Walrus, and in this instance the Type 221 Southampton IV.

The prototype Southampton IV was built alongside the last batch of Southampton IIs destined for the RAF and McLean offered it to the Air Ministry in lieu of the final one of the contract and at the same price. It was an offer difficult to decline so McLean's proposal was accepted. Air Ministry Specification R.20/31D was then written around the aircraft in November 1931.

The Southampton IV flew on 8th July 1932 and was transferred to the MAEE in October for official trials, gaining type approval in April 1933. Thereafter the RAF embarked on a lengthy, and somewhat

The Southampton IV prototype under construction in a wood jig alongside two Southampton metal hulls

leisurely, assessment involving a succession of long distance flights in and around the British Isles and the Mediterranean. Eventually, in August 1933, over a year after the prototype had flown, a contract for 12 production examples was awarded. These production aircraft were to be renamed Scapa.

The Air Ministry's perception of the requirements for general reconnaissance flying boats had wavered considerably since the time of the aborted Specification 9/23. The optimal range, bomb load and type, and defensive capability all remained uncertain and resulted in a diverse stable of flying boats of various types and sizes entering service for evaluation, usually in small numbers.

Supermarine came out of the first cycle of contracts somewhat better than its competitors. The Southampton was favoured with multiple repeat production contracts – there were 66 unique service registrations plus two experimental aircraft and 15 export sales, but it did not end there as at least 25 of the wooden hulled aircraft in RAF service saw their hulls replaced by metal ones as they wore out. Contrast that with Blackburn receiving orders for just five Iris, Shorts one each for the Singapore and Singapore II, plus six for the Rangoon.

The RAF was getting a better grip on how best to structure its flying boat force by 1931. Notwithstanding the order for Scapas, a quick and simple means by which to keep the UK-based squadrons equipped as the Southamptons aged, shortly afterwards it issued Specification R.20/31D – covering the prototype Southampton IV. A further new requirement was then drawn up for the next generation of two-engine general purpose flying boats. Specification R.24/31 called for an aircraft with much the same capability, but while R.20/31D was 'bespoke' for the Southampton IV, R.24/31 would be issued to tender.

Supermarine received the specification and invitation to tender in April 1932, a few months before the Southampton IV prototype flew. This, perhaps, was the appropriate time to ditch the incremental improvement approach and to propose a new tailored design, but by now Supermarine was well advanced with further development plans of the Southampton IV type that could be tweaked to meet R.24/31.

In true evolutionary style, the first move was no more than a simple refinement of the Southampton IV; Type 226 of May 1932 replaced the Kestrel engines with the new Bristol Pegasus radial, an engine with the same cylinder dimensions as the aging Jupiter but expected to deliver more than 700hp at first with plenty of potential for a large increase beyond that. It then became apparent that

the higher load requirement of the new specification suggested the design of a slightly larger hull, and so in mid-June 1932 the Type 226 was effectively stretched – resulting in the Type 227.

Models of this new hull at 1:12 and 1:24 scale were prepared for evaluation in the water tank. The topsides dispensed with the two staggered open gun positions in the rear, replacing them with a single gun behind a retractable windscreen and a new gun position in the extreme tail. All of the guns could be retracted inside the hull and the apertures closed. As weight had now risen considerably, both wingspan and chord needed to be increased – raising the wing area to 1,560sq ft, compared to 1,300sq ft on the Scapa. At the same time the aerofoil was changed to a 12% thickness-to-chord (t/c) section from the new NACA 2400 series. This was a significant moment as previous Supermarine projects had tended to stay with well-known types such as Clark Y and the British aerofoils in the RAF family.

The initial layout drawings, dated 16th June, show the same Pegasus installation as designed for the Type 226 but Mitchell wished to reconsider his favoured Rolls-Royce Kestrel V MS as the better engine and had the team adapt the design for either water cooled or evaporatively-cooled installation under a new project of the same date, Type 230. This, in all other regards, was identical to Type 227. Both types were given the generic name 'Twin Engined Boat Seaplane to Spec R.24/31' although some drawings under Type 230 carry the name 'Southampton Mk IV Modified to Spec R.24/31'.

By this time the Air Ministry had selected Saunders-Roe's A.27 London to fulfil R.24/31, awarding the contract in late 1932. The London's main strength was its corrugated plate hull, which was considered simple to build and maintain. The experimental hull A.14, the Severn and Cloud had all contributed to the development of this type, although problems were still to be encountered. It was in all other respects no great improvement over the Scapa.

On a layout drawing dated May 1933, the Type 230 is shown with wings with the section reduced further to 9% t/c, a small increase in span and decrease in chord. With the adoption of this thinner wing the bracing was now in two bays. The hull had been revised in detail, around the planing bottom and tail gun position in particular. The engines are identified as Rolls-Royce Goshawk IIs, the new name given to the latest evaporatively-cooled development of the Kestrel. Yet the final choice of engine remained uncertain.

The weight of the cooling system, whether water or evaporative, was giving Mitchell cause for concern and the power output of the Rolls-Royce engine was looking a little low for the aircraft. A contract for a prototype was awarded by the Air Ministry on 28th August 1933, just as the production contract for the Scapa was received.

The Air Ministry had considered the development of fuel-efficient and low fire risk diesel engines for use in airships during the late 1920s and had been in discussion with the German company Junkers regarding licence production of its six-cylinder vertically-opposed piston engine, the type 204. Vickers, then building the R.100 airship, was contemplated by the Ministry as the possible manufacturer for the engine before negotiations transferred to Napier, which accepted the contract and licence in 1933.

Napier intended to name its version of the Junkers engine, now named Jumo IV, as the Culverin. Following the announcement of this deal there was a brief flurry of interest in the engine. Its fuel efficiency looked attractive for long range military and commercial aircraft where high speed was not a specific requirement and for a brief period several manufacturers considered the engine for their aircraft, especially those building flying boats.

In the late summer of 1933, Mitchell initiated a project to look at a possible installation of the Jumo IV in the latest version of the Type 230, probably in response to an Air Ministry request. This was formalised as Type 235, and retained the title 'Southampton IV Modified to Spec R.24/31'. The six-cylinder engine, with six pairs of opposed pistons and vertical cylinders was not by any means an ideal configuration for installation in an aircraft of this type; its height was about four times its width with the mount points positioned towards the top.

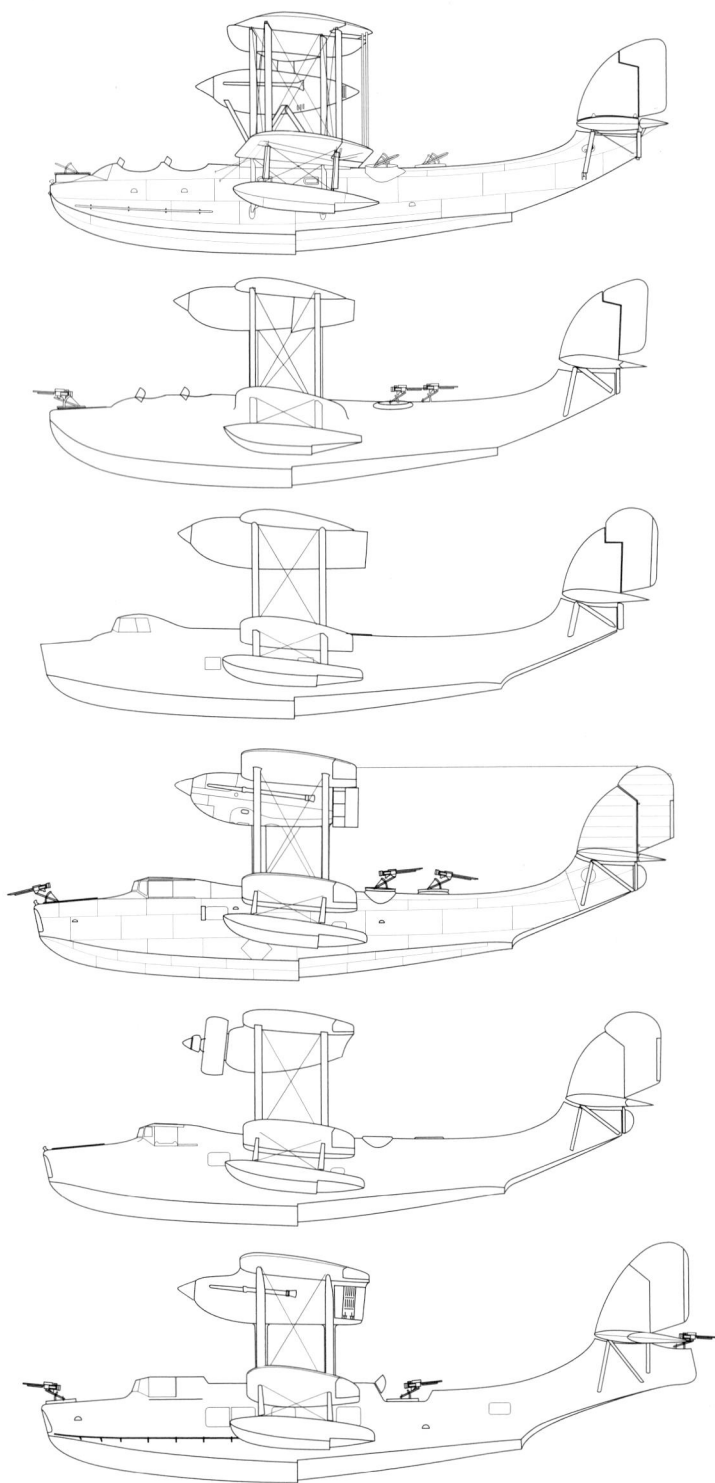

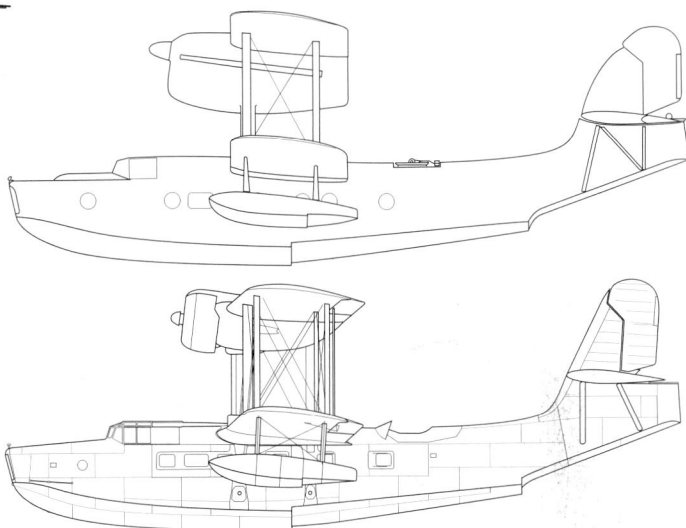

The evolution of the Southampton-Stranraer family. From top to bottom, Southampton II with Kestrel engines, project from 1931, civil Southampton IV 1931, Scapa 1932, Type 226 Scapa Development 1932, Type 230 1932, Type 235 with Junkers Jumo engines 1933, Type 237 Stranraer 1934

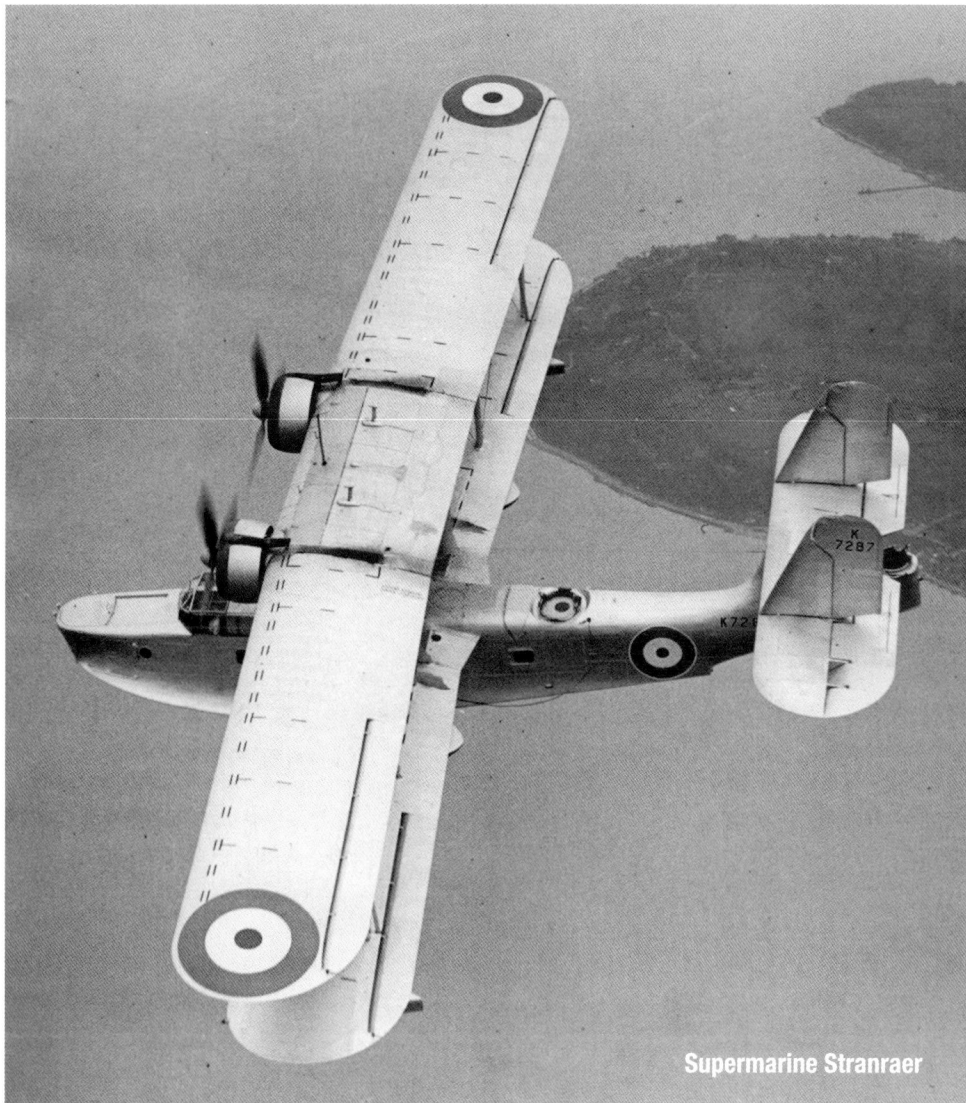

Supermarine Stranraer

Mitchell was less than enthusiastic about the arrangement and pointed out that while the Jumo's attachment points were well engineered to fit in the front of a deep fuselage they were not so for installation in a nacelle without a great increase in frontal area. The semi-monocoque engine mount arrangement for the Kestrel, which distributed the weight of the engine on the 'scoop' of the lower nacelle, could not be applied with the Jumo and a new form of frame had to be designed, suspended from the top wing and braced by the wing struts. Despite Mitchell's reservations, it was a neat solution to a complicated problem. However, the brief enthusiasm for diesels faded away and Napier gave the Culverin project low priority.

Development effort was then focused on the Type 230. The Rolls-Royce engines were dropped once again and the Pegasus reinstated. The shift in weight resulted in the need for four degrees of sweep to be applied to the wings to restore balance. The project was named Southampton V, although

that name does not appear on any drawing, and construction started in late 1933. The aircraft was flown on 27th July 1934 and went to the MAEE in October. A production contract for 17 aircraft, under the name Type 237 Stranraer, was finally awarded in July 1935 – a year having passed before the decision to proceed.

It questionable whether the Southampton V/ Stranraer was the best that Mitchell could have achieved at this point. Certainly the specification's emphasis on simplicity and ease of construction acted as a bit of a brake on trying something new, but it is disappointing that the aircraft selected to replace the Stranraer in service in 1939 was the Consolidated Model 28 Catalina – the prototype of which first flew just a year after the Stranraer, with both entering service around the same time in 1937.

While the Stranraer design was being finalised the design staff were preoccupied handling a great many projects, some very advanced, that may help explain why the Stranraer was kept simple.

11 CHAPTER

Four Engine Military Flying Boats

The Air Ministry planners found themselves in a difficult position in 1932 and for the following two years. The Conference for Reduction and Limitation of Armaments had convened in Geneva on 2nd February 1932 after more than a decade of negligible progress on the issue by the League of Nations. It was chaired by Arthur Henderson, Labour Member of Parliament and former Foreign Secretary. The British Government of National Unity, an alliance between parties headed by Prime Minister Ramsey MacDonald, formerly Labour Prime Minister but expelled from the party when the Unity government was formed, stood behind the aims of the conference while also moving to ensure that Britain's status on the world stage was maintained.

Naturally there was a great deal of scepticism, and not a little opposition, but Government policy was to hold back on any visible major rearmament efforts while the conference was in session. It was they, in fact, who tabled a proposal to limit the unladen size of military aircraft, suggesting just three tons (6,720lbs), and the Air Ministry had perforce to tailor its requirements to respect that initiative, however much the ministry itself and the aircraft companies objected.

Reconnaissance flying boats, conveniently, fell outside the scope of this proposal so development of them could, to a large extent, proceed without too much concern regarding constraint. So, when considering what type of aircraft should form the larger, long range element of the coastal defence force it was possible to raise a specification for an aircraft which would, had it been a bomber, fall way outside the restrictions that the government had proposed. That the development of such a type could all too easily be reworked as a bomber was discretely ignored. Such is the nature of Machiavellian politics.

Specification R.2/33 was issued for tender in November 1933. The operational requirement,

OR.8, was for a long-range Four-engined General Purpose Boat Seaplane capable of carrying an offensive load of either four 500lb or eight 250lb bombs or depth charges. As an interim measure the Air Ministry also issued Specification R.3/33 to cover the construction of four examples of an improved version of the Short Singapore II prototype, with a further 33 ordered the following year. The Singapore III was powered by four Rolls-Royce Kestrels in tandem pairs and was larger overall than the Stranraer – yet its bomb load was no greater and performance was generally inferior. Essentially obsolete even as it entered service in January 1935, it was very much a stopgap until the new designs became available.

Before any serious work had begun on a design to meet R.2/33, Mitchell had visited his doctor in August for advice as he was experiencing bouts of abdominal pain. After being referred to a specialist he had been diagnosed as suffering from colon cancer and was advised that it required immediate surgery. For more than half a year after the operation he was unable to work from the office but during this period of convalescence he kept himself involved in all key decisions through daily meetings with his deputies at his home.

R.2/33 had not specified whether the aircraft should be a biplane or monoplane but the performance required, and the general design trend within the industry, strongly suggested that a monoplane was the appropriate choice. Neither did the specification dictate the choice of engines, the only instruction being that any British engine could be selected subject to it having passed its 100-hour service endurance tests or would likely have done so when the aircraft flew.

Prior to the issue of the specification, Supermarine's main competitors had already embarked on design schemes that could be revised to meet the requirement. Saunders-Roe had been busy working with General Aircraft Limited to fit a monospar wing to an A.29 Cloud flying boat and also to equip this with sponson stabilisers, the experimental project covered by Air Ministry spec 18/32. Blackburn had in hand a number of variations of a civil or military sesquiplane powered by Junkers Jumo diesel engines and had submitted models for testing in the wind tunnel at the RAE. Short Bros was perhaps a little less prepared but flew the S.18 'Knuckleduster', an experimental monoplane design to meet R.24/31, in November 1933 and had another twin-engine monoplane flying boat design on the drawing board to form the lower component of the Mayo Composite Aircraft project, covered by Specification 13/33, but was actively contemplating a major change in direction for flying boat design.

Supermarine was in a very strong position to design the wing for a large monoplane flying boat. It had built and flown one design of wing on the Air Yacht in 1930 and the RAE had undertaken strength tests on a sub-scale model to assess the torsional strength of the cantilever single spar wing for the Type 179 Giant. A smaller cantilever wing of this type had been built for the Type 224 fighter, then nearing completion in the works.

It was almost a given that this single spar type of wing should be part of the design for the R.2/33 project as this then enabled Mitchell to specify the Rolls-Royce Goshawk as his preferred engine, once again utilising the 'D' leading edge spar box as the steam condenser. Despite Mitchell's experience with sponson stabilisers having been less than positive on the Air Yacht he must still have felt that the concept offered advantages that made them preferable to wing floats and that the numerous problems encountered with the Air Yacht had been resolved to the point where he was prepared to include them in the new design.

In the first layout drawings, which were produced in April 1934, the lower hull form was not dissimilar to that of an enlarged Stranraer but with the addition of an upper deck that housed the cockpit just ahead of the attachment for the wing roots. The enclosed cockpit, set some way back from the nose, placed the pilot a few feet behind the plane of the propeller discs and close to those of the inner engines, which one would have thought less than ideal and potentially distracting from strobe effect on a long mission.

The navigator's spotting position was in the lower main hull directly below the plane of the propeller discs, generally a position subject to maximum noise, but his navigation chart table was placed behind in a control room located below the wing and alongside the engineer's station. A staircase led from this control room to the cockpit but the navigator was sitting out of sight of the pilot and therefore not in direct visual contact. There were four berths for the crew with lockers beneath.

The defensive armament was comprised of an upper gun behind the wing root trailing edge, which had a field of fire upwards and to the rear, and two lateral firing positions at opening observation windows in the rear hull. A further gun in the extreme tail was shielded by a helmet type cowl that could be closed when the gun was not in use. In the nose a rotating turret could house either a Lewis machine gun or a COW cannon. The latter, a 37mm cannon, found favour with the RAF at this time for patrol flying boats since it enabled them to engage small boats and submarines on the surface. A single COW gun installation was evaluated in the bow position of a Blackburn Iris III before the concept was dropped. Beneath the turret there was the usual Supermarine top-hinged hatch for the use of the bomb aimer, a simple system installed in the Scapa and Stranraer

The sponsons were slightly tapered in plan and thickness and had an increase in incidence outboard, a feature seen on the Air Yacht after modification. Unlike the straight-cut tips of the Air Yacht the new design had blunt rounded tips. As on the Air Yacht, the main fuel tanks were housed within the sponsons

To ensure that the propellers were raised well clear of spray, the inner portion of the wing with the engines attached had significant dihedral. This also benefited the drainage and pooling of the condensate from the cooling system. The inner wing featured reverse taper and had a t/c of about 10% at the root rising to 18% at the outer engine nacelle. The outer wing then tapered to the tips. The Goshawk engines were positioned on the inner wings ahead of the leading edge and slightly above the mean chord line, installed in cantilevered nacelles that also enclosed the fuel and water header tanks and the oil tank.

Curiously the wings were not designed as full cantilever, which would admittedly have been difficult given the thin section and reduced chord at the root, but were supported by struts. These ran from the outer edge of the sponsons, the rearmost of the struts secured to the main wing spar and the other to the mount of the outer engine. For additional strength, the strut pairs had conventional diagonal wire bracing between them and the front struts were similarly wire braced to the hull by lift and landing wires.

As in the Type 179 'Giant', the entire wing leading edge back to the spar at around 30% chord formed the steam condenser of the cooling system and had a

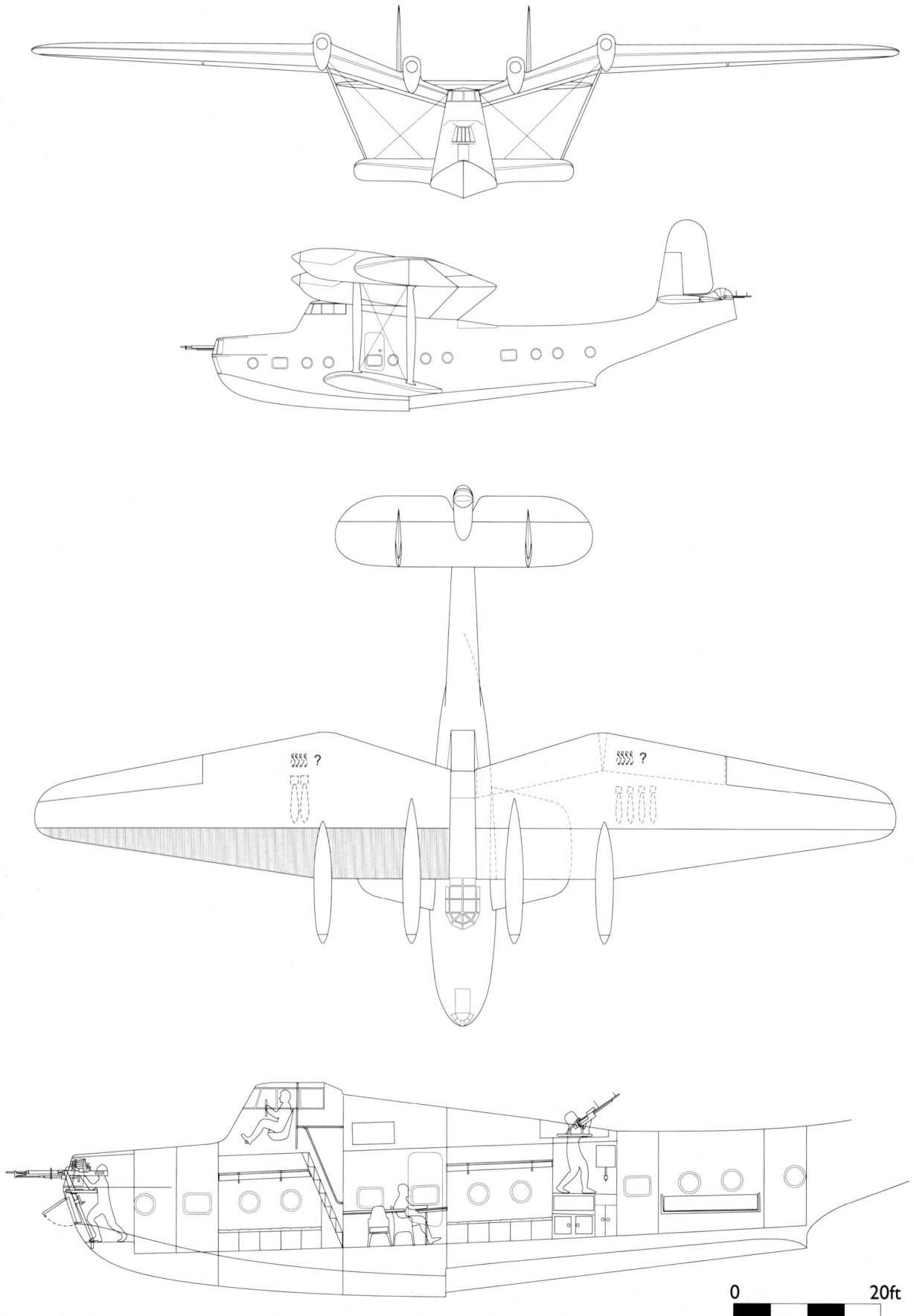

The Type 232 four-engine reconnaissance flying boat for Specification R.2/33

corrugated skin. Steam from the engines entered the condenser directly behind each engine and from there was expected to fill the whole span through natural expansion and turbulence, although whether the outer reaches of the condenser would have contributed materially to the cooling appears questionable.

Condensed water then flowed by gravity down to pool in the hot well in the wing root from where it could be returned to the engines. This looked to be effective in principal, and small scale tests had indicated no issues, but experience with the Type 224 fighter, which had commenced test flights in February 1934, had soon shown that having the hot well located below the level of the water intake for the engine could all too easily result in problems as the pressure drop created at the intake end of the water pumps could cause spontaneous re-boiling of the hot water if it had not cooled sufficiently. Steam in the pumps would then result in a breakdown in flow and possible airlocks if air had been drawn in with the steam.

The bomb bays were fully internal and located outboard of the engines behind the wing spar. On each side these could house two bombs/depth charges in the 450-550lb range or four of 100-250lb. Behind the main bays were smaller ones for the carriage of four 20lb bombs.

The performance estimates for this initial project

must have proven disappointing as in July it underwent a thorough overhaul and was decreased in size. While the hull maintained much the original shape it was reduced in length and the planing bottom narrowed. In a similar way the wing was reduced in both span and chord although the span of the inner portion had to be maintained in order to preserve the appropriate spacing of the engines. Split flaps were added inboard of the ailerons on both the inner and outer wings.

Drawings for the project included many showing field of fire, internal arrangement, details of the engine installation, beaching gear and so on – implying that a formal brochure to accompany a tender had been intended, but no records have been located to show that the Air Ministry received one.

While the original set of layout drawings were being prepared a second set, under the designation Type 239, show the same design scaled up to be powered by Rolls-Royce Merlins, also evaporatively cooled.

Finally, Supermarine hedged its bets by considering a biplane to meet the same specification. Type 238 was in essence a scaled up Stranraer powered by four Bristol Perseus radial engines.

In 1934 the Air Ministry awarded contracts for prototypes to Saunders-Roe for the A.33 and to Short Bros for the S.25, which would be named

The Type 232 would have flown long range patrol missions over the North Atlantic to protect the convoys of merchant vessels (© Matt Painter)

Sunderland. Both were powered by four Bristol Pegasus radials. Shorts was on a roll regarding large four-engine flying boats, gaining contracts for the S.20 lower component of the Mayo Composite, the S.23, which would enter Imperial Airways service as the 'C' class Empire flying boat and now the S.25 Sunderland. All three types were derived from the same basic template, a suite of innovative ideas developed by the team under Arthur Gouge. Each had a version of a tall, narrow hull, a full cantilever box-spar wing with large area-increasing flaps, and shock-absorbing wing floats. It would prove to be a winning formula for the next ten years and resulted in multiple orders.

Saunders-Roe had followed up on its monospar-winged, sponson-stabilised flying boat concept and produced the A.33. The parasol wing was supported by struts from the inner edge of the sponsons providing a parallelogram bracing, with no connection at all to the top of the hull. This allowed the hull to be of shallow profile, and hence of low drag form. However the aircraft was plagued by porpoising problems and on its fifth test flight was thrown into the air after hitting the wake of a boat. It stalled and the wing collapsed in the ensuing hard landing, the same fate as had befallen the Supermarine Air Yacht. Already a year behind the Sunderland in its test programme, it was abandoned.

Had Supermarine built and flown the Type 232, it is inevitable that it would have had to be re-engined before completion. The Goshawk had proven to be disappointing in its intended role as a fighter engine and development was abandoned by Rolls-Royce in early 1935, years before Supermarine could have completed the aircraft. Evaporative cooling for other Rolls-Royce engines was discontinued in favour of glycol or water/glycol mixtures at the same time.

In a Daily Mirror article published in October 1934 on the subject of 'What is happening now in air transport?' Mitchell wrote: "The evaporative cooling of engines is another development with great possibilities… The advantages of this are so obvious that the system is bound to be used largely in the future, but its practical application has been long delayed." Within a few months he was to be proven wrong.

In any head-to-head competition the Type 232's wing, supported by struts and bracing wires, would surely have proven aerodynamically inferior to that of the Sunderland and there were no other features to the design that look likely to have proven superior. Following the aborted Type 179 'Giant', it was a second poor foray into the world of large monoplane flying boats and Mitchell and the team

would need to up their game considerably if they were to regain their position as a prime producer of the type.

Before looking at Supermarine's next attempts to win in a competitive tender situation we should pause and consider a commercial success running in the background.

Replacing the Seagull part 2 – Seagull V

Following the failure to garner any interest in the Type 181 for the civil market, and the RAAF having declined to place an order for its military stablemate, it would have been wholly understandable for the company to quit that line of development. But Mitchell was loath to drop what he had long perceived as a useful class of flying boat, and the RAAF requirement was still there and unfulfilled. While the primary focus of the design team remained on developing an attractive Southampton replacement he continued to keep active the RAAF Seagull III replacement projecct.

After the Vickers takeover and the cutbacks resulting from the onset of the depression, MacLean set about pruning the Supermarine organisation to bring it more into line with Vickers' practice. Even some of those who worked for the company during this period have conceded that it had grown in a rather shambolic manner since the war. In the drawing office there was no systematic catalogue, drawings were just numbered sequentially in the order they were produced so that retrieving all those associated with a particular project was tedious as they were stored interleaved with those relating to others.

The parts bins for aircraft under construction were equally illogical in their arrangement, relying to a certain degree on the memory of the store manager. Many Supermarine staff resented the arrival of Vickers and were not fully cooperative, resulting in several cycles of lay-offs, including some from within Mitchell's departments. As business began to improve a round of recruitments commenced, targeting designers and draughtsmen with experience working for other companies. Among those who joined the design team at this time was William Munro, a naval architect trained at Vickers' Barrow yard who had worked subsequently on float designs for Gloster's racing seaplanes before moving first to Canada to join Vickers' Canadian division and then to the USA where he worked as chief engineer with the US company Towle on their monoplane flying boats – aircraft similar in style to the Saunders-Roe Cloud.

Munro had produced a couple of layout drawings for civil and military monoplane flying boats when he arrived in 1931, probably on a speculative

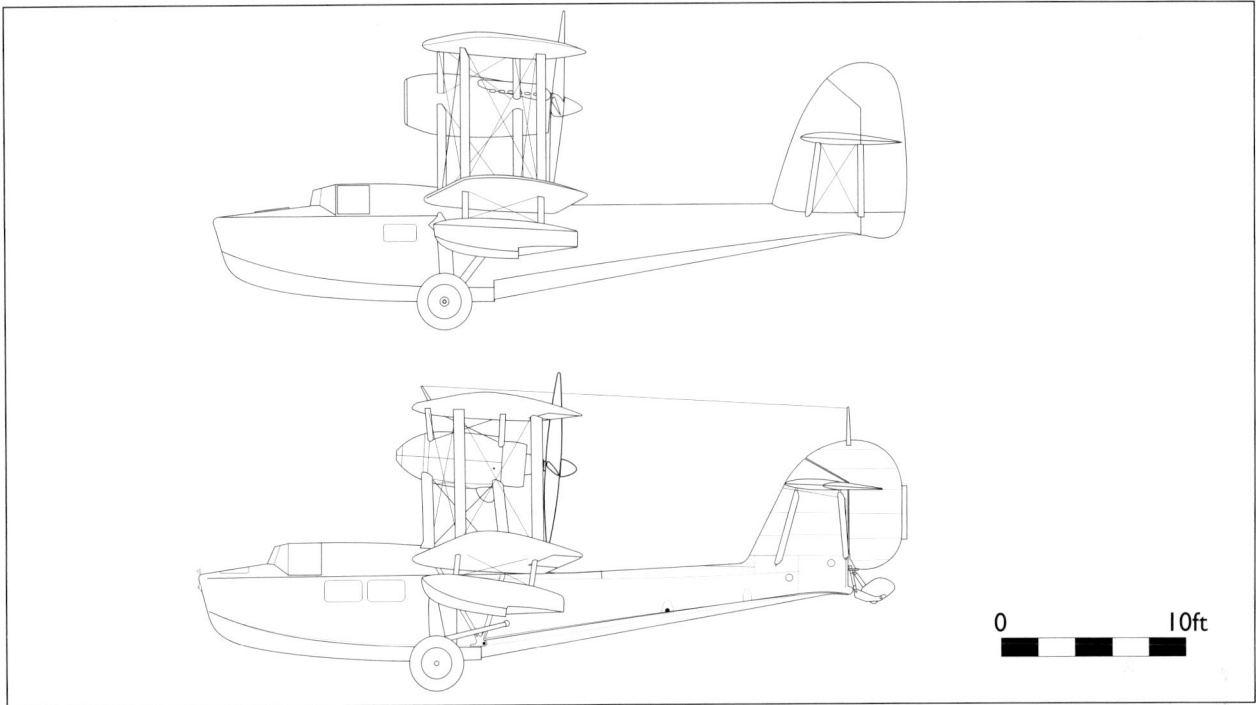

The Seagull V was a simple military amphibian and not well suited for airline use. Nevertheless two variants were offered, one a Kestrel-powered Seagull V in 1932, the other an adaptation of the Walrus that was offered to Jersey Airways in 1934

basis and to demonstrate his capabilities, and was assigned to the Seagull III replacement team where his knowledge and experience were to have a major influence on the direction that the design was to follow. Rather than take the easy option to modify the Type 181, the team opted to start afresh and, although adhering to the basic single pusher engine biplane formula, developed an extremely simple metal hull that avoided all but essential curved panels.

The planing surface was itself composed of flat panels based on patents held by Saunders-Roe. The hull was stressed for catapulting. The rearward folding biplane wings were of mixed metal and wood construction in a single bay. There was a single fin with the tailplane attached near the top. The engine, initially a Rolls-Royce Kestrel in pusher configuration, was positioned mid-gap with the supporting struts also doubling as the support for the wing centre section. The engine nacelle was angled slightly to port to compensate for the torque effect of the propeller slipstream on the tail. A completely new, and simple, form of retractable undercarriage was designed for the project with a single braced oleo leg pivoted at the top that rotated the undercarriage leg through 90-degrees outwards so that the wheels retracted to lie flat within wells in the lower wing. Before the aircraft was built the choice of engine was changed to a Bristol Pegasus radial. Thus was

born the Type 223, Seagull V.

Once again this raises the question of nomenclature; what was the Seagull IV? This was most likely a name given unofficially to the Type 181, although there do not appear to be any records to confirm that.

The Seagull V was another project given the personal support of Sir Robert McLean when he approved expenditure on the construction of a prototype before having received an order from the RAAF, who were as yet uncertain as to the merits of the design. This proved to be another shrewd move as once the prototype had proven itself, including trials on the catapult at the RAE, an order was received for 24 aircraft, the first entering service in June 1935.

Although sceptical at first, the RAF had been impressed by the performance of the Seagull V prototype and in May 1935 an order was placed for an initial batch of five covered by Specification 2/35 under the new name Walrus. A further 36 were ordered later in the year.

It was inevitable that civil versions of the Seagull V would also be considered, although as a simple spartan metal box the interior did not really lend itself to civilian use. The Kestrel-powered Type 225 was the first offering in 1932 and there was a later Pegasus-powered adaptation in 1934 aimed at a requirement of Jersey Airways. Neither were built.

CHAPTER 12
Flying Boats for Imperial Airways

The chairman of Imperial Airways, Sir Eric Geddes, submitted a memorandum to the British government in early 1933 which outlined a plan for the carriage of subsidised mail throughout the Empire and mandated territories using a fleet of fast flying boats configured for passengers and freight. The summary stated: "The Board thinks that, in great measure, the future of air communications within the Empire lies in Marine aircraft, and that we should return or, rather, lean more and more to our national heritage, the Sea. The influence of our Naval power in the past centuries has provided us with marine airports, on a scale to which no other country can aspire. Such a policy as is forecast has many political, economic and technical advantages, which cannot be equalled in the development of land-aircraft".

An overseas mail scheme along these lines had been under consideration within Government for some time so Geddes' recommendations were accepted as the basis for the Empire Air Mail Service (EAMS) which would be initiated a few years later. The funding was approved for a substantial fleet of large, fast flying boats.

With the government on board, Imperial Airways management requested that their technical advisor, Robert Mayo, formulate a specification that could be circulated to industry for an appropriate medium range flying boat. In November 1933, a draft specification called for a flying boat with an all-up weight of 60,000lbs, payload of 8,000lb, a cruising speed of 150mph and a range of 500 miles against a 40mph headwind. It seems unlikely that this was ever issued to industry but it may have formed the basis for discussions. However, a revised formal outline specification for a Four Engine Flying Boat was prepared and approved in March 1934. The preamble stated:

"Nature of Tenders now required. Tenders are invited for the supply of :-

a)   Two flying boats conforming to this outline Specification.

b)   Two flying boats generally in accordance with this Specification but having –

i) Four engines of the next larger size – i.e. between 540 and 600 continuous cruising horse-power.

ii)   The capacities for passengers, freight and mail raised in proportion to the increase in paying load excluding crew.

General

a)   This outline has been prepared for the guidance of those who are invited to submit tenders and it should be noted that it is a confidential document, and that the basic principle observed in its preparation is a desire to give manufacturers the greatest possible freedom for the expression of their own ideas while requiring greatest safety and lowest cost of operation.

b)   We have, in consequence, specified only those essentials which arise from (i) study of general characteristics of the type of aircraft for which we now desire tenders and (ii) our own experience in the operation of aircraft.

c)   Tenderers are especially invited to offer alternatives which they may consider superior to any suggestions or equipment mentioned in this outline Specification."

The flying boat would have a crew of five; weight allocation 1,000lb, and passengers, mail and cargo totalling 7,200lb. The interior needed to allow for various configurations; space for 6,200lb of mail, accommodation for 24 day passengers at 165lb each plus 85lb baggage, or 16 night passengers.

The cruising speed at full load should be not less than 130mph at 5,000ft, and range at cruising speed is to be 500 miles against a 40mph head wind. Stalling speed at full load could not exceed 68mph at sea level.

An unusual aspect of the requirement was that the flying boat should be capable of operating as a landplane for 7-10% of its operating life, so provision had to be made for the fitment of a land undercarriage.

There was plenty of scope, and indeed encouragement, for innovative designs, which could have set the ground for an interesting competition.

It has been written that Short Bros received a copy of this outline specification on 1st March 1934 and that a tender for the S.23 design was submitted to Imperial Airways as early as 29th June. It is also a matter of record that a patent application made by Short Bros in July for "Improvements in or connected with the Construction of Cantilever Wings and other Aircraft Structures", another for wingtip floats submitted in June that year and others to be applied for shortly thereafter were all directly relevant to the S.23 flying boat project.

The conclusion that can be drawn from this is that Imperial Airways and Short Bros had developed a particularly close relationship, built up through the successful operation of Calcutta and Kent flying boats and the design work associated with the Mayo Composite aircraft, and that the new specification had in fact been drawn up with Short Bros' new concepts in mind.

The S.23 project must surely have been well under way when the specification was finalised. Indeed, it is quite conceivable that the specification could have received input from the company based on the work it already had in hand. Short Bros received an Instruction to Proceed with the S.23 project on 24th January 1935, with a formal contract following on 19th February.

Where did this leave Short Bros' competitors? It is not known when Supermarine and Blackburn were informed of the specification or, indeed, whether they ever actually received copies, but both initiated projects appropriate to Imperial Airways' requirement. That both only commenced work in mid-1935 after Short Bros had been awarded production contracts for the S.23 'off the drawing board' surely indicates that neither were ever in the running – although they may well have been unaware of this at the time.

The only yardstick by which to judge a modern medium range commercial flying boat project in late 1934 was the Sikorski S-42. The prototype of this aircraft, ordered by Pan American Airways, flew in April 1934 and was reported in detail in the press, neither Igor Sikorsky nor Juan Trippe of Pan American being averse to publicity. After completion of manufacturer and airline acceptance trials, the S-42 entered service in August and Sikorsky released a blizzard of surprisingly detailed data covering the main design aspects of the aircraft and its performance.

During its trials the aircraft had set a number of international class records for speed, range, altitude and load carrying, all homologated by the F.A.I. to dispel any doubt that they were simply sales hype. The overall performance of the aircraft was in the words of an article in *Flight* "startling". Sikorsky was then invited to lecture to the Royal Aeronautical Society, which he accepted and on 15th November 1934 he presented his paper on 'The Development and Characteristics of Long Range Flying Boats', the greater part of which reiterated the data previously published and extolled the virtues of the S-42. The flying boat did indeed seem to be a hard act to follow and among those listening were representatives of a couple of British investment trusts who were sufficiently impressed to acquire a licence to build the type in the UK. In early 1935 they registered a new company, British Marine Aircraft, and acquired land at Hamble on Southampton Water where they commenced construction of a large factory and slipway.

In summary, the S-42 was an all-metal parasol monoplane with the wing mounted on a pylon atop the hull and braced by substantial struts on either side. It was powered by four 670hp Pratt & Whitney Hornet radial engines on the leading edge of the 114ft span wing. The tailplane held twin fins and rudders. Gross loaded weight, carrying 32 day passengers, was 38,000lb. Maximum speed was 188mph and cruise in the range 150-160mph for 1200 miles. In Pan American service the S-42 ran on routes along the eastern coast of the US and around the Caribbean to Central America.

The Sikorsky S-42 was never directly comparable to the Short S.23 as they were optimised for different routes and operations, yet the overlap was considerable and certainly influenced, and indeed worried, Imperial Airways management as to the competition they would encounter on international routes. The Imperial Airways specification was modified on several occasions in discussions with Short Bros – in particular the requirement for a land undercarriage was dropped and the range requirement extended to 700 miles for the Empire routes.

One variant was added to provide a service from New York to Bermuda and there were experimental aircraft to trial trans-Atlantic flights. The arrangement of fuel tanks in the wings of the S.23 made it a simple operation to add extra when required. It is reasonable to assume that Supermarine and Blackburn, commencing work later than Short Bros, even if they had not received a copy of the Imperial Airways specification, should have been mindful of the rough outline of Imperial Airways' requirements and were more than aware of the competition in other markets from Sikorsky,

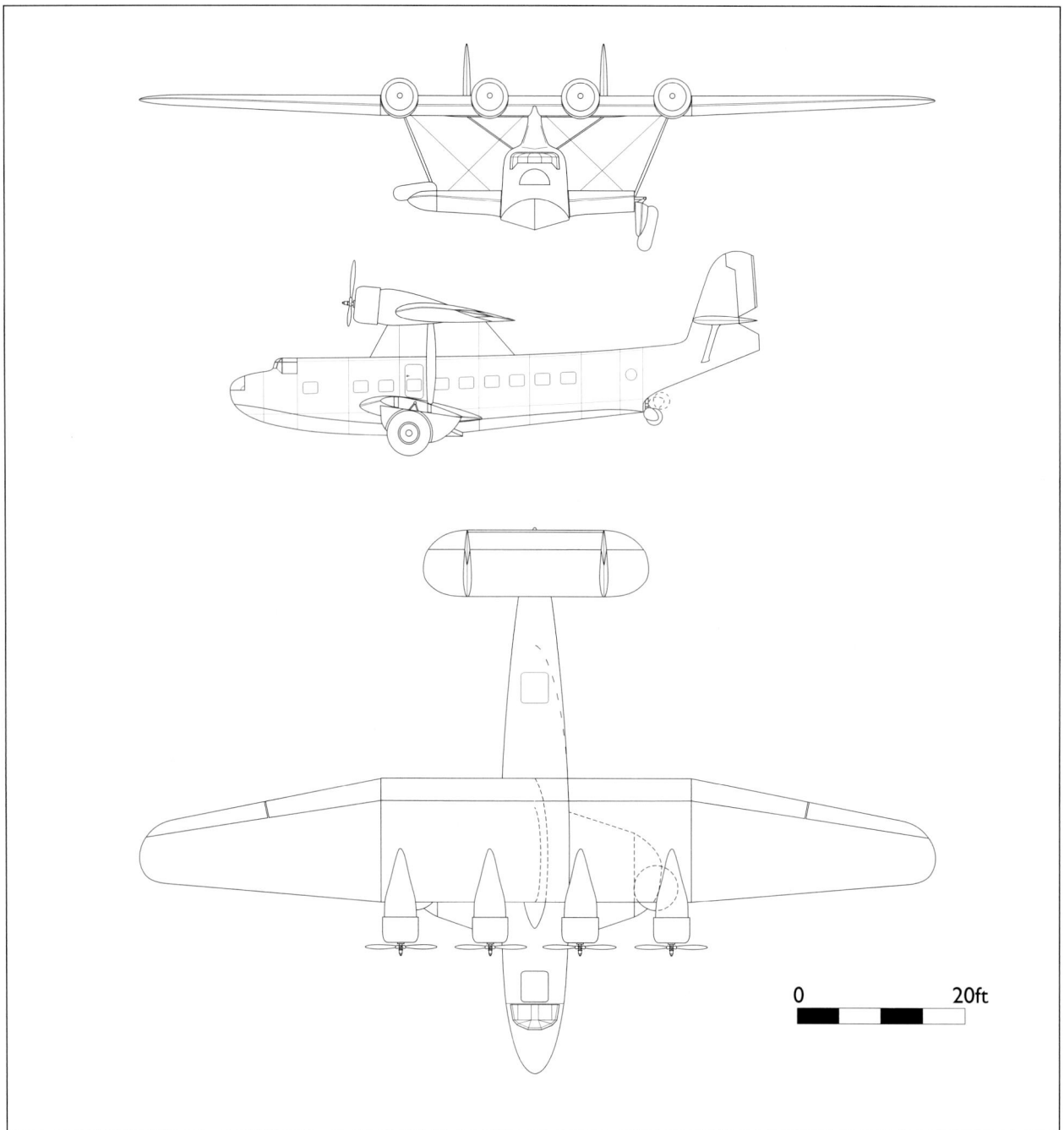

One version of the Type 302 was a 24-passenger amphibian with partially retractable wheels on the tips of the sponson stabilisers

especially as it was now anticipated that S-42s would be constructed in Britain.

Mitchell commenced work on the Type 302 around April 1935 and the first rough schemes were sketched by the team in May, two of which were biplanes. By July the project was taking shape as a strut-braced monoplane with the wing mounted on a streamlined pylon above the hull and a twin-fin tail – closely following the layout championed by the S-42.

Three alternative arrangements were suggested, one a flying boat with wingtip floats, another with sponson stabilisers, and a third as an amphibian with retractable wheels at the sponson ends to address the early Imperial Airways requirement for the fitment of a land undercarriage, although as mentioned that requirement had been discarded months before.

The initial scheme with sponsons had a hull of almost rectangular section; vertical sides and a relatively flat top. The planing bottom was of simple 'V' form with the main step of chevron type, that is to say in plan it was angled rearwards to a point on the centre line. The sponsons were of the form

The Type 302 as it could have appeared in service with Imperial Airways

suggested for the Type 232, tapered with rounded tips and increasing incidence outboard. The parallel chord wing centre section was mounted above the hull on an aerodynamically shaped pylon and braced to the outer edge of the sponson by a single strut each side, implying that the wing was of the single-spar type, and further braced by wires. The outer wing panels were of straight taper. Simple split flaps ran along the centre section and on the outer wing panels inboard of the ailerons. Accommodation was for 24 day passengers.

Mitchell tackled the requirement for a land undercarriage in a novel manner, transforming the sponson flying boat into an amphibian. The main wheels were to be fitted, semi-recessed, to the top surface of the tips of the sponsons outboard of the bracing strut. The entire sponson tip and wheel assembly could rotate through 90-degrees to bring the wheels into a vertical position. The tailwheel, also retractable, was located just behind the rear step. Presumably this system would have required considerable strengthening of the sponson structure to allow it to carry the load and landing stress.

A second design was developed in parallel to this which had the same basic layout but with wingtip floats substituted for the sponsons. The design differs so much in detail from the previous scheme that it would appear to have been drawn-up by a different hand, with little or no direct reference to the other. The hull was wider at the chine and more rounded across the top. Accommodation was again for a maximum of 24 day passengers. The planing bottom had the novel feature of a reflexed edge ahead of the main step. While the inner part formed a simple 'V' the outer edge curved sharply over to turn slightly downward, effectively forming a narrow channel which was presumably an attempt to minimize spray. The main step was conventional and ran straight across rather than being of chevron form.

The wing centre section appears to be identical with that of the earlier scheme but the pylon on which it was mounted had been shifted to port of the centre line, but it is not at all clear why this was necessary or what advantage this was intended to confer. The outer panels were double elliptical in plan, in effect a scaled-up version of that selected recently for the Spitfire. The tailplane, fins and rudders are strongly reminiscent of the Type 230, the initial scheme for the Stranraer. The wingtip floats were of the standard fixed type.

Later in the design process one drawing was prepared that showed a deeper slab-sided hull, eliminating the need for the wing support pylon. Because of the greater width of the hull at the

Mail and/or Baggage
450 cu.ft.

No.1 Cabin

No.2 Cabin

No.3 Cabin

No.4 Cabin

Mail and/or Baggage
170 cu.ft.

0   20ft

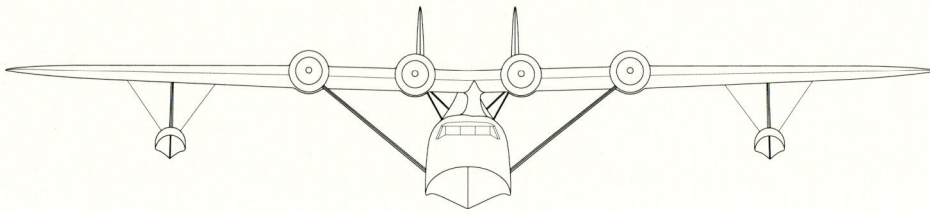

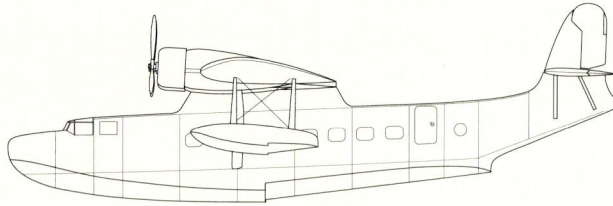

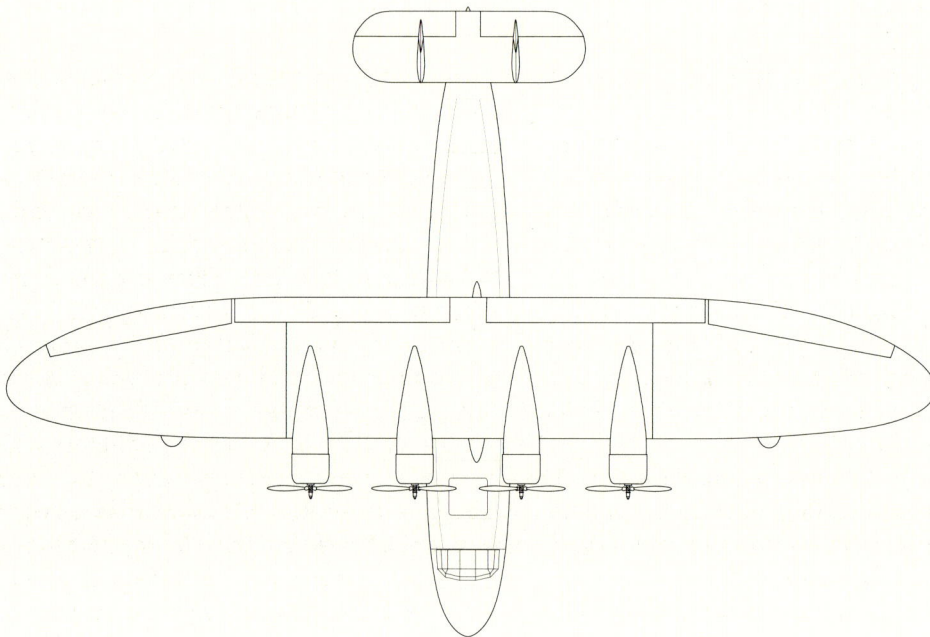

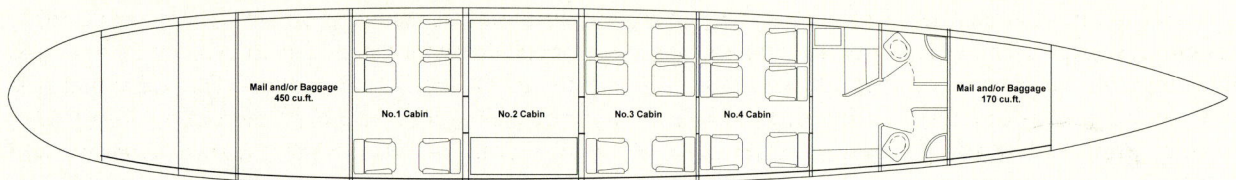

The redesigned Type 302 with wing floats

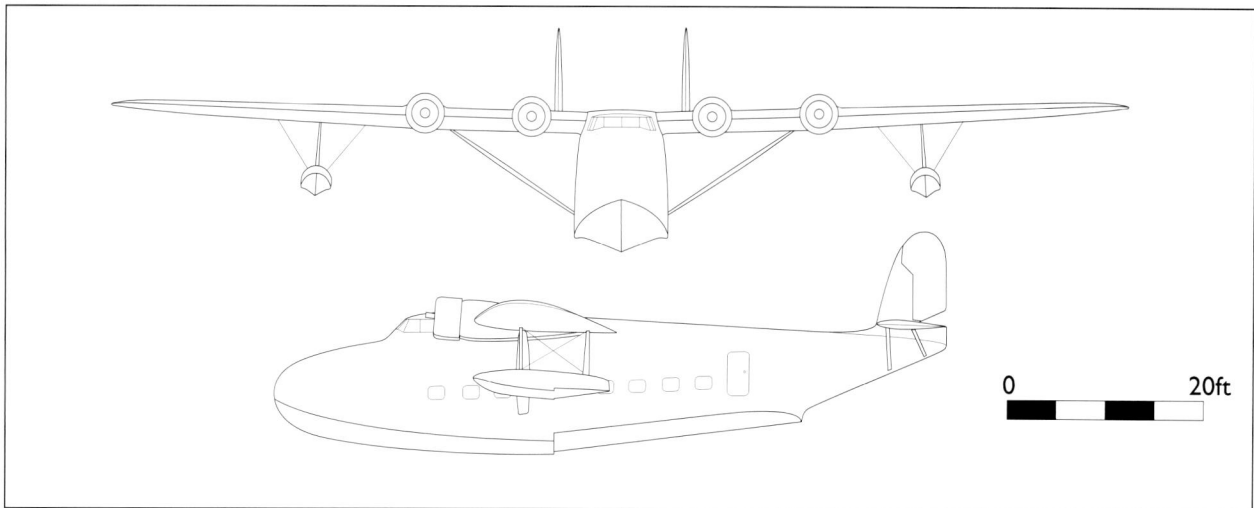

The Type 302 with tall 'Short-style' hull

wing root the engines had to be moved outboard to ensure clearance for the propellers. The cockpit had been moved to a top deck ahead of the wing. Although the changes to the hull resulted in a considerable increase in volume and height, the cabin layout appears to have remained unchanged. It is just possible that this last minute adjustment was a response to the Shorts S.23 design.

None of the surviving Type 302 drawings are of the style or standard usually associated with an official Supermarine tender document, which may suggest that no formal proposal was sent to Imperial Airways. For the record, Blackburn's broadly equivalent project, designated B.B.4, dates from September 1935. The aircraft was very similar in style to the Short S.23 and would have carried up to 32 day passengers. Loaded weight was 45,000lb. There does not appear to have been an official tender associated with this design either.

To put the whole episode into context the record-breaking, much admired Sikorsky S-42 was not destined to be the great sales success that many expected as only ten were produced, all for Pan American. Compare that with the near 200 Douglas DC2s sold around the world at about the same time. Flying boats were a niche market.

In Britain, British Marine Aircraft failed to build a single aircraft. The investment fund backing it failed to secure support or significant work, collapsed and was wound up. The business was salvaged by Alan Goode, an investment entrepreneur, who bought the ailing company and then sold 50% of the shares to a second group of investors fronted by Henry Folland, previously chief designer at Gloster. The restructured company was renamed subsequently as Folland Aircraft.

Once Imperial Airways had issued contracts for the Short S.23 it turned its attention to an aircraft

to be designed specifically to tackle the difficult North Atlantic route. Juan Trippe had been urging Imperial Airways and the British government to establish the legal framework for this service, which would involve the cooperation and approval not just of the British and US authorities but also those of the Irish Free State and the Dominion of Newfoundland (self-governing until 1934, then administered from Britain by a committee after its finances collapsed) as the only practical direct service was on the shortest great circle route and would have to stage through both territories.

The distance entirely over the ocean was almost exactly 2,000 miles. This added a further complication as Newfoundland suffered from severe winters and the harbours were prone to icing over for several months. An alternative southerly route for use over these winter months, via the Azores (an autonomous region of Portugal) and Bermuda (a self-governing British Overseas Territory) also need official approvals. There were many fingers in this particular pie and it would take a fair amount of negotiation to get all interested parties aligned and to establish a work plan that was economically viable for the airlines. Nevertheless it was inevitable that a way forward would be found in time.

On 2nd December 1935 the delegates at the Transatlantic Air Mail Conference, representing Canada, Britain and the Irish Free State, reached unanimous agreement on the framework for a service and then proceeded to Washington to seek their acceptance of the terms. The US concurred and it was agreed that the contract for westbound mail would be awarded to Imperial Airways and eastbound to Pan American. The situation regarding the operation on the Azores and Bermuda route was also discussed. With the main agreements in place, the door was now open to make arrangements

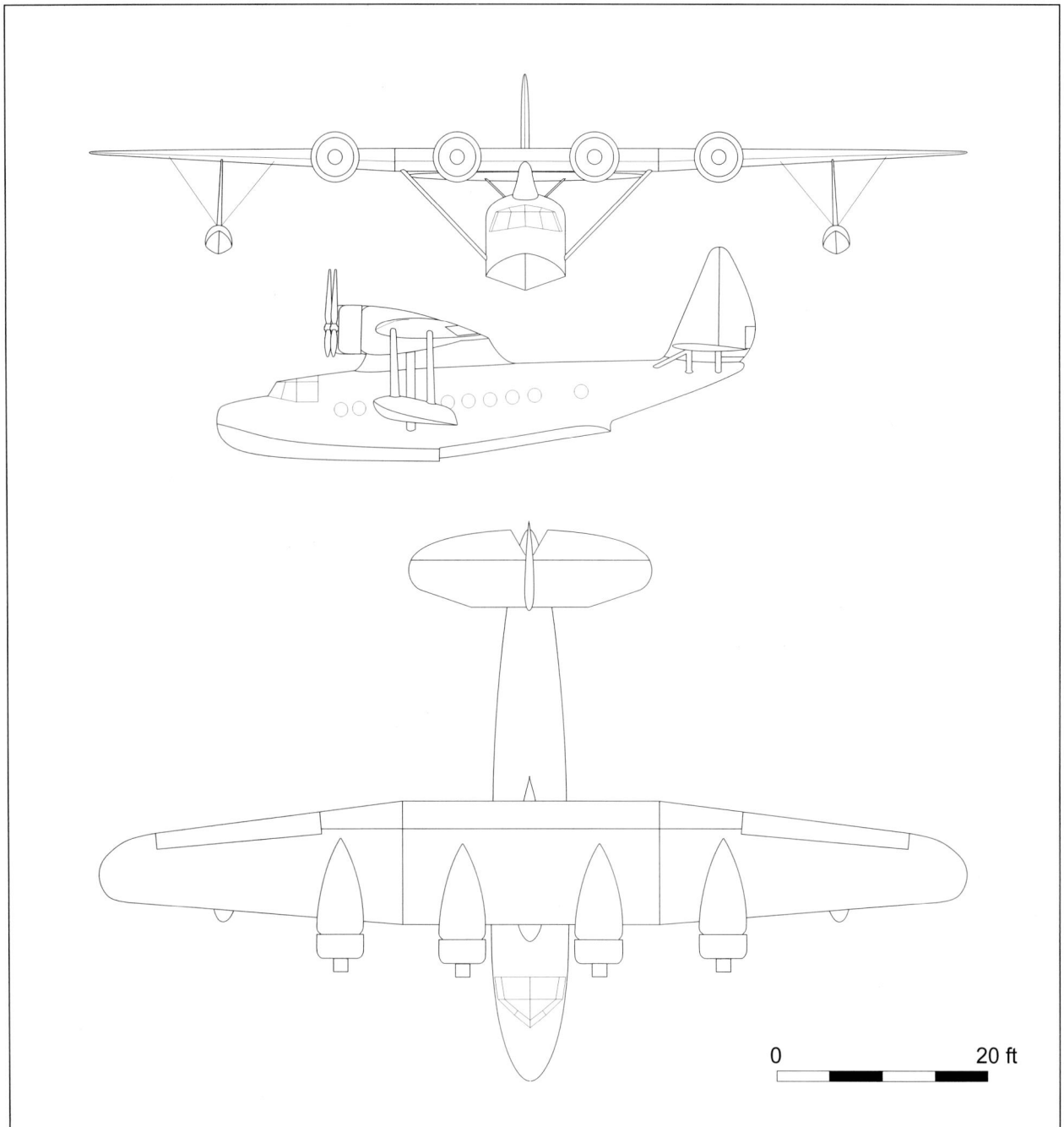

An unnumbered Supermarine project for a dedicated flying boat mail plane designed for catapult launch

for the essential meteorological, navigational and communication systems, plans for flights to prove the routes and, last but by no means least, set the specifications for the aircraft types required to fly the service.

In anticipation of an agreement, in the summer of 1935 Imperial Airways sent out a brief specification asking for designs of a dedicated transatlantic mail plane flying boat configured for catapult launching. This was basically a back-up option for comparison with the Short-Mayo Composite Aircraft, both components of which had been designed by Short Bros and were under construction alongside the

Short S.23, and the inflight refuelling system pioneered by Alan Cobham and his company Flight Refuelling Ltd, which was soon to become a subsidiary of Imperial Airways.

Supermarine prepared a preliminary scheme for a mail plane flying boat under Type 306, dated 26th August 1935, that was a simple revision of the Type 302 passenger flying boat with wingtip floats. A second scheme, dated 23rd September 1935, was for a smaller flying boat of unique design that was not given an official type number.

The following year the Imperial Airways requirement was formalised under Air Ministry

Specification 35/36, but there is no indication that Supermarine responded. Short submitted the S.27 'Civet' flying boat project, looking like a scaled-down C.23 'C' class, but the specification was soon withdrawn and no further action taken.

In parallel with the request for mail plane designs, Imperial Airways also issued a Specification for a Trans Atlantic Passenger Flying Boat, written in very general terms in order to obtain the industry's views on what was technically feasible. Operations on both the northerly and southerly routes were to be considered. The specification called for a flying boat that could carry six passengers and 1,000lb of mail at a cruising speed of not less than 150mph, and with a range of 2,500 miles against a 40mph headwind.

Supermarine developed its concepts under Type 306 in September 1935 and a full brochure and tender specification was presented to Imperial Airways on 10th October. Mitchell was surprisingly cautious in his response, although it has to be said that Imperial Airways' requirement was certainly demanding for the era.

Looking at the southern route, essential if an all-year service was to be provided, Mitchell was less than enthusiastic about the harbour facilities available at Horta in the Azores, which he judged to provide inadequate shelter for the take-off of a heavily laden flying boat that would need a run of, at the very least, 30 seconds. He concluded that some form of catapult launch would be highly desirable – one that would not exceed 1.33g acceleration, which was considered the maximum acceptable for passengers.

Imperial Airways had specified, as usual, that the aircraft should be powered by four engines. When considering the powerplants available, Supermarine's calculations indicated that the higher drag of air-cooled radial engines resulted in the need for a very high fuel load, and this led to a take-off run of more than 40 seconds which would not meet the specification.

Fitting four Rolls-Royce Merlin engines satisfied most requirements, but even then the take-off limit of 40 seconds could not be guaranteed. A design powered by six Merlins was considered but if these were all installed as tractors, spread along the span of the wing, the seaworthiness was compromised, and if two were installed as pushers in a tandem arrangement with the tractors, this reduced efficiency and raised cabin noise to an unacceptable level. Therefore a second design, basically a scaled-up version of the first, was to be fitted with the new Rolls-Royce Vulture 'X' configuration 24-cylinder engine. The tender document also included

performance calculations for the smaller airframe fitted with Vulture engines, which would be for catapulting only and gave a higher cruising speed.

A careful investigation of wing loading and structural variation showed that the minimum fuel load and take-off time was met best by setting wing loading between 28 and 32lb/sq ft, which was at the high end of current practice for civil aircraft but quite feasible.

The layout followed that established for the version of the Type 302 fitted with wing floats with particular attention paid to refinements of the aerodynamic form of the hull. One surviving drawing was amended in pencil to suggest that consideration had been given to increasing the height of the hull in order to produce an aerodynamically clean hull shape enclosing the pylon supporting the wing and reshaping the cockpit glazing to conform to the lines of the nose. The planing bottom had a straight main step and a knife-edge step at the rear while the wingtip floats were of a basic aerodynamic shape with a minimal planing surface and no step.

The mail compartment was located behind the cockpit in the hull, in line with the plane of the propeller discs, with the navigator and radio operator stations immediately behind. Next came the galley and lavatory, with the six passengers in a cabin to the rear. Each passenger was provided with an individual compartment, three on each side, separated by partitions and by a curtain adjacent to the central aisle. The compartments would be converted for sleeping at night; a 2,000 mile journey at a cruising air speed of 150mph against a 40mph headwind would take about 18 hours.

The parallel chord inner wing section included the mounts for the engine nacelles, as in the Type 302, with intakes in the leading edge inboard of each engine for the internal radiators. The system of single-strut bracing of the wing as designed for the Type 302 was retained. A single central fin and rudder supported the tailplane, which was strut braced to the hull. Twin fins and rudders were mounted outboard on the tailplane.

In summary, design A.1, powered by four Merlins, would weigh 54,000lb loaded and cruise at 150mph while design A.2, with four Vultures, would weigh 71,000lb and cruise at 175mph. In both cases the cruise speed was maintained with the engines running at 42% of their maximum power.

Mitchell then stated that if the estimates of structural weight and engine performance were realised then the smaller design was capable of carrying 12 passengers and the larger 26 passengers while conforming to the Imperial Airways standard of 120cu ft per passenger. However, he cautioned

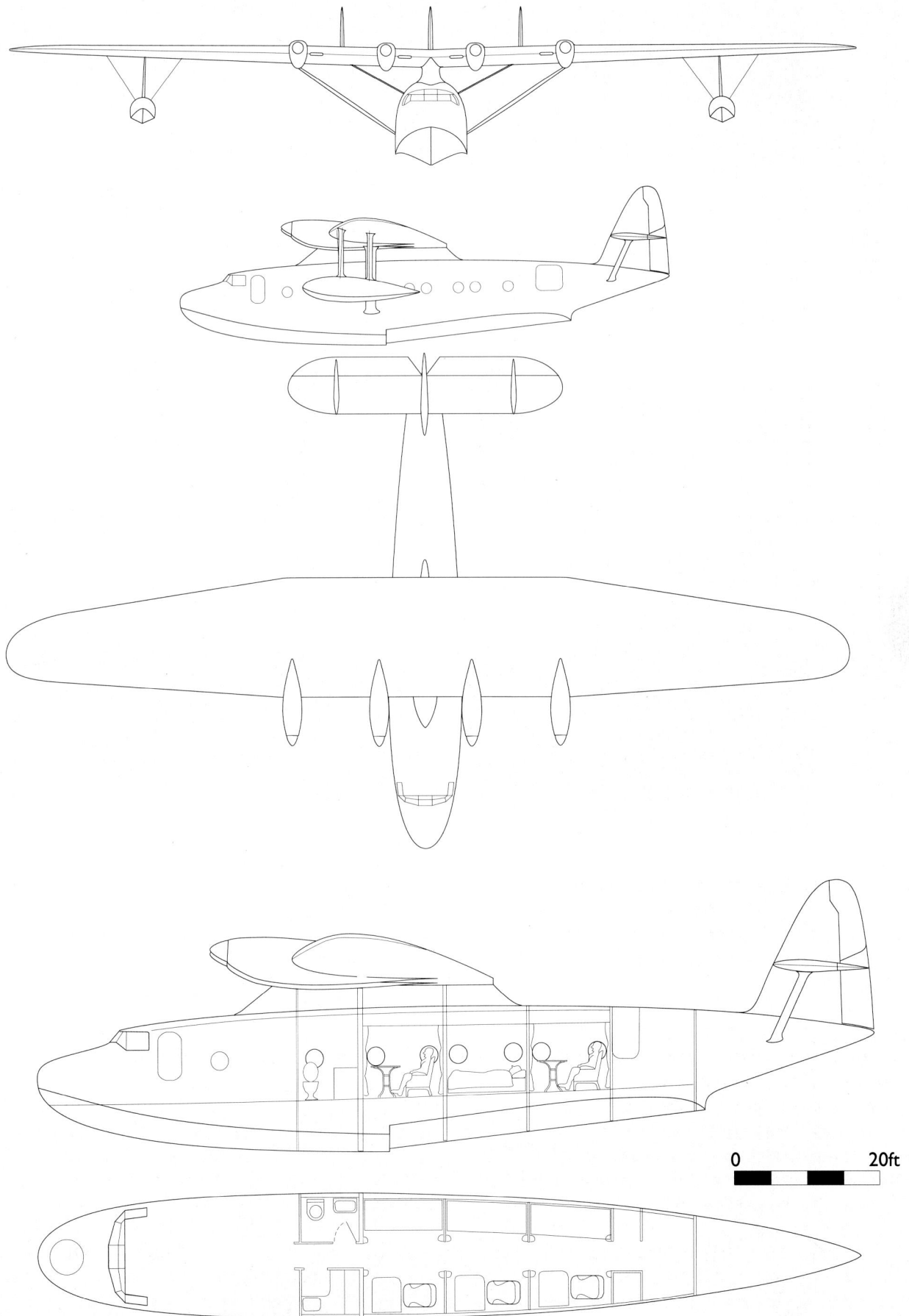

Type 306 Merlin-powered transatlantic flying boat for six passengers

0   20ft

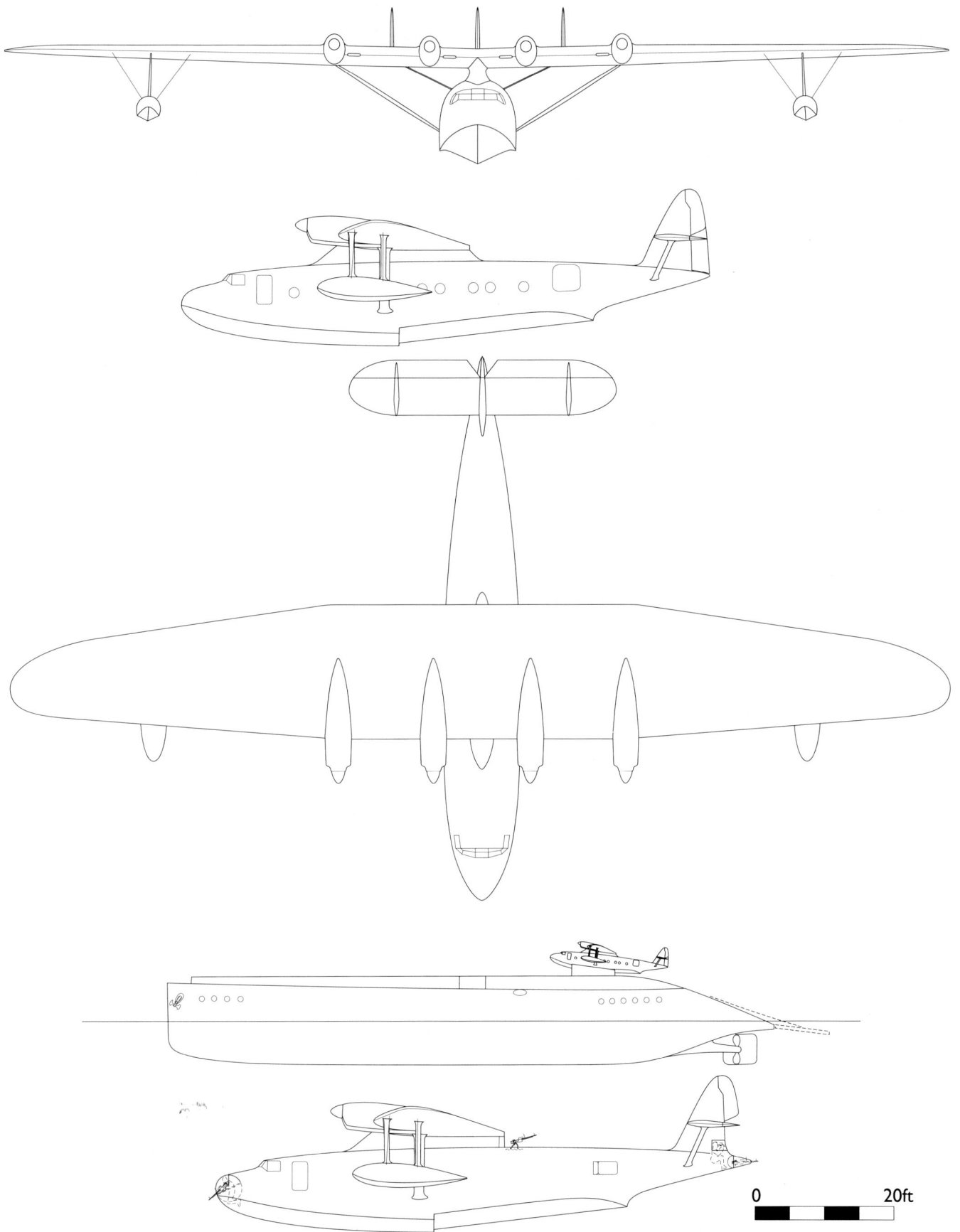

The larger Type 306 powered by four Vultures. The Type 306 was designed for catapult or accelerator launch from a converted barge or ship. A militarised version was also offered, featuring a machine gun enclosed in an aerodynamic shroud in the tail

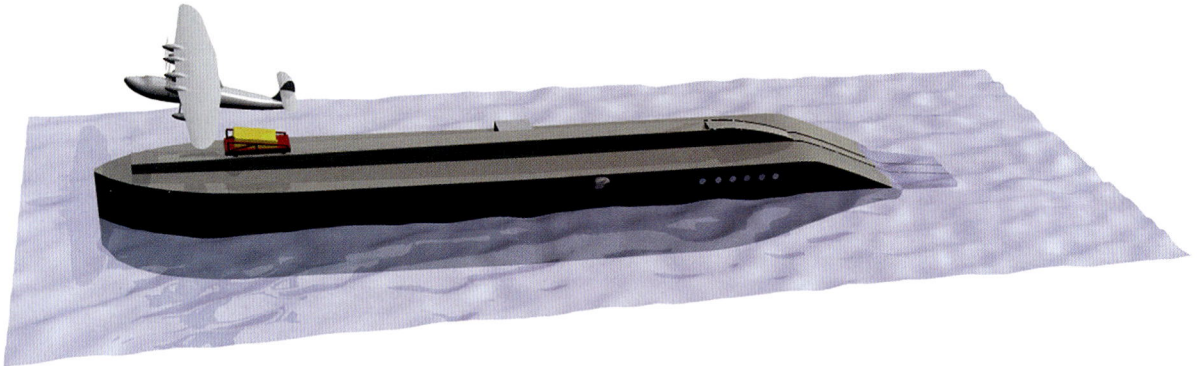

A ship-mounted catapult accelerator as proposed for the Type 306 gained the approval of the Air Ministry but was never trialled

"that the effect of small variation in assumptions is very large in a long range design and a margin is therefore required to cover the following points:-

1) Difficulty of forecasting accurately the weight of structures and also accommodation and equipment.

2) Lack of information regarding the characteristics of three-bladed metal airscrews, particularly during take-off.

3) Lack of experience regarding take off of aircraft of this type."

The tender document then went on to discuss two possible forms of floating catapult.

In both cases, the catapult was to be powered by compressed air, with an acceleration run of 225ft which would enable the aircraft to be launched with no headwind at a speed of 94mph without exceeding 1.33g. With a 10mph headwind the acceleration could be reduced to 1.06g.

The simple option was to mount the catapult on a barge, which had the advantage of having a relatively low deck which would facilitate loading the aircraft from the water, and the disadvantage that it would need to be towed into position and oriented into the wind. The alternative of utilising a converted ship of around 5,000 tons had the advantage of being self-powered for manoeuvring and capable of being used as a depot and rescue ship, and the disadvantage of the deck being higher above the water and hence more inconvenient for loading the aircraft.

The loading operation involved the flying boat taxiing into position over a submerged trolley that ran on rails down from the catapult onto a retractable apron. Once the aircraft was engaged on the trolley, both would be winched up onto the catapult carriage. The flying boat was positioned on the carriage at a pre-set angle of incidence. The catapult then accelerated the flying boat to the take-

off speed of 94mph, at which point it would pull free from the carriage and trolley. These would then decelerate to standstill over a distance of 45ft.

The Director of Scientific Research at the Air Ministry issued a report entitled 'A Consideration of the Methods of Assisted Take-off now available for Trans-Atlantic Services' in July 1936 which addressed both passenger and mail planes. This was a detailed review of the pros and cons associated with in-flight refuelling, the Mayo Composite Aircraft scheme, and accelerators (catapults) of all types.

In-flight refuelling had been tried experimentally, with success, but had yet to prove itself as viable for routine operation. Imperial Airways and Flight Refuelling were to commence test flights with an S.23 flying boat in late 1937. As a commercial transatlantic aircraft would benefit from a high wing loading, the speed at which such an aircraft would need to fly while transferring fuel was considered a cause for concern. To date, the process had only been carried out at around 100mph in calm weather. The report was pessimistic about the practicality of the scheme based on current methodology.

The Mayo scheme, which used a lightly loaded aircraft to assist the take-off of a highly loaded aircraft on its back, was reviewed alongside the opposite scheme, championed at that time by Boulton-Paul, where the relative positions of the two aircraft were reversed. The Mayo system was considered the better of the two from the load and structural weight point of view and the detailed evaluation then focused on this.

The weak point was that the size of the upper component would be limited both by the need for it to be lifted into place and also by the need to prevent the lower component from becoming excessively large. Various scenarios were evaluated, adjusting size, wing loading and distance flown before separation. While there were many advantages, especially for the carriage or mail, there were equally several operational and cost issues.

The bulk of the report considered accelerators of various types. There was plenty of data on their use since the RAE had been experimenting with several types for many years with aircraft of up to 20,000lb in weight. At this time the RAE was reviewing methods for launching flying boats of 80,000lb. For passenger aircraft, it was found to be more important that the rate of acceleration should be increased gradually rather than to restrict the maximum to 1.5g, as had been assumed previously.

Optimising wing loading for high speed at, say, 45-50lb/sq ft, would suggest a take-off speed of 110mph, with full use of flaps, which would be quite feasible with a catapult accelerator. The report then describes the boat-based accelerator of the type proposed by Supermarine, which was viewed favourably.

In conclusion the report stated "The Mayo scheme and accelerated take-off both show the possibility of successful operation, but the Mayo scheme is considerably more limited in its scope than the use of an accelerator, and shows no marked advantages at any point… The use of wing loading of the order of 45lb/sq ft appears at present to be the best compromise for flying boats of the order of 60,000lb all up weight".

Yet despite this positive report, no further action was taken by either the Air Ministry or Imperial Airways and the concept of large catapults to assist civil aircraft, or indeed military ones, was sidelined.

No contract was awarded to Supermarine for the Type 306, with Short Bros' S.26 being declared the winner. The S.26 leant heavily on the experience the company had gained through the S.23 'C' class and S.25 Sunderland projects. It was powered by four Bristol Hercules radials, Gouge not sharing Mitchell's concerns regarding drag and fuel. The loaded weight was higher than that of the Vulture-powered Type 306, at 73,500lb, but with a smaller wing and hence higher wing loading. Both fuel load and payload were higher. Cruising speed was slightly higher and range, as per Imperial Airways Specification, was 2,500 miles against a 40mph head wind. However, when the S.25 'G' class aircraft entered service with Imperial Airways in the summer of 1939 they were configured as mail planes only, so some of the weight numbers may not be directly comparable.

13 CHAPTER

High Speed Flying Boats

Once the Short S.25 Sunderland and Saunders-Roe A.33 had been selected to compete for the large military flying boat role, the Air Ministry turned its attention back to the smaller types. None of the potential replacements for the Southampton – the Scapa, London and Stranraer – truly met the RAF's growing requirements. They were too slow and lacked the offensive punch for the modern world. Unfortunately, as time would tell, just what the requirement was exactly and how the specification for a new flying boat should be written, remained elusive.

Supermarine would find 1934 another pivotal year. Mitchell was back from post-operative convalescence and his brush with death had given him a new sense of purpose. His surgeon was not in a position to assure him that he was cancer free, which was simply not possible to determine in that era, so he was living under the spectre that it could flare up again at any time. It was during this period that he discarded his disappointing Type 224 fighter and initiated the design work that would lead to the Spitfire.

In a similar way he now accepted that the Stranraer was not the aircraft it could have been and pushed the design team to develop more advanced concepts. As a start, the Type 302 civil flying boat was adapted as a military type and added to Type 232 and an alternative design, but this was too late to attract the Air Ministry. He then initiated Type 303, named as R.24/31 Development. This was essentially a better Stranraer.

Several schemes were sketched around a hull very similar to that of the Stranraer, with aerodynamic improvements especially around the nose. All were to be powered by two Rolls-Royce PV12 engines, the future Merlin. Initially there were two biplane schemes in the style of the Scapa and Stranraer, followed by two more, monoplanes, which followed the form of the Type 302, one with sponson stabilisers, the other wingtip floats. All were simple preliminary drawings and the type was put to one side at the end of 1934.

Sometime around the middle of 1935, the Air Ministry issued Specification R.12/35. Supermarine

commenced work on potential layouts, none drawn directly from the Type 303 project. All the early schemes, six in total, are dated 13th September 1935 and show a diversity not just in layout but also in the number and type of engines, suggesting that the specification was not restrictive on this point.

All were monoplanes, most as cantilever and sharing the same basic hull design. One was equipped with sponson stabilisers in two alternative configurations. The others had conventional wing floats, in one instance these were retractable. Two, three and four engines layouts were sketched, as conventional tractors, a tandem tractor and pusher and as tandem installations driving contra-props. Engine choice was between two Rolls-Royce Merlins, three Rolls-Royce Goshawks, or four Bristol Mercurys. There were plenty of innovative ideas but none were destined to make it into the final choice.

By 1st October, Supermarine had selected a design to take forward – producing the first layout drawing under Type 308. It was described as a Long Range Flying Boat. It is therefore curious that a tender document and brochure drawings produced by Blackburn, also to R.12/35, were described as a High Performance Flying Boat. While Supermarine was designing a flying boat powered by two Rolls-Royce Vultures, Blackburn's design had four Bristol Taurus radials. The wording of the specification must have been somewhat vague as to the requirement and intent, and it is not entirely surprising that it was soon withdrawn and redrafted under a new number.

The Type 308 was a cantilever monoplane with the wing mounted above the hull on a shallow pylon. As with Supermarine's previous reconnaissance flying boats, there was a single gun position in the nose, with the bomb aimer's hatch below, twin guns in the tail and one in the rear of the wing support pylon. The nose and tail gun positions were fully enclosed turrets.

Two Rolls-Royce Vulture engines were installed on mounts suspended from the wing torsion box ahead of the wing leading edge. The exhausts from the lower cylinder banks were run up within the engine nacelle to join that from the upper bank

Many schemes for a high speed flying boat to replace the Scapa and Stranraer were drawn up under Type 303 (top) or as preliminary drawings

and the combined pipe exited above the wing. The engines were cooled by twin radiator blocks located side-by-side within the wing support pylon and the warm air exited on either side through shuttered outlets at the rear. The warm air could also be used to heat the cabin, with provision for five crew, if required.

While it is not absolutely certain from the drawings of the civil Type 302 and 306 what form of construction was intended for their braced wings, the Type 308 cantilever wing definitely utilised Mitchell's single spar and 'D' leading edge torsion box, and to great effect as it housed the fuel tanks in the torsion box itself, with the bomb load and retractable balance floats stowed behind the spar.

Wilfred Kimber, an engineer within the Technical Office had devised a type of wing float that had the form of an aerofoil surface, a hydrofoil, which when extended was set at a small positive angle of incidence and large dihedral. It could be retracted within the wing once airborne, where its lower surface conformed to that of the bottom of the wing.

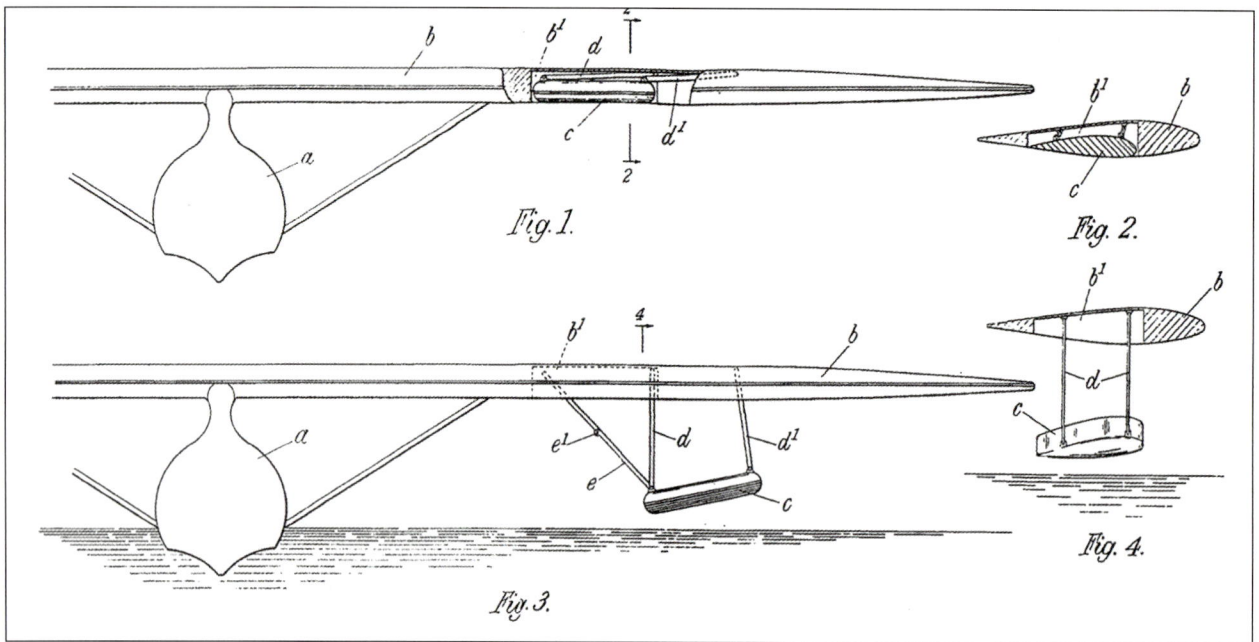

Supermarine 1935 patent for retractable hydrofoil-type wing floats, GB464408A4

The volume of the float was sufficient to provide lateral stability when the flying boat was at rest, and once under way the buoyancy was aided by the set angle of incidence of the float which then functioned as a hydrofoil to maintain stability. The concept was patented in October 1935.

The bomb load was stored behind and outboard of the engine nacelles. The inner two racks on each side could hold either 500lb or 250lb bombs and the outer two held 250lb bombs only. There was also provision for four light bombs, typically 20lb, on

either side. The wing hydrofoil floats retracted into wells outboard of the bombs. Normal fuel load was in two 325 gallon tanks in the torsion box outboard of the nacelles with two further overload tanks, also of 325 gallons, outboard of those.

A revision to the layout drawings in mid-January 1936 shows a number of detail changes, the most noticeable of which were a slight lengthening of the hull, a taller and longer wing support pylon that raised the wing by a couple of feet, and engine nacelles that were a tighter fit around the engines.

The early form of the Type 308

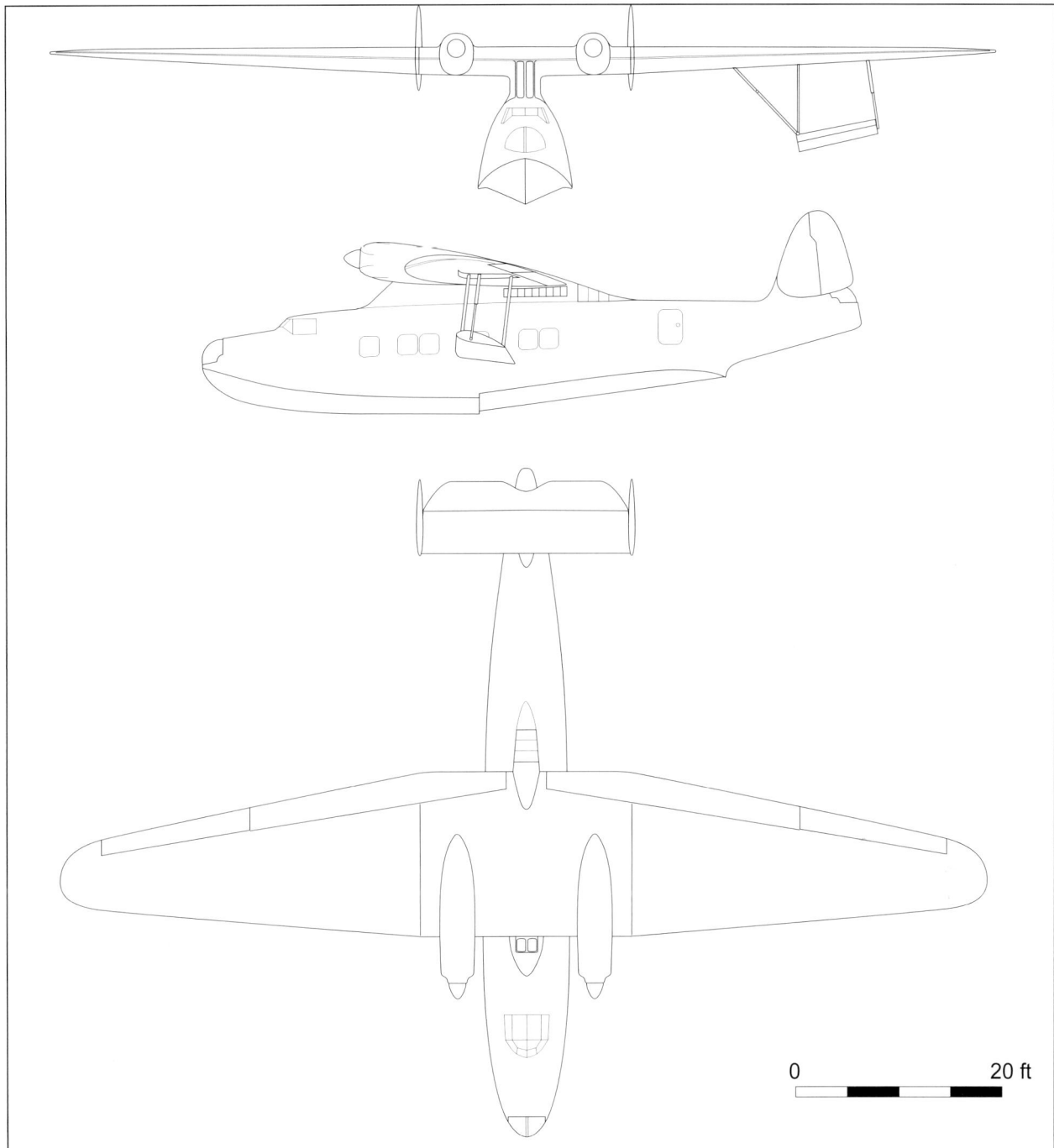

The revised version of the Type 308, January 1936

For reasons that probably relate to the flexible nature of the specification, in December 1935 Supermarine submitted a second design, Type 310, also named as a Long Range Flying Boat, which can be seen as an enlarged Type 308 powered by four engines. Alternative layouts were prepared for four Vultures, or the radial engines Bristol Hercules or Bristol Taurus.

The bomb load had risen dramatically to nine 500lb bombs in each wing, not far short of the load requirement in the forthcoming Air Ministry long range bomber specifications. To put that further into perspective, the Type 308 could carry 3,000lb of bombs, compared to the 2,000lb in the Sunderland. The Type 310 had bomb bays with four times the load carrying ability of the Sunderland, although almost certainly a full bomb load would have come at the expense of fuel, so flying range were likely to have been very different.

After Specification R.12/35 was withdrawn, a revised version was issued. Supermarine and Blackburn were both encouraged to update their projects.

Specification R.1/36, issued to tender on 2nd March 1936, was for a small general purpose High

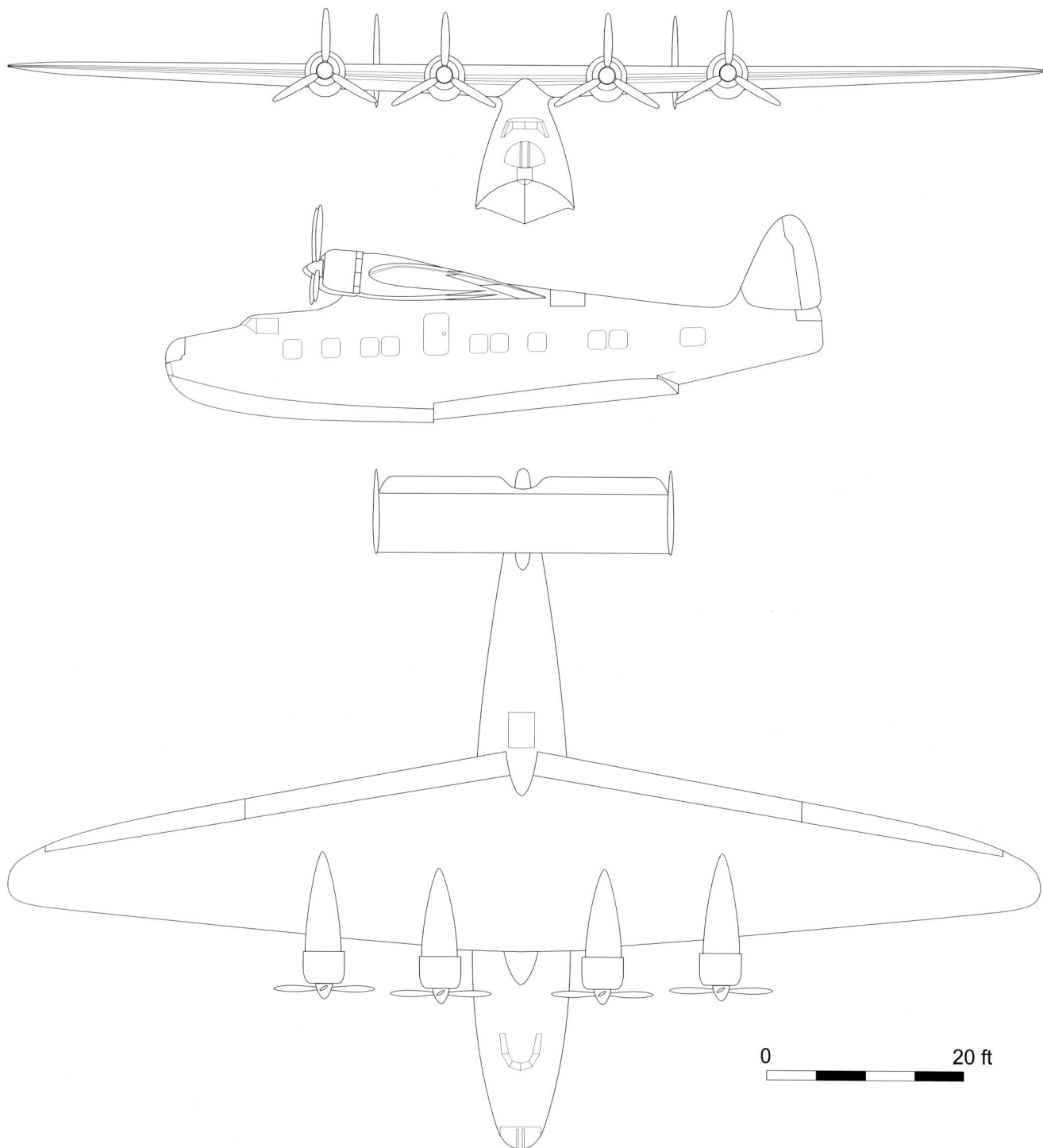

The Type 310 was an enlarged Type 308 design powered by four engines

Performance Flying Boat that was not to exceed an all-up weight of 25,000lbs, the intent being to avoid the projects becoming too large and effectively duplicating the role of the Sunderland. Cruising speed would need to be 230mph or above and at 200mph range had to be at least 1,500 miles. Defensive armament was increased to twin guns in a nose turret, four in a tail turret and two mid-ship – exactly the same as was required in the latest heavy

and medium bomber specifications. Provision had to be made for a surprisingly modest 2,000lb bomb load. Designs were requested along the lines of those prepared for R.12/35.

Supermarine prepared to adapt the Type 308 as Type 314 to meet the new specification. The laden weight of the Type 308 is not currently known but was almost certain to have exceeded 25,000lb as Blackburn's submission tipped the scales at

30,000lbs with a 2,000lb bomb load, albeit featuring a novel retractable hull and four engines. The limit set in the new specification was exceedingly demanding, only 6,000lb greater than the weight of a fully-loaded Stranraer while carrying a 1,000lb greater load of bombs, five more guns, two turrets and substantially larger engines. It seems likely that this restriction was relaxed slightly later.

The changes made by Supermarine to the existing design were not substantial. The cooling system in the pylon was deleted and replaced by chin radiators in each engine nacelle, and the pylon was subsequently reduced slightly in height. Minor modifications were made to the contours of the nose and tail of the hull to fit the turrets. The greatest change came in the plan of the wing where the taper had been adjusted to a more curved form to provide greater length in the bomb bays, a repeat of the process that had produced the two half ellipses of the Spitfire wing.

The retraction mechanism for the hydrofoil floats was also changed to a more robust form. Where previously they had been lowered and braced by a frame of two slender wire-braced struts plus two diagonal struts with hinges at their centres at the inboard end, and an oleo at the tip, the team had devised an improved system that was both far simpler and stronger. Now the stabiliser, still of aerofoil section, simply hinged down from the wingtip end, with the lower end stabilised by a broad panel strut that was articulated at its centre, replacing the two hinged struts of the former design.

The hydraulics that lowered and raised the stabiliser were contained entirely within the wing. As before, the retracted hydrofoil stabiliser sat in a large well and formed the lower surface of the wing.

The new wing design provided for larger bomb bay cells which could accommodate four 500lb and two 250lb bombs each side, exceeding the requirement in the specification by a wide margin.

Air Ministry officials were impressed with the design when it was discussed during a tender conference on 22nd June and were minded to order a prototype, maybe even to award a production contract off the drawing board. However, Supermarine's works was already operating at full capacity to produce the Walrus, Stranraer and Spitfire, which meant that delivery of the Type 314 prototype would take two years. This was too long and the company's proposal therefore had to be dropped with reluctance.

Blackburn was awarded a contract for the B.20, but this was for a much simplified variant of the company's R.12/35 design and not strictly to R.1/36 as it was ordered primarily as an experimental proof-of-concept for the retractable hull system. Wind tunnel and water tank evaluation had indicated that it was effective but full-scale testing was required to be sure.

It has been said that Shorts also submitted a tender but there is no project number in the company's catalogue for such a project. That said, there is no project number either for a bomber design that the firm is known to have developed around the same time for Specification B.1/35. In this case, absence of evidence is not evidence of absence. Given Gouge's economy of design, where projects shared a great deal of features in common, it has to be likely that the twin Vulcan-powered bomber and any twin-engine design to R.1/36 would have been very similar. However Shorts was not to be awarded a contract for either project since it too was already heavy committed to other production contracts, both military and civil.

Thus, to fill the requirement Saunders-Roe was instructed to revise and resubmit its tender. This was then approved in November with some reservations. The aircraft saw the light of day as the S.36 Lerwick in late 1938 – which was ironically no earlier than the delivery date that Supermarine had anticipated for the Type 314. The Lerwick proved to be totally unsatisfactory, dangerously unstable both on the water and in the air, so the small production order placed when the project was approved was cut back. The vacant niche for a small, fast general purpose flying boat to replace the Londons and Stranraers was addressed eventually by ordering the Consolidated Model 28 Catalina from the US – another compromise.

Hiatus

The RAF's rearmament schemes were ramping up by the end of 1936 and large production contracts were being issued with increasing frequency. The shadow factory programme had been initiated the previous year and many, if not most, of the aircraft companies were seeking to expand their works and recruit new staff. Supermarine was no different; a major expansion of the Woolston site was under way and an additional site had been acquired upstream on the Itchen for a second large new assembly works. But then the company was struck by a major tragedy as Mitchell's cancer flared up again and his health deteriorated rapidly.

By February 1937 he was no longer able to visit the office and in May he succumbed to the disease and died. The Vickers management were unsure how they could fill the void at such a critical time and let the decision drift, which caused great uncertainty within the Supermarine design team. Thoroughly competent as they were, there had to be someone who could take key decisions and give them direction.

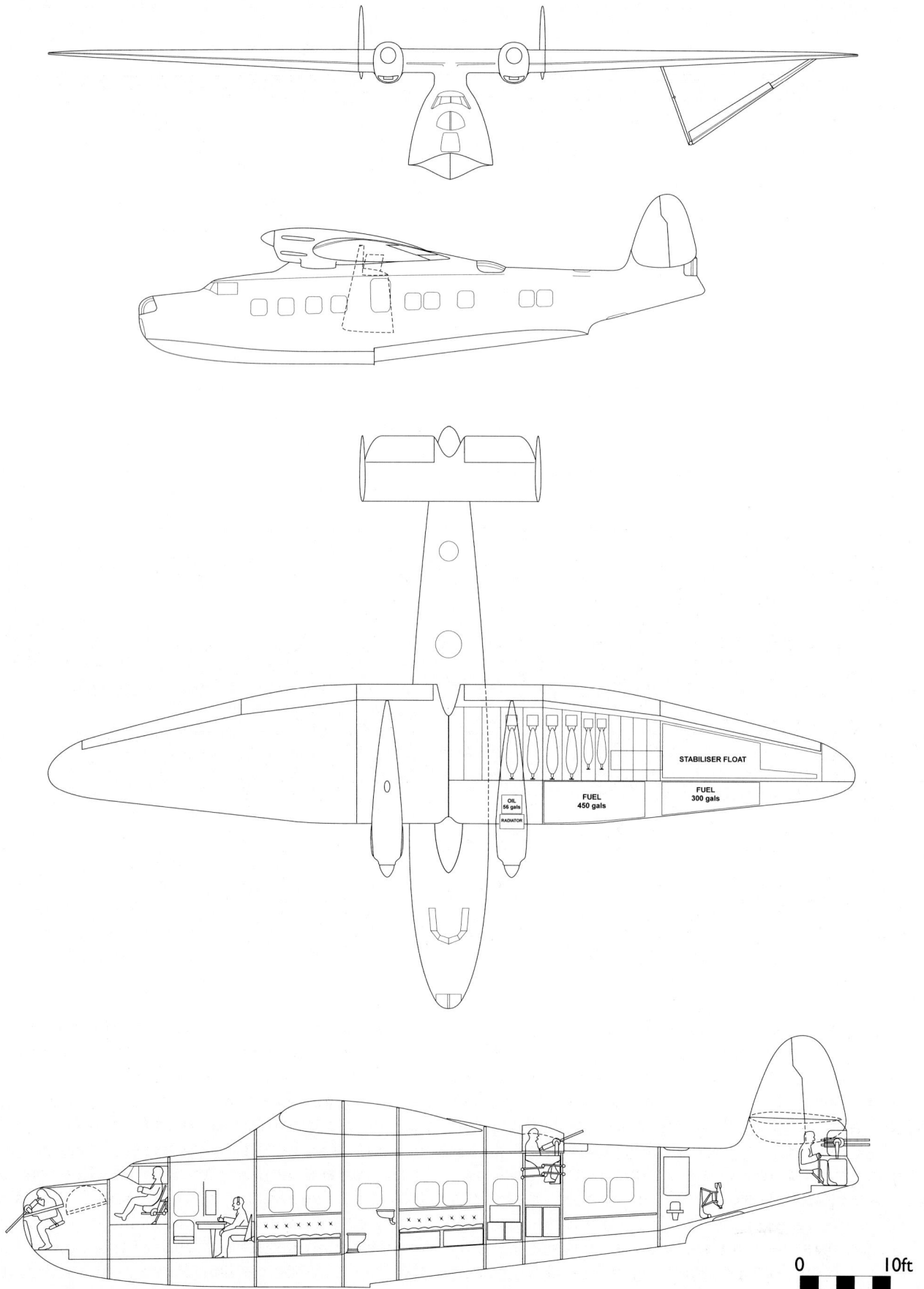

Type 314 High Performance Flying Boat

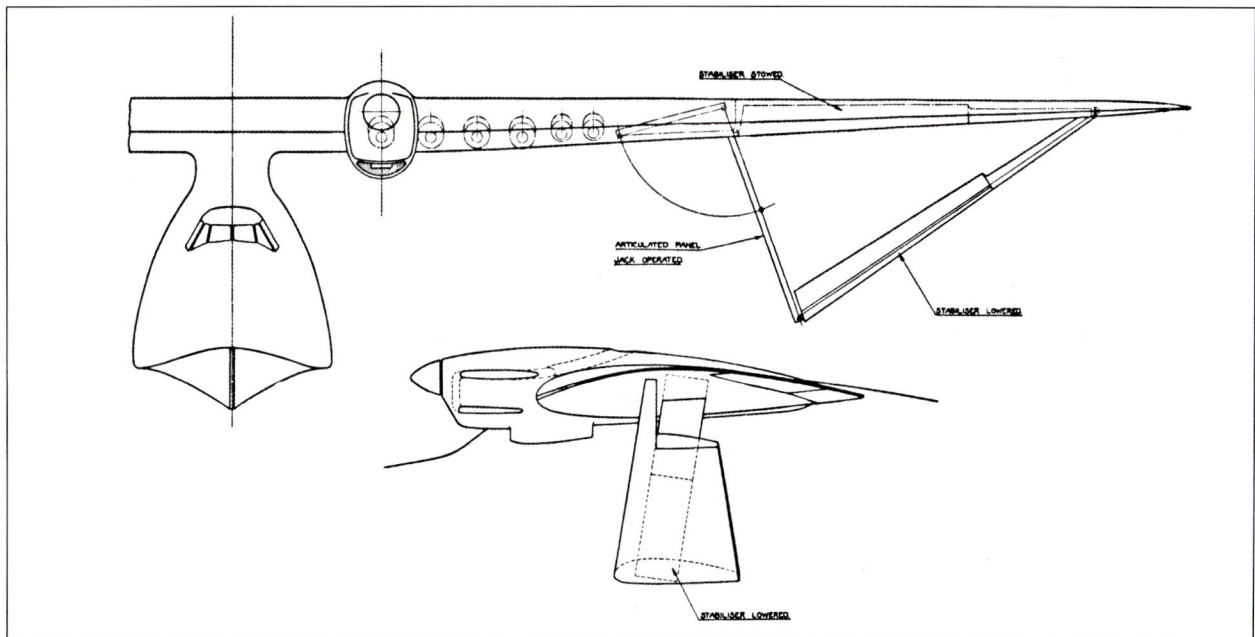

The Type 314 was to be fitted with an improved and simplified form of hydrofoil stabiliser float

A Type 314 as it could have appeared in RAF service in the early days of the war

Mitchell's deputy Harold Payn had joined the team from Vickers in the early 1930s as one of the key staff changes imposed by Vickers to help the reorganisation of the company. He was an ex-RAF pilot and engineer but lacked status as a designer. While he stepped up to take on the role as an interim measure, Vickers' own chief designer Rex Pierson was placed in ultimate control – a far from efficient decision that impacted adversely on both companies' design departments. A while later, as war clouds loomed, someone in the Government noted that Payn's wife was of German decent and panicked, Payn then being removed from the company in the name of national security.

As the industry struggled to keep up with demand, the bulk of available resources – material, manpower and tooling – was prioritised for bombers and fighters. Flying boats were all but marginalised and no new designs were requested for some time. Not that Supermarine was too perturbed, its hands were more than full dealing with the production contract for the Spitfire and the complex issue of organising a network of suppliers and subcontractors. On top of that the last project on which Mitchell had input, the Type 316 bomber, had just received a contract for two prototypes from the Air Ministry with the prospect for major production in the future. Flying boats in many ways seemed like yesterday's news.

14 CHAPTER Replacing the Walrus Part 1

When viewing the Seagull V under construction in 1933, the Air Ministry's Director of Technical Development (DTD) is said to have commented: "Very interesting, but of course we have no requirement for anything like this." The quote was recalled by Alan Clifton, the head of the Technical Office, in the mid-1960s and is usually held up as a typical example of lack of foresight within the ministry, but is this a correct interpretation?

The DTD in 1933 was Air Commodore Henry Cave-Browne-Cave, an RAF officer who had greater knowledge than almost anyone of flying boats in military service. Starting as an engineer with the RNAS during the war he had been based at the flying boat and seaplane test establishment on the Isle of Grain and had risen to the rank of wing commander by the time of the armistice. Post-war, he served in the technical training division before working as the RAF's Deputy Director of Design.

In 1926 he was promoted to group captain and appointed to be Deputy Director of Technical Development. In 1927 he took the post of Officer Commanding with the Far East Flight, the three Southampton II flying boats that paved the way for routes to the Far East and proved the RAF's capability to send reinforcements to remote areas. On completion of the mission he became Officer Commanding RAF Base Singapore before returning to Britain in 1931 to become DTD. This was no reactionary officer lacking vision and unable to see the potential of the aircraft and his comments should not be perceived that way. It was a statement of current RAF procurement priorities and not an indication that these would not change. It is not at all improbable that he would have argued in favour of the aircraft within the ministry.

Behind the scenes, the RAF and Navy had in fact taken more than a passing interest in the aircraft as they evaluated the prototype's capabilities at the MAEE and A&AEE on behalf of the RAAF. MacLean was keen to secure orders from both the RAAF and RAF, as he had staked Vickers' money on the prototype. He therefore pushed the Air

K5772 – The first production Walrus for the RAF

Ministry on the matter whenever the opportunity arose. Officially they hedged their bets, saying that while they wished to be kept informed of progress with these tests they still did not envisage any role for the aircraft with the RAF or Navy.

That there was more interest in the aircraft's capability and potential than they we prepared to divulge at the time became clear in early 1934 when the prototype was sent to Gibraltar for evaluation with the fleet and then to exercise with a battleship off the islands of Scotland. The RAAF ordered 24 Seagull Vs in August 1934 and the RAF followed suit in May 1935 ordering 12, renamed Walrus, with more to follow. The first RAF order was pushed up the queue too – displacing some of the RAAF's Seagull Vs.

The first Walrus aircraft were assigned to the Fleet Air Arm's (FAA) catapult flights – deployed on various capital ships that had short catapults installed on their gun turrets. As a flying boat it was far more capable on the water than a seaplane and less limited by sea conditions. Yet the Navy was somewhat sceptical about carrying either, since both flying boats and seaplanes had to be collected by the host ship, a process which involved stopping and manoeuvring. Under combat conditions this could prove extremely risky.

The Seagull V had been designed to meet a specification first raised by the RAAF in 1929 and did not meet entirely those of the expanding FAA, so a new Air Ministry specification was written for an improved version. Following discussions with Mitchell, Specification 5/36 was issued on 25th April 1936 for an Improved Walrus Development for the FAA. This required an aircraft with the same overall dimensions and construction method as for the Walrus but with improved overall performance; an economical cruising speed not less than 115mph and a range of 800 miles.

It also had to be capable of carrying two 250lb bombs and provide a twin-gun mounting in the rear fuselage. No nose gun position was needed. It was also suggested that the retractable hydrofoil stabilisers of the sort planned for the Type 314 should be considered as an alternative to wing floats. Some parts of the specification were more specific than was the norm; for instance it required the fitment of a fully-cowled Bristol Perseus engine installed as a tractor rather than leaving the choice of engine and installation to the discretion of the designer. This most probably indicates that the discussions held between Mitchell and the DTD in February 1936 had centred on a scheme already under discussion at Supermarine.

A contract for two prototypes is said to have been awarded on 17th April, a week before the specification was issued – further evidence that the specification had been drawn up around Mitchell's proposal.

The project was established as Type 309, which would date its initiation to mid-1935, but it was pursued as relatively low priority and there do not appear to be any surviving drawings earlier than 1938. The aircraft would be named Sea Otter and the prototype flew in September 1938. Although its performance did improve on that of the Walrus, the test programme encountered unexpected problems such as difficulty finding a suitable propeller and cooling issues with the Perseus engine. These resulted in the latter's replacement with a Bristol Mercury. Other changes to FAA requirements meant that performance overall failed to meet the original specification. Nevertheless it was ordered into production in 1940, with all work subcontracted to Saunders-Roe. The search for a true Walrus replacement continued.

Replacing the Sunderland

Throughout the mid and late 1930s it had become common practice for the Air Ministry to issue a specification for a new aircraft type around the time that the one it was intended to replace was entering service. Therefore Specification R.3/38 for a large flying boat to replace the Sunderland was issued in September 1938.

Prototype Sea Otter K8854 on the new slipway at Woolston – circa September 1938

The aircraft designs produced for Specification R.12/35 and R.1/36 had raised questions as to whether the Sunderland was possibly too large, too slow and lacking in offensive capability, and it appeared to be feasible to achieve more with a substantially smaller aircraft. Whether this would have proven to be true or not is a moot point as the Supermarine Type 314, which was the preferred design, was never produced.

The Sunderland Mk 1 had a loaded weight of 50,000lb and the Lerwick 28,000lb, so when R.3/38 called for a flying boat with a loaded weight of about 45,000lb the inference could be that the intent was to tackle both roles with a single design. A similar attempt at a rationalisation process was then under way at the Air Ministry with the latest specifications for large and medium bombers; the proliferation of designs and types on order was cause for concern and there was a desire to reassess operational requirements so that several roles could be fulfilled with a single airframe type.

The first result of this thought process was seen in Specification B.1/39, which called for a large four-engine type that is often referred to as the 'Ideal Bomber'. For flying boats it would appear that the Air Ministry had taken a similar approach, and so it was that R.3/38 was withdrawn, rewritten and reissued as Specification R.5/39 at the end of March 1939, again seeking a large four-engine flying boat to replace the Sunderland.

Cruising speed was to be not less than 235mph at the engines' maximum rated cruising power, and range at this power was to be 1,500 miles at 5,000ft. The bomb load was 4,000lb. The most significant feature, and one shared with the bombers to meet B.1/39, was the provision of a four-cannon defensive armament. The standard 0.303 calibre machine gun was now considered inadequate, both in fighters

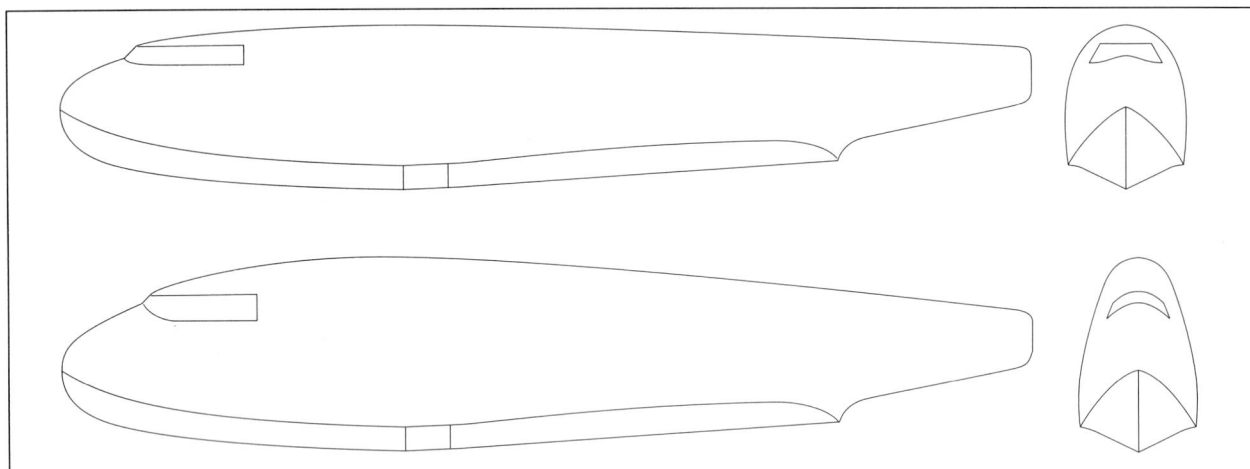

Initial models of the Type 328 hull as tested in the wind tunnel: Model A (top) Model D (Bottom). Neither was destined to be used for the final layout

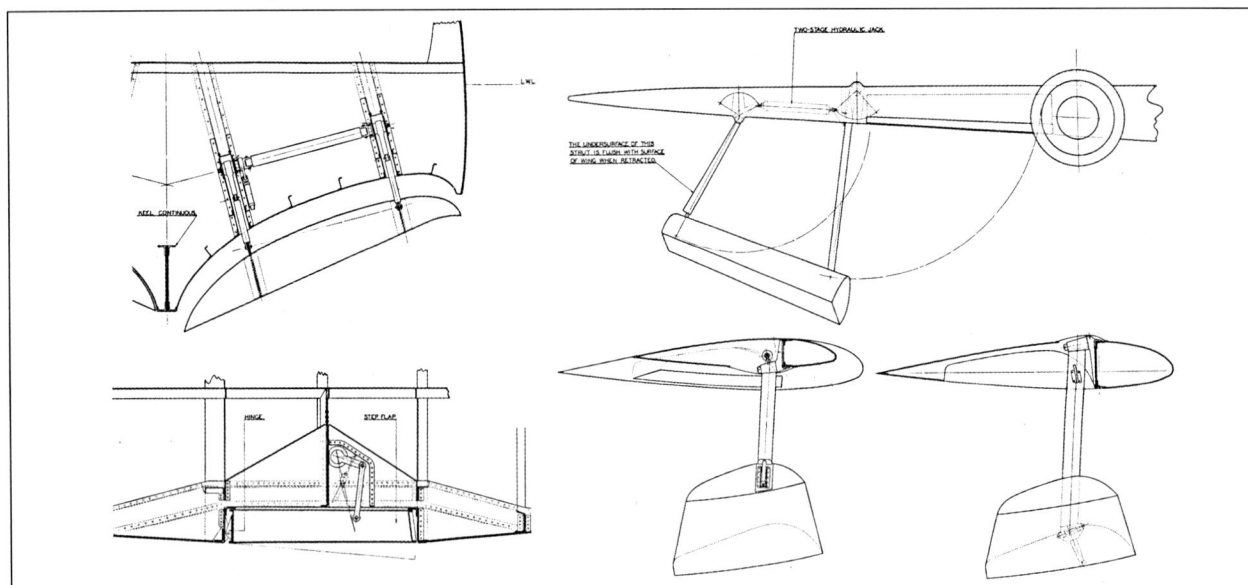

The retractable planing bottom step and wing hydrofoil floats for the Type 328

and in bombers, and the weapon of choice with which to replace it was the 20mm Hispano cannon.

For defensive purposes in large aircraft the favoured installation was for four of these cannon in a shallow cupola turret, and designs for such a turret were in hand at both Frazer-Nash (Parnall) and Boulton-Paul. For R.5/39 the armament requirement was for one upper turret of this type plus a single cannon in the tail. There was no requirement for a forward-firing gun.

Short Bros, now up to its eyes in development and production work on variants of the Sunderland and the new Stirling bomber, offered a smaller, faster Sunderland style design that also drew on work done for a Stirling-derived bomber project to B.1/39, but once again this was not assigned an official project number. Blackburn submitted the B.32, with B.20-type wings and wing floats that retracted to form the wingtips.

Saunders-Roe had been stung by the double failure of its recent flying boats, the structural collapse of the A.33, competitor to the Sunderland, and the below par performance of the Lerwick. Determined to rectify the situation, work commenced on the S.38 as the company's contender to R.3/38, which included a flying sub-scale testbed to refine the hydrodynamic and aerodynamic properties.

Supermarine assigned its R.3/38 project the designation Type 328. The team considered several alternative hull types and in the closing weeks of 1938 two were prepared for testing in the wind tunnel, with models built at 1:16 and 1:24. These two shared a common planing bottom and lower portion of the hull but differed in height. Model 'A' was relatively shallow while Model 'D' was considerably taller and narrow at the top, giving it a 'whale back' profile. However this tall hull appears to have been side-lined early on as further evaluations concentrated on the Model 'A', the form of the wing root being the subject of particular attention.

The design and drawings were all updated after the issue of R.1/39, with the final set of layout drawings dated June 1939.

Once again the heart of the design was to be the single-spar wing, which had now reached its ultimate form. All interior space with the exception of the outer leading edge and tip were utilised for stowage. There were eight bomb cells in each wing, the inner four holding 500lb or 250lb bombs and the outer four holding 250lb bombs. Three fuel tanks were placed within the leading edge torsion box, inboard and outboard of and between the engine nacelles. A fourth overload tank sat inboard of the bomb cells.

The aerofoil float stabiliser, closer to the original design used for the Type 308, retracted into the outer wing. It was supported by just two robust struts with the hydraulic rams in the wing. Retraction of the single leg struts involved a variation of the system developed for the wheel retraction mechanism in the Spitfire. The wing type selected after wind tunnel evaluation was of moderate 'seagull' form with the portion from the centre line of the fuselage out to the inner engine nacelles, essentially the centre section root, set with dihedral.

The definitive hull design was more akin to the tall Model 'D' evaluated in the wind tunnel although not quite so tall. It was of half elliptical section with the longitudinal taper and nose form optimised for aerodynamic cleanliness, benefiting from the absence of a nose turret. The cockpit sat at the front of a large fully glazed cabin housing the stations for the engineer, observer and navigator. The company constructed a mock-up of the nose and cockpit.

To reduce aerodynamic drag the planing bottom was fitted with a retractable step, a step-flap on either side of the centre line that hinged at the front. When extended the rear end dropped by about six inches to form the step and when retracted they lay flat so that the bottom presented an almost continuous gentle curve.

The four-cannon Boulton-Paul cupola turret was positioned on the hull top just to the rear of the wing trailing edge with its axis of rotation angled slightly to the rear. The four cannon could be elevated from horizontal to vertical when facing rearwards, but with the turret rotated to face the front the minimum gun elevation was limited both by the tilt of the turret axis and by the wing centre section. The dihedral did provide some clear view forward though. The turret was manned by two: the gunner, with his head in a semi-circular transparent dome, and a loader below the gun. Boulton-Paul had designed a twin-engine day and night fighter to Specification F.11/37 armed with this turret, project P.92, and in 1939 initiated a plan to test a half-scale experimental aircraft, P.92/2,0 to assess the practicality of the cupola. However the whole project was given low priority after the Air Ministry and Ministry of Aircraft Production wielded the axe on a large number of experimental types in mid-1940.

The rear gunner fired from the kneeling position with his head also within a transparent dome located behind the tailplane. The single cannon had a field of fire of 45 degrees in all directions from centre. There was no provision for defence from attack coming from below.

The primary choice of engines was four Bristol Hercules with the option to fit Rolls-Royce Griffons. The nacelles were similar to those designed for the Type 317 bomber and exhausted cooling air from slots towards the rear under the wings rather than through gills around the cowling. The submissions offered by other companies were based around the same choice of engines.

The Type 328 was estimated to have an all-up weight of nearly 50,000lbs with fuel for 1,500 miles when carrying a standard 4,000lb combat load. In common with all the other contenders, Supermarine had found it impossible to stay within the 45,000lb limit inherited from Specification R.3/38 now that the heavy turret had been added to the requirement. With Hercules engines the top speed at 17,500ft was estimated at an impressive 323mph, with a cruising speed of 268mph at 5,000ft. With full overload fuel the range could be extended to 5,000 miles.

At a tender design conference held on 28th July the Air Ministry reviewed the technical assessment made by the RAE and agreed that Supermarine's design was the best overall, with Saunders-Roe second and Blackburn and Short judged as inferior. The Short submission was deemed conservative, a legacy of its Sunderland origins, and the Blackburn had poor arrangements for bomb stowage.

Although the Type 328 design was accepted, the conference believed that it would benefit from a larger wing and retractable wing floats of the Saunders-Roe wingtip type rather than the unproven hydrofoils. It was also felt that the engines should be fitted with propellers of greater diameter – they were currently about 12ft 9in – which would necessitate moving the inner nacelles further outboard to keep the propeller tips clear of the hull.

Saunders-Roe had shown considerable enterprise by opting to build a half-scale version of its S.38

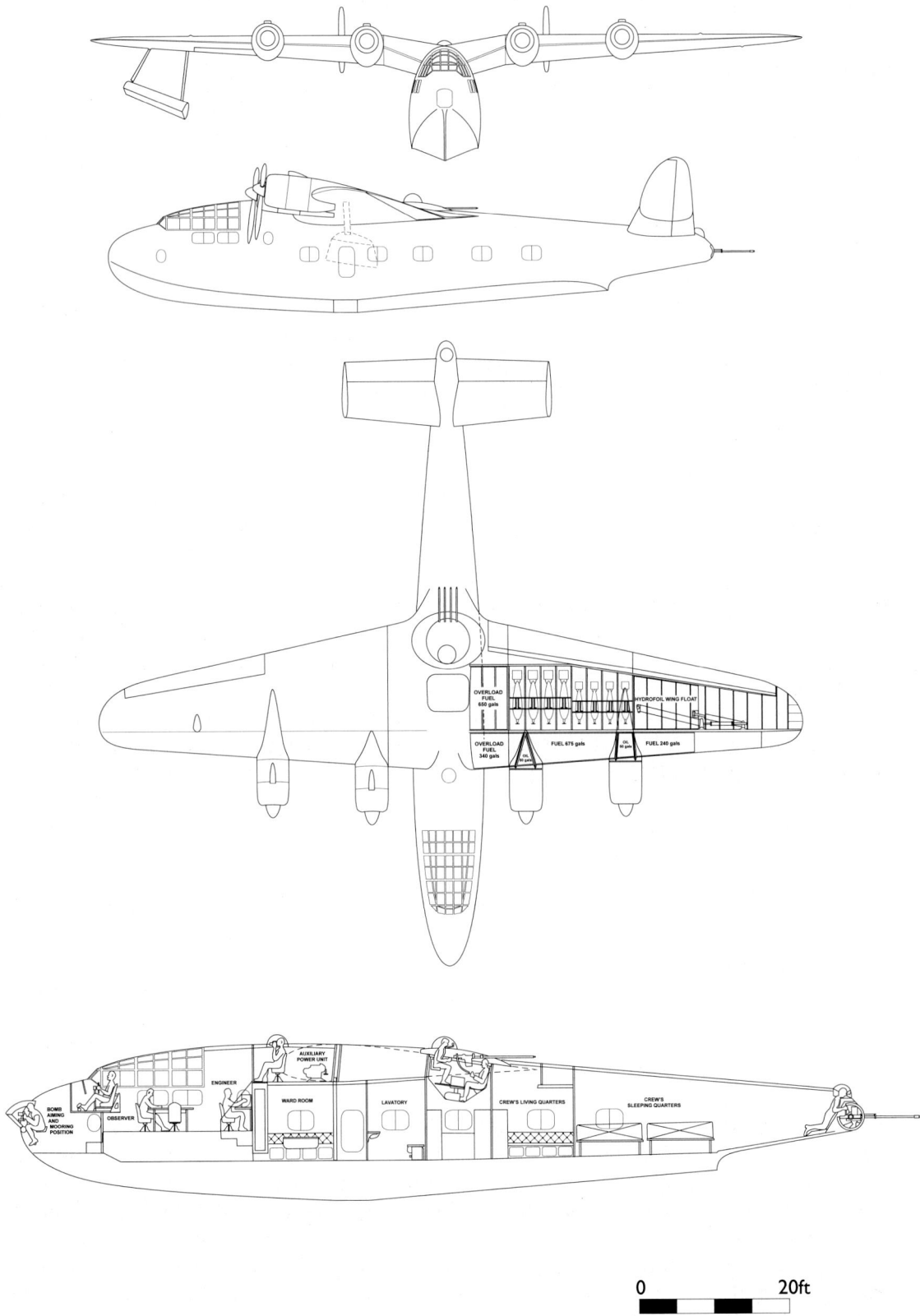

Type 328 showing stowage within the wing and the internal layout of the hull

project to test design ideas, in the same way as Short Bros had done in the mid-1930s utilising the Scion to evaluate planing bottoms and wing flaps with notable success. It was felt that Supermarine should be encouraged to do so too. It was agreed within the Ministry in August that a contract should be issued to Supermarine but by October continuing uncertainty among the Air Staff led to the decision being revoked and the entire specification was dropped. Not only did they now foresee no pressing need to replace the Sunderland, for which progressive improvements were already being introduced or were making their way across the drawing board, but the whole notion of low profile cannon turrets had been abandoned, that decision also taking bomber Specification B.1/39 along with it.

This was not to be the end of the story as the various factions within the Ministry continued to argue about the best way forward. There was grumbling that the constant tweaking of the requirements and specifications had delayed for too long an aircraft that could already have been entering service. Some bemoaned the fact that the ever increasing weight of the projects had undermined the whole purpose of R.3/38 and R.5/39, and those that had preceded them. Yet others felt that the best way forward was to move in the opposite direction and to specify a flying boat of even larger size, perhaps of around 84,000lb or more based broadly on the designs for R.5/39 but powered by the latest generation of engines: the 2,500hp Bristol Centaurus or Napier Sabre. This final view prevailed eventually and Specification R.14/40 was drawn up around this scheme.

By now Supermarine had had enough. It had won two competitive tender reviews on merit, to R.1/36 and R.5/39, and in both cases the contracts awarded had been withdrawn. The design team had put a great deal of effort into the projects, had been judged superior to their competitors and ultimately came away with nothing to show for it. The same had just happened with the four-engine Type 317 bomber project to B.12/36 – cancelled after the half-complete prototype was destroyed by enemy bombing. While it is true that the company was swamped with work, ways and means could surely have been found to accommodate new projects; this was indeed a demoralising time.

R.14/40 was left to Short Bros and Saunders-Roe to fight over, and a lot of good it did them. The Air Ministry could not agree on which of the two rival designs should be supported, so they made the somewhat bizarre decision that the two should collaborate and develop a combined design. This they were able to do and so was born the Short S.35 Shetland. The aircraft flew in December

1944, by which time the RAF had decided that it was unnecessary – the latest development of the Sunderland family would suffice. Supermarine had made a wise decision to stand aside.

Sunderlands, always Sunderlands

What had gone so wrong with the RAF's planning and decision-making process for large general purpose flying boats? From 1935 through to 1944 there had been a dismal failure to agree on operational requirements – specifications being issued only to be withdrawn or rewritten later. Whatever tack they took, the pragmatic solution always seemed to be to fall back on more Sunderlands. Similar doubts plagued much of service planning in the mid-1930s. The rapid advances in aviation technology, ever increasing power of engines, initial restraint imposed by the Disarmament Conference and deep uncertainty as to what kind of war might have to be fought made it very difficult to plot a course forward.

It is all too easy to whisper darkly about anonymous stuffy conservative RAF officers, blinkered boffins, duplicitous politicians, or 'men-in-suits' at the ministry, and blame them for constraining the visionaries in the industry, but that is, of course, a simplistic, not to mention unsubstantiated, characterisation, albeit a very popular one then as now. Yet it has to be acknowledged that while procurement of fighters and bombers made its erratic way forward and managed to produce world-beating aircraft from among the also-rans, the same was not to prove so true for the flying boats, unfortunately.

There is no doubt that the Sunderland was an exceptional aircraft for its time, the multiple design innovations delivering an aircraft with plenty of potential for additions and upgrades that kept it in front line service way beyond the war. It wasn't perfect, its reputation maybe polished a little too much post war, but, like the Felixstowe flying boats of the previous war, it served with distinction.

Was there ever really a need for a smaller, faster flying boat to serve alongside it? Potentially yes, but each time a specification for such an aircraft was written it started to suffer from 'mission creep', growing larger until the original intent was lost. Had the RAF stayed with the ideas first formulated back in the mid-1930s it could have had a medium sized fast flying boat in service before hostilities began and not had to fall back on purchasing Consolidated Catalinas to part-fill the void; the British industry was more than capable of designing and building something comparable or better given the opportunity and support.

15

Replacing the Walrus Part 2

While the whole 'do we? don't we?' saga was being played out for the larger flying boats, the question of finding a suitable replacement for the Walrus also remained unanswered. The supposed quick and easy solution of refining the design layout of the Walrus to create the Sea Otter had taken far more time and effort than anticipated but did result in a fairly good aircraft that served for many years, but one with its design roots firmly in the early 1930s.

By the time the Sea Otter's trials and tribulations had been resolved the FAA had concluded that what it actually wanted was something altogether larger, faster and frankly more sophisticated to operate from carriers. The requirement to be able to catapult from capital ships had been put to one side. Therefore a new Specification for an Amphibian Boat Reconnaissance Aircraft was raised in mid-1939 as S.14/39, then promptly withdrawn, renumbered and reissued as R.12/40 in June 1941. During this brief hiatus control of the FAA had been transferred to the Admiralty.

R.12/40 called for an amphibious flying boat for reconnaissance, observation and shallow-angle dive bombing. In other words not so very different from the duties of the original Seal and Seagull back in 1921. The preference was for the loaded weight to be kept below 12,000lb, with a warning that if it were to exceed 14,000lb the aircraft would be rejected as having no operational value. At a weight of 12,000lb the stalling speed could not exceed 52mph. The range at a speed of 104mph at 2,000ft needed to be 860 miles. In addition, there had to be an option to fit extra fuel tanks, extending the range to 1,150 miles. The aircraft was to be fitted with a turret holding four 0.303 machine guns with clear lines of fire to either side. The maximum bomb load of 500lb could be stowed internally or externally, and the engine was specified as a Rolls-Royce Merlin XXX, a version of the engine developed specifically for naval aircraft.

Supermarine had commenced basic design work to S.12/40 in mid-1940 before the re-written

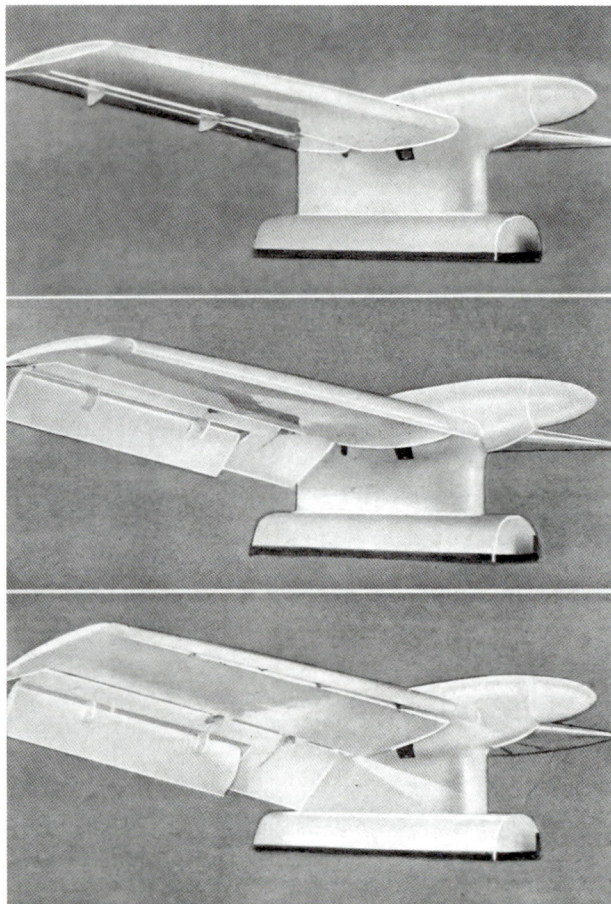

The variable incidence wing, leading edge slots and slotted flaps developed for the Type 381 based on experience with the Type 380 'Dumbo'

specification was finalised and issued, so it appears probable that the new version took the company's work into account. The project was Type 347, for which three alternative layouts were suggested.

The prime proposal was for a monoplane with a slender hull where the wing, Merlin engine and Nash & Thomson turret were supported on a slim pylon. The tail surfaces, attached to a stub pylon at the tail, were to be of the 'butterfly' type; two surfaces that functioned as controls in both the lateral and vertical plane which required differential movement of the moving part of the surfaces to act as both elevators and rudders. This

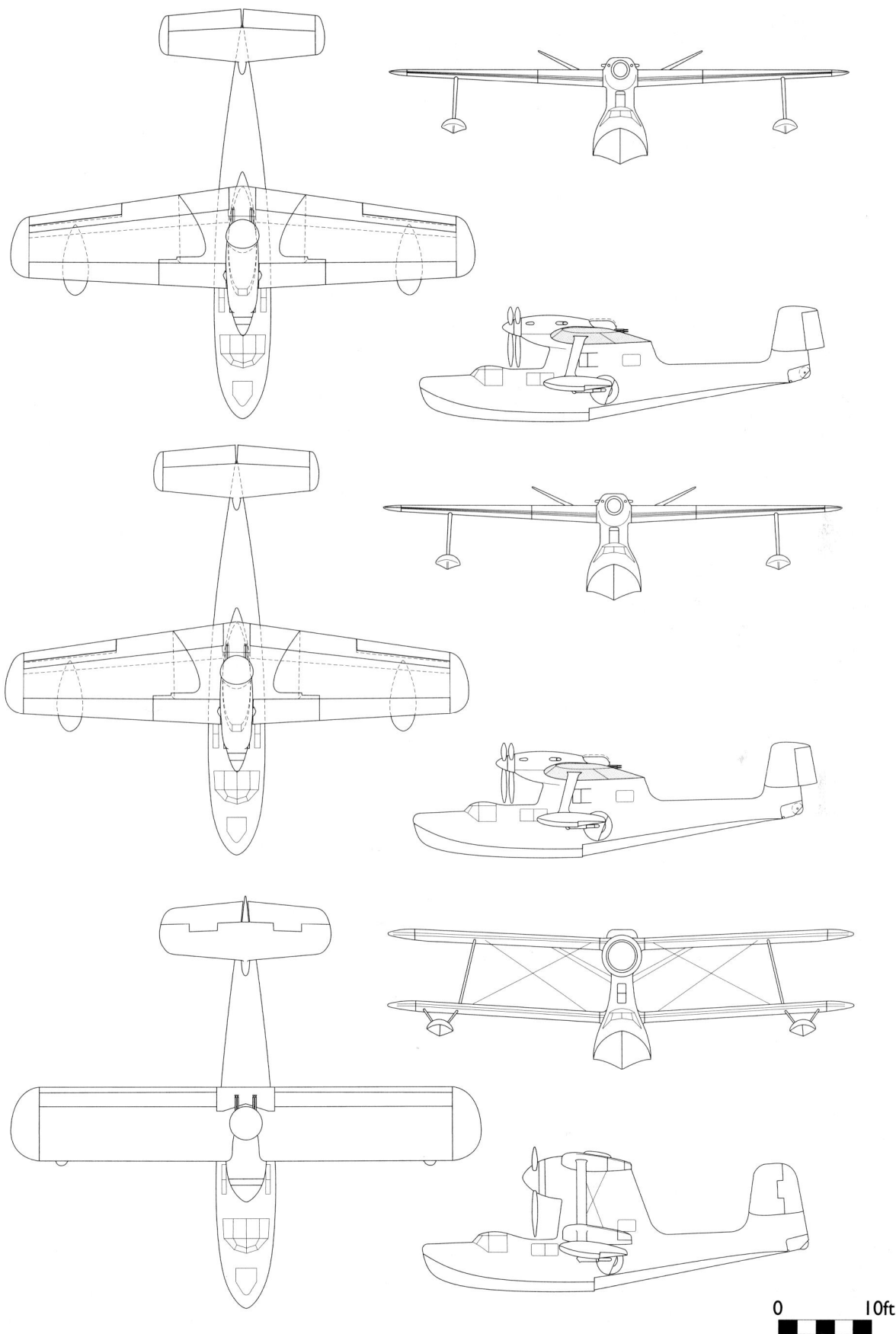

Type 347 – the three alternative layouts

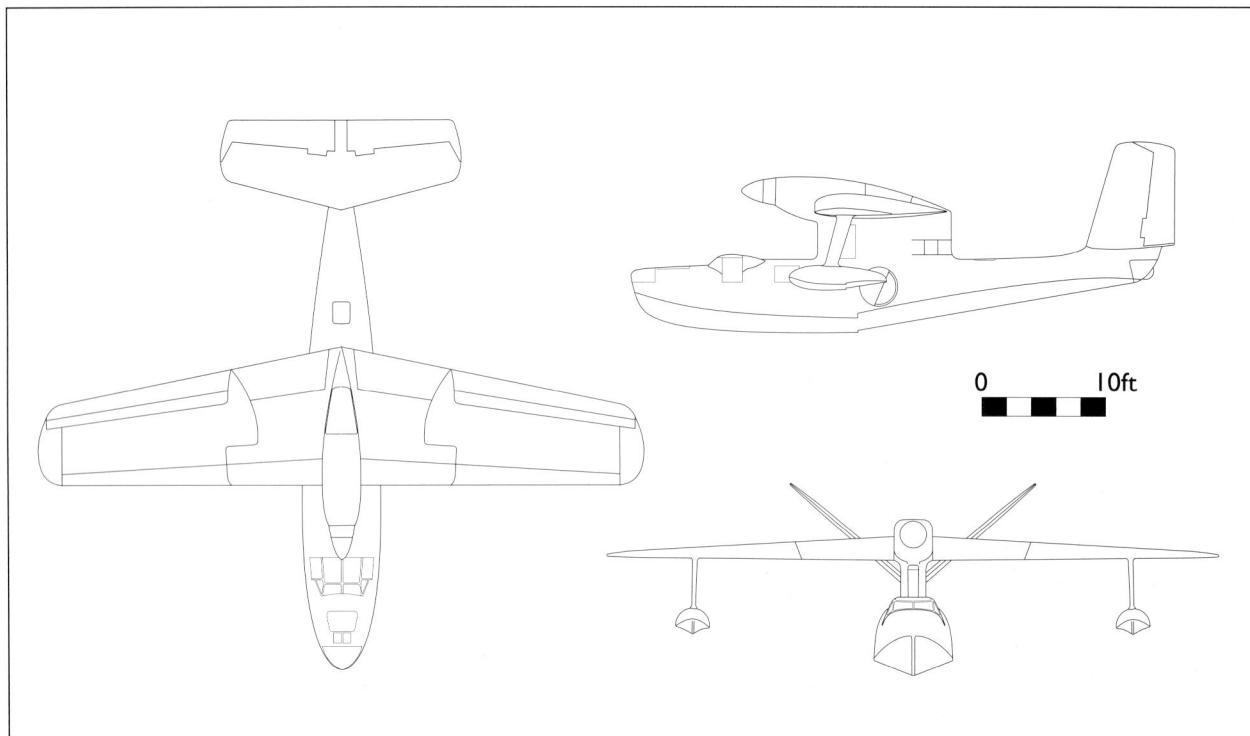

Type 381 – early layout

offered the potential to reduce structural weight and the benefit of keeping the surfaces well away from the sea and spray.

The engine, on cantilever mounts ahead of the wing, drove a tractor contra-prop; one of the first military projects to feature this form of propeller. The low profile gun turret was placed in the rear of the engine nacelle and above the wing. The radiator for the engine cooling system was placed in the front of the pylon with exhaust louvres on either side. The main undercarriage rotated rearwards and upwards to retract into shallow wells in the hull sides. The combined water rudder and tail wheel was also retractable. There would be three crew – the pilot in the nose cockpit just ahead of the propeller arc, the navigator under the front of the pylon, and the gunner in the turret. Interior space was limited and there is no indication that bombs could be stowed within. The aircraft was strengthened for catapulting but had no arrestor hook.

The second option used the same wing and tail, and the same basic hull but with a taller central pylon that now housed the pilot's cockpit at its base. The navigator's position was moved to the nose. The engine was a Bristol Taurus air-cooled radial driving a single 3-blade propeller. A system of reverse cooling was proposed for the engine with an air intake in the pylon above the cockpit channelling air to the rear of the engine and presumably exhausting through gills to the rear of the propeller.

The third option was the most conservative. The hull with the forward cockpit was taken from the first proposal, the taller pylon and Taurus from the second, and it was fitted with single bay biplane wings.

While this project was in the early planning phase, Supermarine were also engaged on work for S.24/37 – a Specification for a Torpedo Bomber Reconnaissance Aeroplane that had been issued in January 1938. For this the company had initiated project Type 322 and designed a novel wing where the angle of incidence could be varied by rotating the entire wing about the front spar. Although the contract for a prototype and subsequent production went to Fairey for the Barracuda, a second contract was awarded to Supermarine for two prototypes only, as experimental aircraft to assess the performance of the wing. Progress was slow, pushed back by more pressing work, so the first did not fly until February 1943, by which time the simplified experimental project had been given the new number Type 380.

Very early in the genesis of Type 347, it was decided that this aircraft would benefit from adopting the Type 322 variable-incidence wing with 12 degrees of movement and this was included in the two monoplanes versions of the initial offering. Wind tunnel models were prepared for evaluation at the RAE during 1942-1943. Supermarine received an Instruction to Proceed letter for three prototypes on 9th April 1943 and the updated project received a

The Seagull ASR in its final configuration with extended engine nacelle, central fin and rudder *(The Aviation Historian)*

new number – Type 381.

The first layout drawings for Type 381 are dated August 1943 and, although still described as being to R.12/40, it is clear that the aircraft was now designed to meet a modified requirement and different role. The turret and guns had been deleted, leaving the aircraft devoid of any defensive armament, and it was to be powered by a Rolls-Royce Griffon 14.SM engine producing around 500hp more than the Merlin in the earlier project.

The increased diameter propeller necessitated raising the height of the pylon. The hull remained essentially unchanged as was the span and area of the wing although it had been swept slightly forward to give a straight leading edge, the change presumably associated with the variable-incidence mechanism adopted from the Type 380 which had a similar wing plan. The RAE wind tunnel tests must have indicated issues with the butterfly tail, a foretaste of problems yet to come, as the surfaces had been almost doubled in area and the dihedral angle increased.

Design conferences with the Admiralty confirmed that service on the older carriers was no longer envisaged, or at least it was not intended for the aircraft to be stowed below deck on them. These conferences must have taken place prior to the initiation of the Type 381 project in August 1943 as the height change

that this decision allowed was already a feature of the design. However, contrary to some descriptions, no change was made to the wingspan at this stage – it remained the same as for the Type 347.

The best configuration for the tail continued to elude the design team. Further tests in the RAE wind tunnel in mid-1944 assessed a variety of differing configurations, including a more conventional T-tail. Not surprisingly, the T-tail was adversely affected by wake turbulence behind the pylon and this turbulence became progressively worse as the wing incidence increased. The butterfly tail was trialled at various dihedral angles between 20 and 40 degrees, and small end fins were added on the lower dihedral tail settings, which proved satisfactory.

In November 1944 a new specification was written around the revised aircraft. S.14/44 was for an Air-Sea Rescue and Reconnaissance amphibian. The aircraft could not exceed 15,000lb loaded and a tail hook was now a requirement.

Like so many non-war critical projects, work on the Type 381, now named Seagull ASR, proceeded at a leisurely pace. The aircraft flew for the first time on 14th July 1948, not so far short of ten years after Type 347 project had been initiated. All was far from well. During company tests a small vertical fin was added between the butterfly surfaces and a dorsal strake added to the hull top

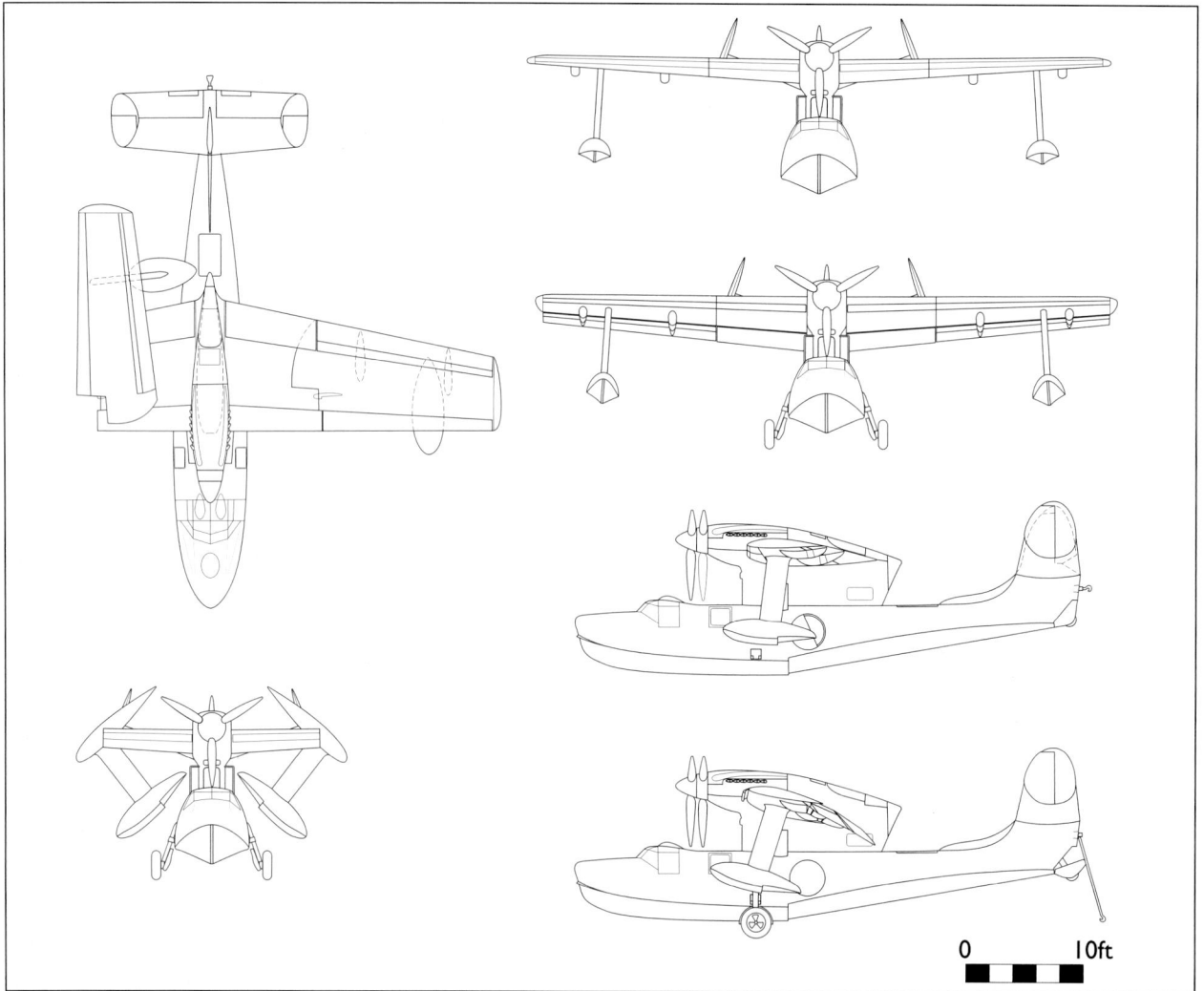

Seagull ASR – technically very clever but a disappointing and flawed aircraft

ahead of the tailplane mounting. The rear of the pylon was extended behind the wing, terminating in a point, to further reduce turbulence. Sometime later the additional fin was increased in size and fitted with a rudder.

When the Seagull was sent for evaluation by the MAEE in mid-1949 the tail region continued to give problems. There was a strong tendency for the aircraft to weathercock in even a light wind, and on the water it proved impossible to make a turn if the wind exceeded 17mph. The layout of instruments and controls in the cockpit came in for criticism, propeller noise was judged to be excessive and the aircraft wallowed and was unstable in yaw when on the approach to land at low speed and with the wing at high incidence. Despite many years of experimentation, research and operational experience, the design of flying boats continued to be somewhat of an art.

There was no prospect for a production order and the aging Sea Otter continued to serve alone in the ASR role until 1955 when helicopters began to take over.

Last of the Line

Back on the saga of the four-engine military marine reconnaissance flying boat two new specifications had been raised in 1946; R.5/46 was for a Marine Reconnaissance Conversion Land Plane, a fairly straightforward derivative of the Avro Lincoln bomber, and R.36/46 for a Reconnaissance Flying Boat, although internal disagreements within the Ministry soon led to the latter being withdrawn.

Thus it appeared for a while that the UK-based marine reconnaissance role was to be taken over by Avro Shackleton land planes alone. But the reconnaissance flying boat was not yet finished, as R.36/46 was reconfigured through 1947 and resurrected eventually as R.2/48.

Although it was becoming pretty much accepted, at least by most of the Air Staff and for some grudgingly, that Shackletons would slowly replace the Sunderlands as these were struck-off charge, there were still those who continued to lobby for a larger aircraft. This, they said, would carry out similar reconnaissance and anti-submarine duties to the Shackleton but for larger radius patrols and especially around overseas territories, a role, they firmly believed, that remained the domain of the flying boat.

So, after a prolonged consultation with industry and much internal debate, Specification R.2/48 was issued in April 1948 calling, once again, for a new flying boat to replace the Sunderland. The advent of radar, sonar and advanced torpedoes would likely require a novel airframe layout, quite different from that of the Sunderland.

The ministry envisaged a large flying boat of around 90,000lb capable of carrying a standard bomb load of 4,000lb on a four hour patrol with a radius of 1,150 miles, or 8,000lb for a 12 hour patrol of 115 miles radius. Weapon load would include a mix of up to 16 x 300lb anti-submarine bombs, 16 x 500lb general purpose medium bombs, 8 x 1,000lb general purpose medium bombs, the latest homing torpedoes; either 8 x 'Dealer' or 2-4 x 'Zeta' (later 4 x 21in Pentanes), plus 8 x 3in rockets with 25 or 60lb warheads and two to four cannon in a retractable Bristol B.17 turret.

Maximum speed was required as at least 400mph with cruise in the range of 150-230mph.

For the extended missions, it was envisaged that the crew would comprise two pilots, four wireless/radar/gunners, one engineer/gunner, and two navigator/radar/bomb aimers.

A lot had changed in the world of the flying boat manufacturers during and immediately after the war. Short Bros had fallen afoul of the Ministry for Aircraft Production in 1942 after a review of the relative efficiency of the aircraft companies had shown them to be one of the least productive and in need of improvement. When this assessment was reported back to the company with instructions to instigate plans for improvement, the company's management had been deemed uncooperative. The Government therefore approved a plan put forward by the Minister, Stafford Cripps, to enact a compulsory purchase of the entire share capital.

In 1943 this brought the company under direct government control, a nationalisation in all but name. The board resigned, including chairman Oswald Short. Arthur Gouge, the chief designer and architect of all Short's successful flying boats from the late 1920s, chose to quit and joined the board of Saunders-Roe. In 1947 the company was merged with Short & Harland, the 50:50 joint venture that the company had launched back in 1936 with a shipyard in Belfast. The company was now renamed as Short Brothers and Harland.

Blackburn lost its prototype B.20 flying boat, with the experimental retractable planing bottom, within the first few days of its test programme in 1940 as a result of aileron flutter. This effectively put an end to any prospect of related projects since the assessment of the merits of the system, which at least had been proven to work, was far from complete. The company concentrated on aircraft for the FAA throughout the war. A second factory built at Dumbarton on the Clyde and managed by William Hargreaves, John Rennie's deputy and ex-Supermarine chief designer, constructed a significant number of Short Sunderlands and maintained their interest in flying boats.

In 1944 the company designed the Clydesman, a large pressurised flying boat powered by six unnamed turbine-propeller engines. It would have

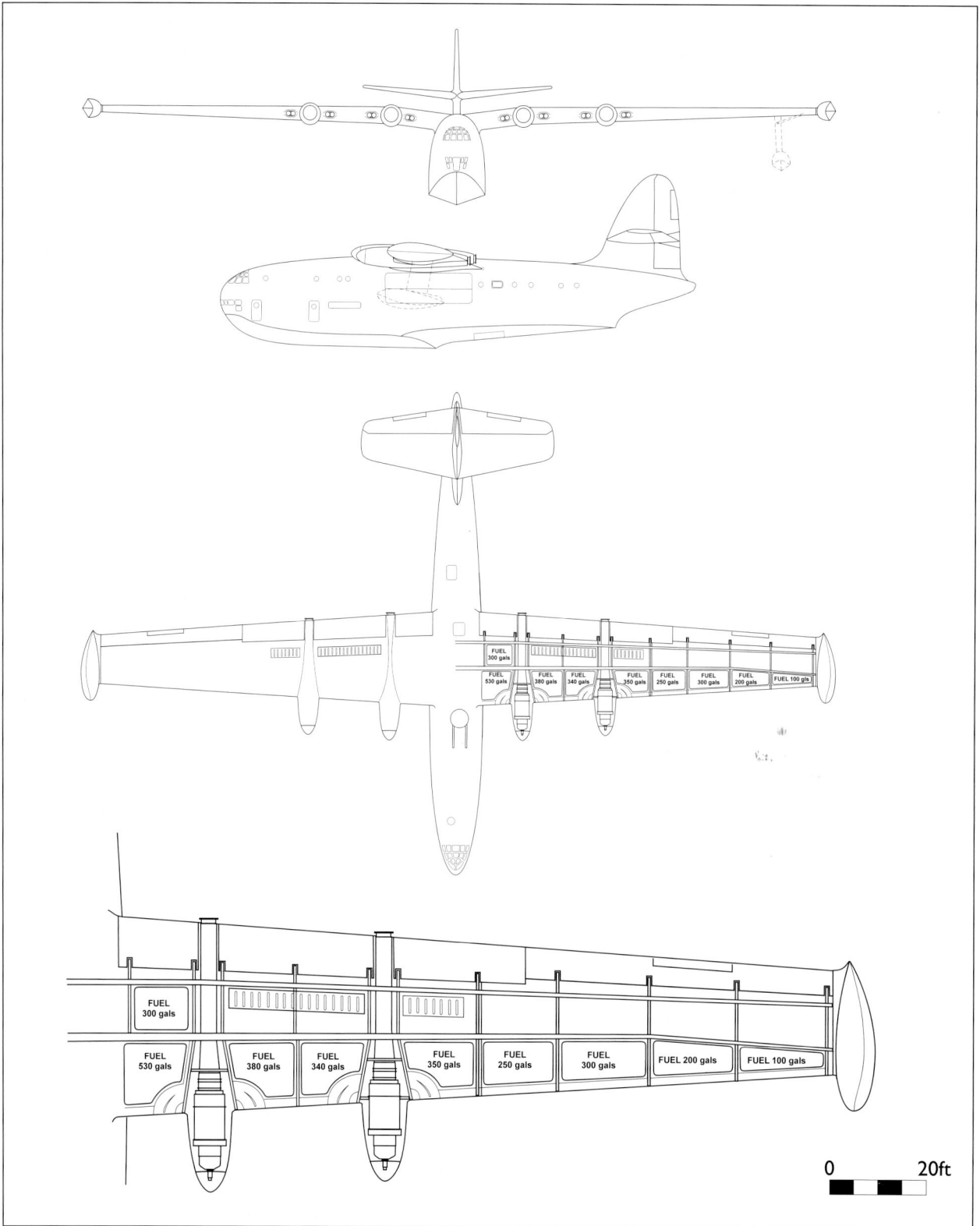

The Type 524 with Bristol Proteus turboprop engines

had sufficient range to fly the Atlantic and was intended primarily for the carriage of cargo. The company placed a lot of advertisements in the aviation press featuring artwork that showed the Clydesman in various forms, and several articles were written about it, but by mid-1945 the project was shelved.

This came about presumably through a lack of support from either the Brabazon Committee, busy reviewing projects for post-war commercial use, or the government. Rennie, now approaching 60, retired from the company in 1946. Blackburn, like many others, suffered in the immediate post-war

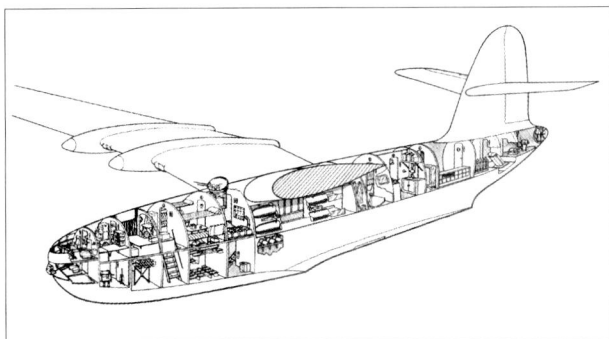

Cutaway drawing showing the interior of the Type 524 hull

years from a lack of orders and by 1948 was deep in the throes of a somewhat acrimonious merger with General Aircraft Ltd. The Dumbarton works was manufacturing metal buildings to keep itself going.

Then there was Saunders-Roe, a company with negligible capacity to build anything other than marine aircraft. All its wartime production had been subcontract work, most noticeably for the Supermarine Walrus and Sea Otter, and it had acted as the UK partner company for Consolidated Aircraft Corporation to carry out maintenance and modification of the PBY Catalina.

Despite the company's less than stellar performance since the relative success of the London and Cloud in the early 1930s, it intended to stay firmly on track as a flying boat manufacturer. To support this vision, and partly in response to the Brabazon Committee having failed to recommend the construction of any civil flying boats, the company commenced with the issue of a brochure in August 1943 written by the design department and titled The Case for the Flying Boat.

After citing various scenarios for future flying boats, it concluded "…It is therefore essential, in the national interest, that flying boat types should be developed concurrently with the selected landplane types… A break now in the development of the flying boat would mean a gap of many years after the end of the war before the flying boat would be able to compete on reasonably level terms with the landplane".

This paper was also published, in revised form, in *Flight* the following November. Written by chief designer Henry Knowler, the paper laid out all the advantages that the company believed flying boats had over their land counterparts, focusing on civil types. It provoked a counter-argument, 'Where Angels Fear', published in *Flight* in December and the spat batted back-and-forth over the following years, with Gouge adding his weight once ensconced on the board at Saunders-Roe. The company's persistence paid off eventually when it managed to secure a contract for the very large SR/45 Princess civil flying boat, but the issue was very far from over.

Which brings us back to Supermarine. Conflict at the top level, largely between Vickers-Armstrong group chairman Charles Craven and Robert McLean, MD of the aviation subsidiaries, flared up regarding McLean's perceived overpromising to the Government and the consequent annoyance at the Air Ministry when delivery targets were not met. At the end of 1938, this resulted in McLean being ousted and the merger of Supermarine Aviation Works (Vickers) Ltd and parent Vickers (Aviation) Ltd; the combined concern henceforth to be controlled directly by Vickers-Armstrong Ltd.

All effort was now to be focused on the rapid production of the Supermarine Spitfire and Vickers Wellington and development of their numerous variants. As the war progressed, the Supermarine team dealt primarily with fighters, to the detriment of other projects, while Vickers concentrated more on bombers and larger types, an arrangement that continued into the post-war period. Supermarine had lost its riverside Woolston Works in a bombing raid in 1940 and the Itchen Works upstream were also badly damaged. Both were abandoned and all production moved to dispersed inland sites while the design office was moved to Hursley Park, a large estate near to Winchester. The company's marine heritage was much diluted, although it was in the experimental department, also located at Hursley Park, that the Seagull ASR flying boats were constructed.

Vickers-Armstrong had been lobbying the Government since the end of the war to sanction the reconstruction of the Itchen Works, writing in October 1945: "I need not tell you that Supermarine first built their reputation on seaborne and amphibian aircraft… Without an erection shop on water frontage with slipway we shall be in the greatest difficulty in accepting such contracts, and may lose not only the particular export trade that offers at the moment, but our established position and reputation as suppliers of this type of aircraft".

The bomb damage to the large hangar, with a floor space of 200ft x 376ft, had been relatively minor, blowing out the doors, roof and wall panels but leaving intact most of the structural framework. The adjacent offices had also survived largely in one piece and the apron and slipway were untouched. The company was granted approval to rebuild and the site was functional from around late 1948. Once again the company was capable of constructing large flying boats.

R.2/48 requested tenders on the basis of a possible production order of 80 aircraft, which in the climate of the time was a very significant number, certainly sufficient to lure designers back once more to the world of flying boats. Short Bros, Blackburn,

Supermarine artwork of the Type 524

Saunders-Roe and Supermarine all prepared designs. The bomb load, speed and, most especially, endurance required by the specification suggested strongly that the better aircraft projects should be powered by the next generation of large fuel-efficient engines, with the current types as a safe back-up alternative. The Ministry of Aircraft Production had approved the development of several such designs in 1944, including the 3,000hp Napier Nomad, a compound engine combining a supercharged two-stroke diesel with an exhaust-driven turbine, and the 3,000hp Bristol Proteus free-turbine. The 2,850hp Rolls-Royce RGT.30.SM Turbo Griffon, also with an exhaust-driven turbine, would be added to the list soon after.

Blackburn is believed to have initiated a project, B.78, but this does not appear to have passed beyond the schematic stage and nothing is currently known of its configuration. Short offered one new design, PD.2, and two cheap-and-quick options, one based around the Shetland, the other on the Seaford. The PD.2 was perceived as a compromise design by the Air Ministry as Short had elected to submit a layout that would be easy to adapt as a transport or civil airliner. Saunders-Roe pushed and pushed, drawing up no fewer than 14 different configurations under project P.104; highly enthusiastic and vocal, but perhaps lacking clarity and focus.

Supermarine Type 524

The Supermarine project was numbered Type 524 and detailed work commenced in late 1948. The designers were well aware of the uncertainty regarding the potential of the new engine types and hedged their bets by choosing to configure the wing and airframe to be adaptable for the installation of any four engines in the 3,000hp class. Three alternative types were suggested; the Napier Nomad, Bristol Centaurus or Bristol Proteus.

The introduction to the tender document laid out the pros and cons for each engine in terms of weight, fuel requirement and development promise. The Nomad was judged the superior type, at least on paper, resulting in a lower fuel load and all-up weight, better take-off performance, and higher service ceiling, at the small expense of slightly lower maximum and cruising speeds. With the Proteus, the unladen weight would be the lowest and speed highest, but would also have the highest fuel load, nearly double that required for the Nomad. It was the version powered by the Proteus that was used for the main illustration.

The watchword in Supermarine's design was economy – economy in construction, maintenance and operation. Consequently, the design introduced few new features. It chose instead to build upon in-house experience and published research, both British and from the US, of which a large volume had become available after the war. It was, in essence, a pragmatic and low risk approach.

Supermarine's long-favoured single spar and 'D' leading edge torsion box had now been dropped, replaced by a torsion box formed between a front main spar at 40% chord and a rear spar at 70%. This torsion box was continuous, tip to tip, and the whole wing was fabricated in five parts; the centre section integral with the hull and with moderate dihedral, the inner wings that included the engine mounts, and the outer wings.

Only the region around the engines required modification to accept the three different engines – the leading edge modified as required to accommodate radiators, intake ducts and so on, and the shape of the adjacent fuel tanks adjusted to fit. The wing floats were retractable and formed the wingtips, an arrangement as used on the Blackburn B.20 and Consolidated Catalina.

The designers settled on a tall hull form with two decks. The shape was selected to minimise drag in the air and approximated an ideal aerodynamic form, with a well faired cockpit that conformed to the contours of the nose. The planing bottom was of the stepless or faired step profile, as adopted by both Short and Saunders-Roe in recent years, and Supermarine made reference to the latest reports issued by the RAE and NACA Technical Report TN1182. The latter, published in 1947, that was a compilation and distillation of over a hundred evaluations of hull design, by NACA and the RAE.

As the aircraft was expected to undertake long patrols and also to be able to operate from remote bases, a wardroom, berths, galley and mess facilities were built in. The cockpit was placed on the top deck in the extreme nose with the stations for the radio operator, radar and sono-buoy operators, navigator and flight engineer immediately behind.

The bombsight was also in the nose on the lower deck beneath the cockpit, and the retractable Bristol B.17 turret was in the hull roof just ahead of the wing and behind the plane of the propeller discs. The main bomb/torpedo bays were located in the hull sides beneath the wing centre section and the munitions were deployed by running them out sideways on lateral rails within the lower wing, much like the well-established system on the Sunderland. The smaller rocket bays were similar and located forward. A large diameter retractable watertight housing was provided for the ASV radar which was deployed through the rear planing bottom.

The Ministry of Supply, which had taken over from the Ministry of Aircraft Production, requested in July 1949 that Supermarine adapt its proposal to accept the Rolls-Royce Turbo-Griffon engine. With limited time, the design team simply reduced the length, span and width of the planing bottom of the aircraft. As a result, fitted with the Turbo-Griffon, the revised Type 524 would have had performance characteristics comparable to the larger aircraft with Nomads.

So, where did that leave the matter? Within the Air Staff, the flying boat supporters were still at loggerheads with those that saw flying boats as yesterday's news. It is all too apparent that vigorous lobbying by Saunders-Roe was having an effect as the arguments put forward in support of the company's project came straight out of the company's play book. After the Short proposals had been side-lined as deficient, it came down to a head-to-head with Supermarine.

Saunders-Roe made great play of the long narrow planing bottom as a significant breakthrough in flying boat design, and had an RAE test report in support of this. Yet this was really nothing new; the beam to length ratio of flying boats had been decreasing for some time. It was, in fact, one of the primary arguments that had been made in support of Gouge's design for the 'C' class and Sunderland back in 1934. Certainly further reduction was always possible, and the potential water and air drag benefits were obvious, but they were not dramatic and came at the cost of restriction to the internal space.

Supermarine was probably more aware than most of the trade-off between air and water drag through the extensive research carried out on the floats for the Schneider racers way back in the 1920s and steered clear of taking this route with the Type 524. But Saunders-Roe's lobbying efforts won out and its project was ranked ahead of Supermarine's, which was judged as conventional, as if that were a weakness for a marine reconnaissance aircraft. It is also precisely the term the company had itself used to describe its own project, a deliberate choice to keep the aircraft simple and cheap without compromising performance. The reason for the criticism would become apparent later.

Supermarine stood back while the Air Ministry continued its internal arguments, juggling political expedience, financial restrictions, and mission requirements, until the whole specification was abandoned a few years later. No further military flying boats were to be built – although the arguments droned on until the close of the 1950s.

17 CHAPTER

The (Oh So Slow and Painful) End of an Era

The demise of the flying boat was an erratic and contentious process that played out over many years. Despite the encouragement from, and active promotion by, a vocal and influential group of supporters, not to mention constructors with much to gain or lose, the flying boat had never managed to achieve the large-scale breakthrough in either the civil or military British markets that they had firmly believed was all but inevitable.

There had not been an obvious, organised rival faction arguing against the flying boat throughout – it was just that when push came to shove the sums simply did not add up and landplanes were judged the better option more times than not.

In Britain, the only significant application of the civil flying boat had been the fleet of Short Calcuttas, Kents and 'C' Class Empire flying boats that formed the core of Imperial Airways' assets in the 1930s. Yet just as Imperial Airways was in the throes of its forced merger with British Airways to form British Overseas Airways Corporation (BOAC), Robert Mayo, former Imperial Airways General Manager (technical) and now a consultant to the airline, wrote a long memo to the board arguing that, after reviewing all the pros and cons of different aircraft types with which to operate services on the Empire routes, he had concluded that the next generation of airliners to replace the Short 'C' class flying boats should, on balance, be land planes.

He wrote: "For the convenience of passengers and the handling of mail and freight, there can be no doubt that experience has shown that the land plane is far superior to the flying boat, while there is probably not a single member of the technical staff with experience of land and marine types, who would not prefer to operate and maintain land planes rather than flying boats, provided their general safety is comparable."

The economic assessment was equally blunt. "After making all necessary allowances, the ton

mile per gallon figure for the land plane has been shown to be 25% better than that of the flying boat over a range of 750 miles, and allowing for the differences in the cost of petrol between the two types (87 and 100 octane) the fuel cost would be even less per ton mile on the landplane."

Obviously not all of Imperial Airways' senior managers were convinced by his analysis but much of his argument was accepted, coming as it did just as BOAC was struggling to reorganise, involving major changes to managers and management structure with key positions going to former British Airways managers who had no experience, or indeed interest, in flying boats.

At the end of 1942, the Government, via the Air Ministry and the Ministry of Aircraft Production, established a committee to advise on the range of civil aircraft types that British industry should build after the war, and on which some preliminary design work could commence before hostilities had ceased. Chaired by Lord Brabazon, and formed entirely from government ministry officers, the committee gathered information on existing aircraft and engine types, reviewed pre-war statistics of passenger numbers and cargo, and solicited the views of selected aircraft companies on what future trends in design could deliver.

Although restricting the committee to ministry insiders could be construed, with good reason, as unrepresentative of the civil aviation business, they were a well-balanced group of experienced technical and organisational advisors as capable as anyone at the time of providing a reasonably objective view. In their report, which was confidential and not distributed outside of the Cabinet, the flying boat did not feature at all, other than as a footnote supporting the civil conversion, as an interim type, of the unwanted military Short Shetland, at that time nearing completion in Short's yard.

Even for the 'big prize' prestigious direct transatlantic service, the recommendation was for a land plane. The government accepted the report as the basis for more detailed planning and established a second committee, also chaired by Brabazon, on which both industry and airline customers were represented. Again, no flying boats were recommended, despite the submission for consideration of various proposals, all unsolicited.

Nevertheless there were various schemes drawn up for new airports that combined runways with a sheltered lagoon or harbour from which to operate flying boats. The pre-war option of Langstone, near Portsmouth, was resurrected. Captain McIntyre of Scottish Aviation proposed an extension to his former airfield at Prestwick, and F. G. Miles of Phillip & Powis commissioned studies from architects and consultant engineers for an airport in the Thames Estuary east of London. The arguments continued.

For the military, the situation was equally uncertain. The Supermarine Southampton had a successful career in both UK and overseas waters and proved difficult to replace. The Supermarine Scapa, Stranraer and Saunders-Roe London all offered improvements yet were always regarded as stop-gaps, worthy aircraft but no great step forward and not in the same league, technically, as the larger Sunderland.

Only one new large flying boat type had entered production since the Short Sunderland, which had been designed in 1934, and that was the woefully unsuccessful Saunders-Roe Lerwick. Despite the circulation of multiple specifications by the Air Ministry, nothing had advanced beyond the drawing board in nearly ten years. A series of entirely successful modifications and upgrades had kept the Sunderland and its derivatives in frontline service throughout the war and beyond. But during the war the long-range maritime patrol and strike role with RAF Coastal Command had been supplemented by a variety of land-based types, among them the Armstrong-Whitworth Whitley, Consolidated Liberator and Vickers Wellington, and their success had demonstrated conclusively that the ability to operate from the sea was not essential.

Yet the advocates continued to argue in favour of the flying boat and achieved a notable success when just post-war the new Labour government sanctioned the construction of three examples of a very large civil flying boats designed by Saunders-Roe, the future SR.45 Princess, despite a notable lack of enthusiasm from BOAC as the potential customer.

BOAC had not been involved in writing the details of the specification and long before the prototype had flown actually expressed the view that as it stood the aircraft would be of no use to

its business at all. It was soon apparent that an internal battle was once more under way among BOAC management regarding the airline's future support for flying boat operations, then run using the sole remaining Short S.26 'G' type, and a small number of Short Hythes (converted Sunderland MkIII) and Short Solents (converted Sunderland MkIV/Seaford).

However with no suitable replacement types readily available and more modern concepts, such as Saunders-Roe's P.131 Duchess jet-powered flying boat, not yet even on the drawing board, those in favour of continuing to use the flying boat rapidly lost influence and the services were slowly run down before the last Solent was replaced by land airliners in 1950. British South American Airways expressed interest in operating the Princess on the route to Buenos Aires, making an offer for the three under construction and suggesting the possibility of an order for a further 20 aircraft, which surely would have proven commercially unrealistic. The issue then became wholly academic in 1949 when the airline was merged with BOAC.

The saga of the Princess had its parallel in the conflict within the Air Staff over Specification R.2/48. Although the argument in favour of flying boats made slightly more sense for service types than it did for civil carriers, the need was not great and they were an easy target for the axe when funds were limited. At this point the probable reason behind the negative comment about the Type 524 being conventional became apparent. Within both the Air Ministry and sectors of industry a large part of the argument in favour of ordering a further large flying boat, and one of perceived advanced design, was concern that without it the country would lose expertise in the type; the advocates still convinced, with little tangible justification, that flying boats still had a great future worldwide and that the US was positioning itself to exploit the market. It was largely fantasy.

The Princess limped on, the first prototype flying in the summer of 1952, the other two remained incomplete, until all flying and development was terminated in July 1954. A project initially tagged at under £3m was estimated to have cost more than £9m when the dust settled.

Despite all the negativity expressed within the military and commercial world, Saunders-Roe refused to roll over and give up without a fight. Several projects were still in progress on the company's drawing boards and lobbying continued unabated. The firm would continue with a strategy of actively placing advertisements featuring flying boats in the press right through until the mid-1950s, extolling the virtues of the type and castigating those who stood against them.

Most of the arguments tabled were the same as those that had been used 20 years previously by Imperial Airways, and experience had shown that these were oversold. To this they now added the prospect of nuclear power, admittedly the subject of an industry review at the Government's nuclear research facility in 1954. **Among a series of pros and cons statements in the advertisements, it was stated that, "They think only in terms of the present and the immediate future. They neglect the almost certain advent of atomic power for aircraft. The implications are highly important.**

"First, only very large aircraft will be able to carry the heavy power plant and shielding. Secondly, since fuel consumption will be negligible, wing loading at landing will be high. Both these facts support the belief that atomic aircraft will have to be large flying boats". They could not have been more wrong.

In February 1954, James V Martin, one of the pioneers of British aviation and a staunch believer in the future of the flying boat, arranged a dinner at the Royal Aero Club 'in honour of the flying boat', for fellow advocates of the type. There was a guest list of just 27, including aircraft designers, test pilots, various aviation experts, consultants, former Air Ministry officers and journalists. Among those present were former and current senior personnel from Saunders-Roe, Short and Bristol, but Supermarine personnel were notable by their absence. After 50 years as one of Britain's premier builders of flying boats, the company had bowed to the inevitable and abandoned any further interest in the type. Henceforth the company would concentrate of jet fighters.

Appendix – How to Construct a Linton Hope Hull

L inton Chorley Hope was a marine architect who had specialised in the design of hulls for racing yachts in the Edwardian era utilising what was described at the time as the 'stressed shell' principle. In order to avoid localised concentration of stress these hulls lacked an internal structure of bulkheads and instead employed a framework of lightweight hoops and stringers to which the skin was attached, the final hull then exhibited a degree of flexibility. Hope's basic structural methods proved to be most suitable for wooden flying boats in the First World War and early post-war period and were adopted immediately by Scott Paine for Supermarine's flying boat projects. The method for the construction was broadly the same for any hull size but is here described for the Southampton.

Each hull was built within a jig around a series of transverse templates known as moulds that defined the shape of the hull. These moulds were assembled in three parts, for ease of removal, and spaced at 3ft intervals, keel uppermost, and braced to form a rigid structure. A long spar, resting on trestles and levelled, ran fore and aft through the moulds to define a datum line for the build.

The keel for the hull was built up from shaped mahogany pieces fastened together by copper rods, with localised strengthening by packing pieces of ash or elm attached with copper nails. The stringers were of spruce or American elm and the hoops, 19 in total for a Southampton, were also of American elm. The Supermarine woodworkers fabricated their own auger drills from bicycle spokes to be able to drill the deep narrow holes required for the copper fixings.

Once assembly of the hoop and stringer framework was completed the first of two layers of skin planks could be attached. The inner layer were cut from cedar planks 1/16 in thickness and were laid diagonally and secured with copper nails and brass screws.

The jig of transverse mould frames and longitudinal spar in the jig for the hull of the Scylla flying boat

The stringers in place over the mould frames for a Southampton hull

The final framework of stringers and hoops for a Southampton hull

The inner skin of diagonal planks for the Scylla flying boat

The completed inner skin was then covered by a layer of fabric that was heavily doped with marine varnish to form a watertight barrier. The outer skin was built up from $\frac{1}{8}$ in thick mahogany planks laid longitudinally, also secured by copper nails and brass screws. The senior Supermarine overseer ensured that all the screw head slots were neatly aligned fore and aft!

The outer skin of the Southampton flying boat at the RAF Museum, Hendon

At this point the mould frames were disassembled and removed from the hull allowing full access within. The moulds were then available for reuse on the next jig.

The interior of the Southampton at the RAF Museum, Hendon looking aft

The planing bottom was a box-like construction consisting of an inner framework of a longitudinal keelson and transverse bulkheads that formed five watertight compartments on each side after the stringers and mahogany planks were secured and varnished. A layer of varnished fabric was placed between the planing bottom and main hull and the bottom then secured in place with copper nails and rods to the keel and longitudinal American elm timbers placed within the hull.

A Southampton flying boat with the planning bottom installed and removed from the jig

Once complete the hull and bottom could be released from the jig, turned the right way up, the cockpit and gun ring apertures built in place and all the fixtures and fittings installed.